PRAISE FOR

Off the Record

"Norman Pearlstine pulls no punches on either journalism or law in this fascinating book."

—**Anthony Lewis**, longtime *New York Times* columnist
and author of *Gideon's Trumpet*

"*Off the Record* is a masterful blend of gripping personal narrative and profound public issues. This no-holds-barred account from a top media executive is the closest thing I've ever read to actually being at the center of a major news organization. After a career editing *The Wall Street Journal* and leading Time Inc., Norman Pearlstine has demonstrated that a legendary editor is also a great writer."

—**James Stewart**, author of *Den of Thieves* and *Blind Eye:
The Terrifying Story of a Doctor Who Got Away with Murder*

"A vivid and engaging account of *Time*'s legal adventures."

—**Adam Liptak**, *The New York Times*

"One of journalism's premier practitioners explores the nature of news sourcing."

—**Seth Lipsky**, *The New York Sun*

"Pearlstine's book is an informed and provocative account of a complicated legal battle."

—**Bob Hoover**, *Pittsburgh Post-Gazette*

OFF THE RECORD

OFF THE RECORD

The Press, the Government,
and the War over
Anonymous Sources

NORMAN PEARLSTINE

Farrar, Straus and Giroux
New York

Farrar, Straus and Giroux
18 West 18th Street, New York 10011

Printed in the United States of America
Published in 2007 by Farrar, Straus and Giroux
First paperback edition, 2008

The Library of Congress has cataloged the hardcover edition as follows:
Pearlstine, Norman.
  Off the record : the press, the government, and the war over anonymous sources / Norman Pearlstine. — 1st ed.
    p. cm.
  Includes index.

  1. Confidential communications—Press—United States. 2. Journalists—Legal status, laws, etc.—United States. 3. Government and the press—United States. 4. Plame, Valerie. 5. Intelligence officers—United States—Identification. I. Title.

KF8959.P7P43 2007
342.7308'53—dc22

                                                             2007002972

Paperback ISBN-13: 978-0-374-53118-8
Paperback ISBN-10: 0-374-53118-8

Designed by Michelle McMillian

www.fsgbooks.com

For Jane

Were it left to me to decide whether we should have a government without newspapers, or newspapers without a government, I should not hesitate a moment to prefer the latter.

—THOMAS JEFFERSON, 1787

ROPER: So now you'd give the Devil benefit of law!
MORE: Yes. What could you do? Cut a great road through the law to get after the Devil?
ROPER: I'd cut down every law in England to do that!
MORE: Oh? And when the last was down, and the Devil turned round on you—where would you hide, Roper, the laws all being flat? This country's planted thick with laws from coast to coast—man's laws, not God's—and if you cut them down—and you're just the man to do it—d'you really think you could stand upright in the winds that would blow then? Yes, I'd give the Devil benefit of law, for my own safety's sake.

—ROBERT BOLT, *A MAN FOR ALL SEASONS*, 1960

Contents

Preface

Before he was a businessman, Time Warner Inc. CEO Dick Parsons was a lawyer, and a very good one. So it was with mixed emotions that I met him and nine other Time Warner officers and attorneys the morning of October 20, 2004, to discuss contempt citations against Time Inc. and Matthew Cooper, a reporter for *Time* magazine. Parsons, who had assisted Rudy Giuliani on complex libel and First Amendment cases when they were young lawyers at the white-shoe New York firm Patterson, Belknap, Webb & Tyler, understood the issues. That was a plus. But his strongly held views were a problem.

A federal district court judge in Washington, D.C., had held Cooper and Time Inc., Time Warner's magazine division and the publisher of *Time*, in civil contempt for refusing to tell a grand jury the source for a story by Cooper, published on *Time*'s website, naming Valerie Plame as a CIA operative. The refusal was the result of a decision I, as editor in chief, had made, in accordance with long practice at the magazine and in American journalism. Cooper had been sentenced to a jail term, and Time Inc. had been fined $1,000 per day. Both sentences had been suspended pending our appeal.

I had learned that Parsons had told his board of directors about the case in a memo two months earlier and had said, "At the end of the day, the company will abide by the final determination of the courts." In other words, he would stand with the courts, not with me and my journalistic colleagues. I was alarmed by his declaration and had sought the October meeting to talk about it.

I told Parsons I thought it unlikely the district court ruling would be reversed on appeal, and equally unlikely that the Supreme Court would agree to hear it if we were to seek its review. Although we agreed to continue to litigate, he repeated what he had told his board: "If we exhaust our legal remedies, Matt should testify and you must turn over our files."

The mood inside the conference room turned as somber as the sky outside when I told him we would do no such thing. "The decision is mine to make," I said, "and if we lose, we shall pay the fines and Matt will do the time."

I was editor in chief of Time Inc. We were the world's largest magazine publisher, and I was responsible for the words and pictures in more than 150 titles, including *Time*, *People*, *Sports Illustrated*, *Entertainment Weekly*, and *Fortune*. I had been brought to Time Inc. in 1994 after a lengthy career in publishing, including nine years in which I served as *The Wall Street Journal*'s top news executive.

I reminded Parsons that he and the rest of Time Warner's board had granted me unprecedented editorial independence in 1997, when it had signed off on a short document I had presented that defined the role of Time Inc.'s editor in chief. I told him that many of our best stories relied on confidential sources, and I showed him where Time Inc.'s Editorial Guidelines stipulated that it was our policy "not to reveal the identity of a confidential source." The guidelines also warned that there might be occasions involving federal grand jury proceedings "in which the only way to keep your promise of confidentiality to a source is to serve a jail term for contempt of court."

I noted the distinction between civil and criminal contempt. In our case, fines and jail terms were threatened to induce cooperation. In criminal contempt cases the punishment, usually resulting from a felony conviction, is for wrongdoing. I cited more than two hundred years of tradition in which reporters went to jail and publishers paid fines to protect their editorial independence. Finally, after more than an hour's heated discussion, during which I never disclosed our source, Parsons grudgingly accepted my position.

We didn't discuss the matter again over the next eight months, while the grand jury case dragged on, as the special prosecutor urged us to reveal our source. But on June 27, 2005, the Supreme Court announced that it wouldn't hear our petition, leaving the adverse appellate court ruling intact.

Two days later I called Parsons to tell him we would turn over our files to the grand jury. "You've surprised me," he said. "I was just getting comfortable with your earlier position." I could hear a chuckle as he hung up the phone.

Both of us knew, however, that my decision was no laughing matter. In nearly forty years working as a reporter and editor, I had never faced such a difficult decision. I knew that many of America's most respected journalists, including some of my role models, would denounce me, often in the pages of their publications. Nonetheless, I thought that we should comply with the court's orders. And the more I learned about the use of confidential sources, the more I came to understand how their *mis*use was undermining the press's credibility.

Since then, of course, the battles over confidential sources have escalated, with important implications for the nation and for the press. The Plame case grew out of George Bush's State of the Union address, in which he asserted that Iraq had been trying to buy uranium in Africa to restart its nuclear weapons program. As a result, the special counsel's investigation became an important part of the fight over the President's decision to invade Iraq and the overall conduct of his war on terrorism.

Bush's detractors say Plame was outed by the administration to punish her husband, Joseph Wilson. Wilson, a retired diplomat who had served in Iraq and in Africa, had visited Niger on behalf of the CIA and had concluded that there was no evidence that Iraq had bought uranium in Africa. That argument buttressed other evidence that there was no basis for going to war with Saddam Hussein, prompting critics to conclude that Bush, Vice President Cheney, and their key aides had deliberately lied to the American public.

The President's defenders see the Plame episode as an example of routine political skirmishing inside the Beltway, and they insist that the revelation of Plame's CIA status should never have led to an investigation, let alone the indictment, trial, and conviction of Vice President Dick Cheney's chief of staff, I. Lewis (Scooter) Libby Jr., and the investigation of Bush's key aide Karl Rove.

Our case developed against the backdrop of the Bush administration's war on the press. The administration has produced video news releases that masquerade as stories, has paid columnists to spout the party line, and has questioned the press's check-and-balance function in society. Special Counsel Patrick Fitzgerald acted independently of and often against the administration, but the courts' support for his tactics has emboldened the Department of Justice, other prosecutors, and civil plaintiffs, leading to the biggest increase in subpoenas since the Nixon era, all seeking reporters' testimony about their confidential sources and about the information gained from them. To cite one example, the Hearst Corp.'s general counsel says it received more than eighty subpoenas in 2005–2006—the vast majority from prosecutors—compared with about half a dozen in the prior two years.

Judith Miller of *The New York Times* served eighty-five days in jail for contempt of court before agreeing to testify and reveal a confidential source in the Plame case. The Bush administration has stepped up its attacks on publications and broadcasters that rely on confidential sources. The FBI demanded that the widow of investigative reporter Jack Anderson turn over nearly two hundred boxes of his papers before the donated files were transferred to the archives of George Washington University. The administration has called for investigations to determine who leaked information to *The New York Times* about warrantless domestic wiretapping by the National Security Agency. President Bush has also denounced the *Times* for printing stories about his administration's secret international-banking surveillance program, designed to track terrorists, calling the paper's disclosure a "disgraceful" act that does "great harm" to the nation. *The Washington Post* has similarly been criticized for its reports about CIA interrogation camps in Eastern Europe. Those stories also prompted radio personality William J. Bennett, a former Republican secretary of education, to pronounce the reporters "worthy of jail" for breaching national security. The editors who judge the Pulitzer Prizes, however, gave awards to the *Times* and *Post* reporters who broke the NSA and CIA stories.

Attorney General Alberto Gonzales, stretching his own department's guidelines, has contemplated draconian measures, including possible criminal prosecution under the nation's espionage laws. Two former lobbyists for the American Israel Public Affairs Committee (AIPAC) were indicted in August 2005 and charged with violating the Espionage Act of 1917 by passing U.S. state secrets to Israel. Although the case involves lobbyists, it is otherwise no different from potential cases against reporters.

And so, a generation after Watergate, the use and misuse of anonymous sources and their most important subset, confidential sources, have again become central to any discussion of the role of the press in a free society. As essential as these sources may be, their misuse has undermined the public's support for and interest in the press, making it more difficult for reporters to get the legal protections needed to do their jobs.

As I made my way through the thicket of our case, I realized how little I understood what I had always assumed were long-standing rules for the press when dealing with sources and the public. In truth, there are no rules, and there is no common understanding of what qualifies as proper behavior. Ask a group of reporters or editors to tell you the difference between "confidential" and "anonymous," or between "not for attribution," "background," "deep background," and "off the record," and you will get a lot of different answers. As screenwriter William Goldman once said of Hollywood, "Nobody knows anything."

I never expected to go where my journey took me. But the journey has been revealing, showing the abuse of anonymity, the incestuous relations between reporters and sources, particularly in Washington, and the far too casual way journalists can imperil their own freedom and even the survival of their publications through the careless granting of promises or through the assumption of promises never explicitly made.

Although my decision to hand over Matt Cooper's notes, thus revealing his confidential sources, has divided reporters, editors, lawyers, legislators, and the public, it is, nonetheless, my hope that the decision will help pave the way for new laws, standards, and guidelines that will improve and protect journalism and that will restore the public's faith in the press.

Chronology

2002

February—The CIA, responding to a request for more information from Vice President Cheney, sends Joseph C. Wilson IV, a retired career diplomat, to Niger to evaluate intelligence reports that Iraq was trying to buy high-grade uranium there. Wilson, who went without Cheney's knowledge, concluded the reports were baseless.

2003

January 28—President Bush's State of the Union speech justifies war with Iraq, in part because "the British government has learned that Saddam Hussein recently sought significant quantities of uranium from Africa."

March 19–20—The United States invades Iraq after Bush seeks and obtains congressional support for the use of force there.

May 6—A *New York Times* column by Nicholas D. Kristof reports that an unnamed former diplomat went to Niger in 2002 and that he told the CIA that there was no evidence to support the reports of Iraqi efforts to purchase uranium.

May 29–June 12—I. Lewis (Scooter) Libby, Cheney's chief of staff, asks the State Department about the former ambassador's trip and is told that Joseph Wilson was the ambassador and that Wilson's wife, a CIA employee, was involved in sending him to Niger. A senior CIA official gives Libby similar information, as does Cheney's communications director, Cathie Martin, who learned it from a CIA spokesman.

June 12—Cheney also tells Libby that Wilson's wife works for the CIA.

June 13—Deputy Secretary of State Richard Armitage tells Bob Woodward that Wilson's wife works for the CIA.

June 23—Libby meets with Judith Miller. (Miller later testifies that Libby told her Wilson's wife might work for the CIA. Libby denies Miller's testimony.)

July 6—Joseph Wilson's op-ed piece, "What I Didn't Find in Africa," appears in *The New York Times*, attacking President Bush for his selective use of intelligence—dubious rumors that Iraq was trying to obtain uranium in Africa—in the State of the Union address to justify war with Iraq.

July 8–9—Columnist Robert Novak interviews Armitage, who discloses that Wilson's wife works at the CIA, and, a day later, White House adviser Karl Rove confirms the story.

July 10—Libby calls Tim Russert, NBC's Washington bureau chief and moderator of *Meet the Press*. (Libby says Russert told him that many reporters knew Wilson's wife worked for the CIA. Russert denies that she was discussed or that he knew her identity.)

July 11–12—*Time*'s Matt Cooper calls Karl Rove about Wilson's op-ed piece. Rove indicates that Wilson's wife, who works for the

CIA, authorized Wilson's fact-finding mission to Africa. Rove doesn't name her. The next day, Cooper speaks to Libby, who says he has heard rumors about Wilson and his wife but doesn't comment on them. George Tenet, director of the CIA, also on July 11, tells the press that rumors about Iraq seeking uranium in Africa shouldn't have been included in Bush's speech.

July 14—In a syndicated column, Robert Novak names Wilson's wife, Valerie Plame, as a CIA operative working on weapons of mass destruction.

July 17—Cooper co-authors "A War on Wilson?" for *Time*'s website, a story confirming Novak's column.

September 26—Federal investigators begin to seek the source of leaks about Plame. Armitage subsequently tells the FBI that he may have leaked Plame's identity to Woodward.

October 14—FBI agents first interview Libby.

December 30—Patrick J. Fitzgerald is appointed special counsel to investigate the leak of Plame's identity.

2004

January—Fitzgerald convenes a grand jury.

March 5 and 24—The grand jury hears testimony from Libby in which he says he forgot about Plame's working for the CIA until he heard it from Russert.

May 21—Cooper receives his first subpoena to testify before the grand jury. Time Inc. then hires First Amendment lawyer Floyd Abrams to represent Cooper. Fitzgerald tells Abrams in a phone call that he will limit the government subpoena to questions about Libby.

August 9—Judge Thomas F. Hogan holds Cooper and Time Inc. in contempt for refusing to give the grand jury testimony or documents. Fitzgerald subsequently serves the *New York Times* reporter Judith Miller with a subpoena seeking testimony about her conversations with administration officials. Abrams is also retained to represent Miller. With Libby's agreement, Cooper gives a deposition to Fitzgerald, but following the deposition, Fitzgerald tells Abrams on August 31 that he needs further testimony from Cooper about another source. Cooper and Time Inc. refuse to provide it.

September 13—The second subpoenas are issued to Cooper and Time Inc.

October 7—The district court denies the Cooper and Time Inc. motions to quash their subpoenas, and again orders Cooper to testify and Time Inc. to turn over e-mails in its possession. Cooper, Time Inc., and Miller are held in contempt for refusal to testify or provide notes.

2005

February 15—The Federal Circuit Court of Appeals for the District of Columbia affirms the contempt orders.

June 27—The U.S. Supreme Court denies Cooper's, Time Inc.'s, and Miller's petitions to review their cases. Time Inc. announces two days later that it will comply with the district court order to turn over Cooper's notes.

July 6—Cooper receives a waiver from Rove, his second anonymous source, and testifies before the grand jury. Miller is jailed.

September 29—Miller is released from jail and agrees to testify after speaking to and receiving a letter from her source, Libby, explicitly waiving confidentiality.

September 30—Miller testifies before the grand jury.

October 28—Libby is indicted for perjury, obstruction of justice, and making false statements.

November 10—Miller resigns under pressure from *The New York Times*.

2006

June 12—Rove learns he will not be indicted.

September 7—Armitage's lawyer admits publicly that the former State Department official leaked Plame's identity to Novak and Woodward. Armitage claims he didn't realize Plame was a covert agent.

2007

January 23—Libby's trial begins with lawyers' opening statements.

March 6—Jurors find Libby guilty on four felony counts.

June 5—Libby is sentenced to thirty months in prison and fined $250,000.

July 2—President Bush commutes Libby's prison sentence.

December 10—Libby drops the appeal of his conviction.

OFF THE RECORD

1

Anonymous Sources

As a young reporter in *The Wall Street Journal*'s Detroit bureau, I often wrote the weekly story about current levels of domestic auto-plant production. A table with estimates for each line of car and truck manufactured by the auto companies would appear at the end of the story. The figures served as a barometer for the industry and, by extension, the economy. The companies didn't issue press releases detailing production schedules, but there were men at General Motors, Ford, Chrysler, and American Motors who would answer my calls and give me estimates for their companies. I would include the estimates in my stories with no attribution. One week, my source at Chrysler said he had been told to stop providing estimates. "That's fine," I replied. "I shall do my own estimate, and I always estimate low." The source called back a few minutes later and said Chrysler would continue to provide the numbers we sought to publish.

These anonymous sources were passed from one generation of *Journal* reporters to the next. In my two years in Detroit, 1970 and 1971, I never met any of them, and I never sought verification from a secondary source at any of the companies, because I didn't have a secondary source. To this day, I have no idea whether the numbers were accurate or whether the companies were using the *Journal* to mislead the public or their competitors.

There is no pride in telling this story. Today, I would refuse to print an article based on that kind of reporting. But it is just one example of the ways in which anonymous sources have become embedded in journalism; they are a critical part of coverage in small towns and large cities, and for national newspapers, magazines, cable news channels, and television networks.

The public is rightly suspicious of anonymous sources. Daniel Okrent, the first *New York Times* "public editor" (the *Times* designation for a position known at other publications as ombudsman), wrote in May 2005, "Since I've been in this job, use of anonymous sources has been the substantive issue raised most often by readers. They challenge the authenticity of quotations. They question the accuracy of the information in the quotations. They believe reporters who invoke unidentified sources are lazy or, far worse, dishonest."

In contrast, most journalists believe information from anonymous sources is more trustworthy than the canned, on-the-record quotes printed in press releases and uttered at news conferences by government officials, executives, and celebrities. If a reporter is doing an on-the-record interview, both sides presume that the source is trying to put the best possible face on every answer. So, if the source asks to go on background at some point during the interview, the reporter naturally reacts, "Aha! After ten minutes of mindless crap, I'm finally going to get something juicy I can use." It rarely occurs to the reporter that the source might be spinning the facts—or that spinning the reporter is really easier on background when the subject doesn't have to take responsibility for a quote.

Especially in Washington, the background briefing has supplanted the on-the-record conversation to such a degree that many reporters assume that *every* interview is on background unless the source stipulates otherwise.

Clark Hoyt, the insightful former chief of Knight Ridder's Washington bureau, recalls a meeting he and a few other news executives had with then White House press secretary Scott McClellan in 2005 to protest the number of background briefings the administration was holding. They met "after a particularly silly briefing on an energy policy speech the President was to give the following day," Hoyt recalls. Not only was the conference call on background, but also the reporters weren't told who the two officials were, even though it was understood that one was the secretary of energy. Knight Ridder and some of the others in attendance had drawn the line, refusing to print anything from the briefing. "Scott explained that no one in the administration wanted to get out in front of the President, stealing his news," Hoyt says. "That was ridiculous, especially since there wasn't any news in the speech anyway." Had the briefing been of substance, however, I believe that protests notwithstanding, the news organizations would have run stories based on it.

Jack Shafer, *Slate*'s media columnist, has pointed out that it is difficult for reporters to break this habit because "the surplus of journalists and the relative scarcity of knowledgeable sources allow the sources to pick the rules of engagement. If a reporter insists that a source put the information on the record, the source can always say, 'Screw you,' and shop it to a publication that will agree to anonymity. If what the source has to say is true and newsworthy, he'll find a market."

Shafer's observations about Washington apply to other areas where reporters compete for scoops, including Hollywood, Wall Street, foreign wars, and sports. As a reporter, I frequently wrote stories that included quotes from anonymous sources. But in three decades working as an editor, I came to resent and distrust the absence of attribution. First at *The Wall Street Journal*, and then at Time Inc., I tried to ban unattributed quotes. But I learned there were limits to my power as editor in chief. Reporters and editors alike pushed back, insisting they couldn't do their work without giving sources anonymity. To see how successful my campaign was, consider this item on Britney Spears and Kevin Federline from a December 2005 issue of *People*:

With the sleepless nights, dirty diapers and high emotions that accompany young parenthood, perhaps the big blowup was inevitable. On Nov. 30, Britney Spears and her husband Kevin Federline had such a heated argument that, a source close to the couple says, Spears dropped the D word and Federline bolted from their Malibu home. "She wanted a divorce," says a friend of Spears's. And, says a source close to Federline, "When she's upset with him, he likes to give her some space. I don't think she's upset with him because of something specific he's done. I think she's overwhelmed with her new lifestyle—being a wife and mother—and sometimes takes it out on the people who she's closest to and who she knows will stick around." Spears's way of taking it out on her husband? By showing up that night at the L.A. club LAX and dancing into the wee hours with friends. "It was definitely a girls' night out," says a source. "Kevin was being punished."

Of course, Federline, 27, didn't seem too tortured during his own marathon weekend of clubbing in Las Vegas: First he and his all-male entourage hit Pure Nightclub, where he caught up with Nicole Richie's fiancé DJ AM, then partied at the club Tao Las Vegas until 4 a.m. In any case, the punishment proved short-lived. After her 25th birthday on Dec. 2, Spears took a quick jaunt to Vegas (where she checked into the Wynn Las Vegas resort, half a mile down the Strip from her husband's suite at The Venetian), then repaired to Louisiana to spend time with her mother, Lynne, and sister Jamie Lynn. But by Tuesday, according to a source close to the couple, she had settled back into her Malibu manse with her husband and their 3-month-old son Sean Preston. "This has happened before," says an insider. "They always work it out."

And thus goes the marry-go-round for the Federlines. While they've had their fair share of tiffs since their 2004 nuptials, a source close to the couple says this fight was the worst yet. And friends from both sides say the two share the blame for their recent strife. Says a source close to Spears: "Kevin can be dismissive of her, but Britney's all over the place emotionally."

Part of her anger, sources say, is her feeling that Federline is more fond of going out to a bumping club than staying home with a burping baby. But his friends scoff at the idea. If anything, says a Federline source, he's "more caring" since Spears gave birth to Sean Preston in September. "All of that is overblown," says the source. "He's only gone out a handful of times. He's tried so hard to help [Britney] after she had the baby."

And now they're each putting in the extra effort to mend their relationship. "Kevin loves her," says a Federline source. "He wants to make their marriage work." But will it? "Britney really loves him," says a source close to Spears. "They're back together." But as for their future, adds the source, "Who knows?"

A 516-word story cited unidentified "friends" or "sources" fifteen times! And this was in *People*, the magazine I thought did the best reporting at Time Inc. It wasn't as unusual an example as it should have been.

I knew from experience that some stories simply couldn't be done without confidential sources. Once, when I was working on a story about organized crime for the *Journal*, a Washington-based source who worked as a government lawyer insisted that I fly from Detroit to Miami for a secret meeting. We talked in a run-down Miami Beach motel for three days, with the shades drawn the entire time. He wouldn't let me photocopy any of his documents, but he allowed me to read them and to take notes in longhand. A Justice Department source for other stories refused to use office telephones when he called me because he assumed that they were tapped. Both of these government lawyers knew that a story in the *Journal* would pressure their superiors to devote more resources to their cases and help them get indictments.

Not all my sources worked behind a desk. While pursuing reports that mobsters were skimming Howard Hughes's Las Vegas casinos, I met a woman I came to call Michelle the Chip Hustler. Stunning and refined in a black dress and pearls, she mimicked Jackie Kennedy Onassis as she stalked the baccarat and high-stakes blackjack tables. Attaching herself to high rollers, "Michelle" cheered them on, making a modest living off their tips. Unlike prostitutes, she was a friend of the house, and she was as determined as the casino to keep the players at the tables. Pursuing her livelihood (and her gambling addiction), she had befriended many important pit bosses and had learned the finer points of skimming. She was also on a first-name basis with many of the shady characters who regularly flew into town for a few days of action. "Michelle" rightly feared for her livelihood, if not her life, were I to reveal that she was a source for my exposé. (That is why, more than thirty-five years later, I don't use her real name here.) Every reporter I know could tell a similar story.

So, I thought it routine when, on July 17, 2003, *Time*'s website ran a story by Matt Cooper identifying former ambassador Joseph Wilson's wife, Valerie Plame, as a CIA agent and attributing the information to "government officials." *Time*'s editors hadn't thought the story important enough to put into the magazine.

2

The Plame Episode

f Watergate began as a "third-rate burglary," the Valerie Plame episode began as something even less significant, a bit of Beltway politics played rough. A mean-spirited administration, less competent but more secretive than most, had been shown to be fiddling with the truth about its rationale for going to war. It responded by undermining its attacker's credibility through leaks that impugned his wife, revealing her CIA status in the process.

War with Iraq: George Bush and Dick Cheney wanted it. Paul Wolfowitz, the deputy secretary of defense, was pushing for it before and after September 11, 2001. *Time* reported that in March 2002 the President, referring to Saddam Hussein, told a group of senators, "We're taking him out," and Cheney told other senators that the question was no longer if the United States would attack Iraq, but when.

Saddam had tried to have Bush's father assassinated when the former President visited Kuwait in 1993. Although Cheney had been secretary of defense during the 1991 Gulf War, he subsequently came to believe that the United States should have toppled Saddam after chasing Iraq's military from Kuwait. Bob Woodward wrote in *Plan of Attack* that Wolfowitz favored war because it was "necessary and relatively easy."

President Bush, in his 2003 State of the Union address, gave three justifications for an attack on Iraq. First, he alleged that Iraq was developing weapons of mass destruction. Second, he charged that it supported terrorism and had ties to the terrorist group Al Qaeda. And third, the President claimed that "the British government has learned that Saddam Hussein recently sought significant quantities of uranium from Africa."

All three assertions were at best shaky and unproven, but the sixteen words asserting that Iraq had sought to buy uranium in Africa initially prompted the most suspicion. Beginning in October 2001, U.S. and British intelligence agencies had reported rumors that Niger had agreed to annual exports of as much as five hundred tons of "yellowcake," a widely available milled uranium concentrate that, when combined with fluorine and then converted into a gas, could eventually be used to create weapons-grade uranium. The reports were largely based on dubious assertions from various third-country nationals, including Rocco Martino, an Italian with suspect connections to his country's military-intelligence service, who had been trying to peddle a package of cables, memos, and letters supporting the reports about Iraq and Niger to the agencies. Some of the materials were obvious forgeries. (London's *Sunday Times* subsequently asserted that two employees of the Niger embassy in Rome had faked the documents, hoping intelligence agencies would pay for them.) In any case, the U.S. embassy in Niger gave the rumors little credence, in part because all of the yellowcake produced in Niger was controlled by an international, French-led consortium that had assured the embassy the reports of prospective sales were bogus.

Nonetheless, in February 2002 Vice President Cheney asked the CIA for additional analysis. Later that month, without Cheney's knowledge, the CIA sent Joseph C. Wilson IV, a retired career diplomat, to Niger, where he had served in the mid-1970s, to provide the agency with a fresh evaluation of the intelligence reports. Wilson knew Africa and he knew Iraq. He had served as chargé d'affaires in Baghdad in 1990. He next served in Gabon after receiving an appointment from President George H. W. Bush, then worked on Africa policy at the National Security Council under President Bill Clinton.

While in Niger in 2002, Wilson heard reports of an Iraqi trade mission to Niger several years earlier—presumably it was seeking yellowcake uranium, since Niger has little else to export. But after eight days spent meeting "dozens of people," including former Niger government officials, Wilson concluded it was highly unlikely that any transaction had taken place. After returning to Washington, he gave the CIA and the State Department oral briefings on his findings. There is no indication that his findings were restricted or classified.

Six months after Wilson's trip, the British government published a White Paper (a public, official document) asserting that Iraq had been trying to buy uranium from an unnamed African country a few years earlier. The CIA attached little credence to the British report, assuming it was based on Martino's documents, which it knew to be fake. Members of Bush's National Security Council, nonetheless, continued to assert that the Iraqis were trying to buy uranium to rebuild their nuclear capabilities—Israel had destroyed them when it bombed Iraq's Osirak nuclear reactor in 1981—and the British report's allegation ended up in President Bush's State of the Union speech. Less than two months later, on March 19, the United States attacked Iraq.

Wilson, upset by Bush's assertions about uranium in the address, believed that the preemptive war was based on false pretenses. On Sunday, July 6, he went public with his criticism. In an appearance on NBC's *Meet the Press*, in an interview in *The Washington Post*, and, most notably, in a signed opinion piece in *The New York Times* entitled "What I Didn't Find in Africa," Wilson attacked President Bush and

Vice President Cheney for their selective use of faulty intelligence to justify war with Iraq. Wilson's charges prompted many Democrats to accuse Bush of burying important intelligence, and it led reporters to seek comment from the administration. "There is zero, nada, nothing new here," White House spokesman Ari Fleischer told them.

But on July 11, CIA director George J. Tenet said in an official CIA statement that while the CIA had signed off on the passage in the President's State of the Union address in advance, the allegation that Iraq was trying to obtain uranium in Africa "should never have been included" in the speech. Tenet, apparently taking the heat for Bush, asserted that the CIA had found six reasons to believe Iraq was reconstituting its nuclear weapons program but that "the African uranium issue was not one of them."

And there Wilson's story might have ended, an incendiary but modest incident in the larger conflagration of the Iraq war.

Except that somebody decided to go after the man's wife.

The war over confidential sources first surfaced three days after Tenet admitted that the uranium claims shouldn't have been made—and three days before Matt Cooper and Time Inc. published our story online. On July 14, Robert Novak asserted in his column, which is syndicated in more than three hundred newspapers, including *The Washington Post*, that Wilson's wife, "Valerie Plame, is an agency operative on weapons of mass destruction." Furthermore, he wrote, "Two senior administration officials told me his wife suggested sending Wilson to Niger" to investigate the reports that Iraq was trying to buy uranium there—thus implying that Wilson's trip (and his challenge to the president) was not an act of government service but a politically motivated bit of nepotism.

Novak's story appeared just as the Washington press corps was giving intense scrutiny to Bush's rationale for attacking Iraq. The press had been accused of sleepwalking through the buildup for war, but with the invading force's failure to find those weapons of mass destruction on the ground in Iraq, everything was open to question.

Time had run a tough cover story, "Untruths & Consequences: How Flawed Was the Case for Going to War Against Saddam?" that appeared the same day as Novak's column did. The *Time* cover story described Wilson as someone who "seemed like a wise choice" to send to Niger on the CIA's behalf.

It was no surprise that the administration fought back after Wilson questioned its motives. By tipping off Novak and others, it was doing what it could to undermine Wilson. Given the laws of supply and demand, it wasn't surprising that reporters from many publications were chasing every aspect of the Wilson story.

On July 11, the day of Tenet's apologia for the CIA and three days before Novak's piece was published, Matthew Cooper, *Time's* White House correspondent, had learned that Plame worked at the CIA. Six days later, on July 17, *Time's* website ran a story by Cooper and two other reporters, Massimo Calabresi and John F. Dickerson, titled "A War on Wilson? Inside the Bush Administration's feud with the diplomat who poured cold water on the Iraq-uranium connection."

The Time.com piece, written and primarily reported by Cooper, began, "Has the Bush Administration declared war on a former ambassador who conducted a fact-finding mission to probe possible Iraqi interest in African uranium? Perhaps." The story asserted, "Administration officials have taken public and private whacks at Wilson," after he publicized his criticisms. It said that some government officials have noted "that Wilson's wife, Valerie Plame, is a CIA official who monitors the proliferation of weapons of mass destruction." The story went on to raise the issue of possible misconduct by the administration officials, asserting that they had hoped to undermine Wilson's credibility by revealing his wife's alleged support for his trip.

I. Lewis (Scooter) Libby, Cheney's chief of staff and a crucial named and unnamed source for the story, agreed to be quoted saying, "The Vice President was unaware of the trip by Ambassador Wilson and didn't know about it until this year when it became public in the last month or so."

On July 22, *Newsday* reported that Plame worked undercover in the Directorate of Operations "alongside the operations officers who asked her husband to travel to Niger." *Newsday's* Washington bureau chief, Timothy M. Phelps, quoted Novak as saying of his Plame scoop, "I didn't dig it out, it was given to me," by sources who thought it significant.

Those stories prompted calls for an investigation from Democrats in Congress, notably Senator Charles Schumer of New York, who demanded that the FBI launch a criminal investigation to determine who had leaked Plame's identity. Schumer noted that under the Intelligence Identities Protection Act "the unauthorized disclosure of information relating to the identity of an American intelligence official is a crime punishable by fines and up to ten years in prison."

There things stood at the beginning of the fall. Then, on September 28, *The Washington Post* confirmed an MSNBC report that CIA director Tenet had asked the Justice Department to investigate whether the publication of Plame's name and the nature of her work at the CIA violated federal laws. The *Post* also reported that two top White House officials (whom it did not name) had called half a dozen Washington journalists in the days before Novak's column was published, disclosing (or "leaking") Plame's name and occupation to each of them. Echoing Cooper's assertion in the Time.com story, the *Post* reported that an unnamed senior administration official acknowledged that the leaks were "meant purely and simply for revenge."

Rumors spread through Washington that Karl Rove, then President Bush's chief political adviser, was among the leakers, but Scott McClellan, who had replaced Ari Fleischer as White House press secretary, said it was "simply not true" that Rove was involved, adding that any administration official who leaked classified information "would no longer be in this administration."

Following publication of the *Post*'s story, the Justice Department told the White House on September 30 that it had opened an investigation. Eleven hours later, Alberto R. Gonzales, then White House counsel, directed all White House employees to preserve all documents concerning the Plame episode, including electronic and telephone records, from February 1, 2002, onward. That same day President Bush said, "If there is a leak out of my administration, I want to know who it is. And if the person has violated the law, the person will be taken care of."

Senator Schumer and other Democrats, including Congressman John Conyers Jr., the ranking minority member on the House Judiciary Committee, said they distrusted an administration-led investigation, arguing that conflicts of interest precluded Attorney General John Ashcroft, then head of the Justice Department, from conducting a thorough and unbiased investigation of the White House. They also complained that the eleven-hour delay in the issuance of Gonzales's directive had given employees plenty of time to destroy their notes. Senator Hillary Clinton, who had questioned the motives of Kenneth Starr, the independent counsel who had investigated her husband during the Whitewater and Lewinsky scandals, joined other Democrats in demanding that Ashcroft recuse himself and that the Justice Department appoint an outside special counsel to run the investigation.

Not unlike a general calling for air strikes on his own troops, *The New York Times* joined the chorus advocating an investigation of leaks to the press. An editorial published on October 2, 2003, cited Justice Department guidelines that would permit Attorney General Ashcroft "to appoint an outsider" who could make "independent decisions." I could not find another time that the *Times* had editorialized in favor of an investigation of leaks to news organizations.

Despite these demands for outside investigators, the FBI and the Justice Department continued their own investigations for almost three months. They did so in part because several senior CIA officials had asked them to do so, citing their concern about the way Plame's identity had been disclosed. Those officials worried that once Plame's undercover status had been revealed, her contacts might be endangered and other secrets might become public. In early October, Walter Pincus and Mike Allen had reported in the *Post* that disclosure of Plame's name had exposed the identity of Brewster-Jennings & Associates as a CIA front company. The company's identity became public because it appeared on a form Plame had filled out when she contributed a thousand dollars to Al Gore's presidential primary campaign.

In November 2003, an FBI agent, Christopher Kay, called Matt Cooper at the magazine's Washington bureau. Kay asked Cooper if he would disclose the sources for his story. Cooper referred the call to Time Inc.'s lawyers in New York, who rejected the request. Kay's conversation with the lawyers was cordial, but the agent ended it on an ominous note when he asked what address should be used should the government want to issue a subpoena.

Then, on December 30, the Justice Department made an announcement that stunned Washington: Ashcroft had recused himself from the investigation, and Patrick J. Fitzgerald, the U.S. attorney for the Northern District of Illinois, had been appointed to continue it as a special counsel.

Following Fitzgerald's appointment, the *Times* wrote another editorial, "The Right Thing, at Last," praising Ashcroft's recusal from the investigation, cheering on Fitzgerald's appointment—and inadvertently undermining the press's efforts to protect a reporter's confidential sources. It was a harbinger of how strange this story would become.

3

Patrick Fitzgerald

Surprising as the appointment of a special counsel was—it suggested that the investigation involved high-level administration officials close to the attorney general—there was no faulting the choice of Pat Fitzgerald. Still in his early forties, he had gained a reputation as one of America's toughest, smartest, and most apolitical prosecutors.

Fitzgerald was born in 1960 to Irish immigrants in Brooklyn's Flatbush neighborhood. He attended Regis High School, a prestigious Jesuit secondary school in Manhattan, and majored in mathematics and economics at Amherst, where he received his bachelor's degree in 1982, before getting a degree from Harvard Law School. His father had worked as a doorman at an apartment building on the Upper East Side of Manhattan, and Fitzgerald had also worked as a doorman in the summer while attending college and law school.

Fitzgerald was a lawyer in private practice for three years before becoming an assistant U.S. attorney in New York in 1988. Over the next thirteen years, he helped prosecute Mafia boss John Gotti, tried and convicted Sheikh Omar Abdel-Rahman and others charged in the 1993 World Trade Center bombing, and investigated Osama bin Laden. Fitzgerald was appointed U.S. attorney for Northern Illinois in late 2001. Two years later, he indicted former Illinois Republican governor George Ryan in a bribery case. The indictment led to Ryan's conviction. He also made his mark in cases involving organized and white-collar crime, and he chaired a committee on terrorism for the U.S. attorney general.

Along the way, Fitzgerald developed an idealistic view of government service. In an interview with the Regis High School newspaper, he noted that in private practice "if your client wants to do something, you have to take that position even if it's a position that you don't agree with." But as a federal prosecutor, he said, "My job every day is to do the right thing."

Peter Fitzgerald (no relation), the former Republican senator from Illinois, told *The Washington Post* that he pushed Pat Fitzgerald's nomination for the U.S. attorney's job in his state after then FBI head Louis Freeh told him that Fitzgerald was "the best assistant U.S. attorney" in the country. The senator added that he wanted someone for the job who was free of taint and couldn't be unduly influenced. The Justice Department official who announced his appointment as special counsel called him "Eliot Ness with a Harvard law degree."

Despite Fitzgerald's reputation, I didn't immediately see any problem for *Time.* The leaks about Wilson's connection to Plame seemed typical of the conversations between reporters and government sources that had been essential to the way Washington had functioned since the founding of the republic. As President John F. Kennedy, columnist James Reston, and others have famously observed, "The Ship of State is the only ship that leaks at the top." Plame's outing might have been nasty, but it was hardly out of the ordinary. "Who cares and so what?" I asked myself.

The Justice Department had appointed Fitzgerald pursuant to regulations that require a special counsel be named whenever a criminal investigation by the DOJ "would present a conflict of interest." I understood that Fitzgerald would be given a broad mandate and a big budget, and that he had a proven ability to make waves. I had thought the first Independent Counsel Statute, passed in 1978, made sense in the aftermath of President Nixon's firing of Archibald Cox, the Watergate special prosecutor. But Kenneth Starr's investigation of Bill Clinton and Monica Lewinsky in the 1990s, and Lawrence E. Walsh's earlier Iran-contra investigation, had burned through tens of millions of dollars, failing any cost-benefit analysis. In addition, thirteen of the twenty independent counsels appointed under the statute had failed to bring criminal cases at all. I thought Congress had done the right thing when it let the act expire in 1999.

I realized that it was often impossible to identify a leaker without testimony from the reporter who received the leak. But Justice's own guidelines imposed tight restrictions on when reporters could be interviewed.

Fitzgerald convened a grand jury in early January 2004. Grand juries, in theory, are critical to the American system of jurisprudence. They are used to determine if a prosecutor has enough evidence to go to trial. They meet in secret and they can compel witnesses to testify before them. Although first used in twelfth-century England, grand juries exist today only in the United States. The Fifth Amendment to the Constitution states, "No person shall be held to answer for a capital, or otherwise infamous crime, unless on a presentment or indictment of a Grand Jury." Although originally intended to impose a check on the prosecutor, in modern practice grand juries rarely oppose a prosecutor's wish to indict. As disbarred former New York State chief judge Sol Wachtler once said, "A grand jury would indict a ham sandwich."

Because prosecutors are forbidden to discuss grand jury proceedings with the press or the general public, Fitzgerald wouldn't need to explain what he was investigating or why. A few days after his

4

Subpoenas and Secrecy

Matt Cooper is a stand-up guy, in more ways than one. A journalist with more than twenty years of experience, he is a respected member of the Beltway's press establishment, having edited *The Washington Monthly* in the 1980s, covered the White House for *U.S. News & World Report* in the mid-1990s, and worked as a national correspondent for *Newsweek* for three years before being named deputy Washington bureau chief of *Time* in 1999.

Matt is the very model of the "Washington insider." Bill and Hillary Clinton attended his 1997 wedding to Mandy Grunwald, a media adviser who had done advertising spots for Bill Clinton's presidential campaign. (Mandy is the daughter of Henry Grunwald, one of my predecessors as editor in chief of Time Inc.)

He is also a stand-up comedian of some renown, having been voted "Washington's Funniest Celebrity" in 1998. As a kid, he would entertain his classmates doing impersonations of his teachers. In later years his takes on Presidents Bill Clinton and George H. W. Bush were pitch-perfect, as was his impersonation of S. I. Newhouse, the idiosyncratic owner of the Condé Nast magazine group, which includes *Portfolio*, the new business magazine where Matt now works. After John Kerry called himself a "rebel," Cooper quipped,

"Kerry's idea of rebellion is having red wine with fish." And when Howard Dean proclaimed himself in favor of gay rights and against gun control, Cooper praised him for locking up the "gay hunter vote." When asked what it is like to do stand-up, Cooper replied, "It's about as close as you can get to that dream you have of walking into class naked."

When he wrote his Valerie Plame story, he had been on the White House beat for a short time, having moved back to writing from his deputy's job in the *Time* bureau. So it's understandable that—in the neurotically competitive community of the Washington press corps—he was less than perfectly discreet after he got Karl Rove on the phone on Friday, July 11, 2003, to talk about Plame. Shortly after ending the conversation, he wrote an e-mail to his bureau chief, Michael Duffy, and to Jay Carney, Matt's replacement as deputy, as follows:

> Spoke to Rove on double super secret background for about two mins before he went on vacation . . . his big warning . . . don't get too far out on Wilson . . . says that the DCIA didn't authorize the trip and that Cheney didn't authorize the trip. It was, KR said, wilson's wife, who apparently works at the agency on wmd issues, who authorized the trip. Not only the genesis of the trip is flawd ans suspect but so is the report. He implied strongly there's still plenty to implicate Iraqi interest in acquiring uranium fron Niger . . . some of this is going to be dclassified in the coming days, KR said. Don't get out too far out in front, he warned. Then he bolted . . .

Later in the day, in an e-mail exchange with Adi Ignatius, an executive editor in New York, Cooper again named Rove as his source, stating that the conversation was on "deep background."

Cooper reached Libby the next afternoon, a few hours before *Time*'s issue for that week would close. Cooper would later write that he was "wet, smelling of chlorine" after an afternoon of swimming at friends' "fancy Washington country club." Since the club didn't allow the use of cell phones, Cooper kept "running from pool to parking lot to try to reach Libby, who was traveling to Norfolk, Va. with Vice President Dick Cheney for the commissioning of the U.S.S. Ronald Reagan. Eventually I raced home without showering in order to take Libby's call."

Libby and Cooper spoke for a few minutes. His notes show that during that short conversation, Libby gave Cooper an on-the-record quote, distancing Cheney from Wilson's fact-finding trip to Africa for the CIA. On deep background, which Matt defined as meaning "you can use in your voice but without quotation," Libby told Cooper that Cheney hadn't asked that the yellowcake line be put in the president's speech. Libby then went off the record to charge that Wilson had omitted from his criticisms of Bush a key fact that suggested the Iraqis might in fact have been trying to buy uranium from Niger.

Matt had called Rove and Libby seeking comment for the cover package, "A Question of Trust." After speaking to Libby, Matt wrote his editors, "The pissing match with Wilson is where the whole story could be by Mon or Tues so suggest we play it with prominence." He was right, but his editors thought the information tangential to the cover package.

So Cooper recycled the information he had received in a follow-up story for the website. That story appeared on Time.com on July 17, six days after Cooper had first learned about Plame from Rove. By then, more than two dozen Time Inc. employees—in *Time*'s Washington and New York offices, at the website, and on various IT staffs—had had access to e-mails in which Matt had named Rove as his source. Cooper's notes and memos from the Libby interview were less problematic. There was no mention that, in response to a question from Matt, Libby had said he too had heard rumors Plame had been responsible for sending Wilson to Niger.

At the time the grand jury was convened six months later, however, I hadn't seen Cooper's e-mails and I wasn't aware of how many people had seen them. Nor did I know the identity of his sources, the information they had provided, or the ground rules for the interviews. Only after Matt received a subpoena from Fitzgerald many months later did I learn he believed he must keep Rove's identity confidential. There was also the off-the-record portion of Matt's interview with Scooter Libby that he said should also be treated as if it were confidential.

There is a big difference between anonymous sources, whose identity we would pledge to keep out of our publications, and confidential sources, whose identity we would protect in the face of court orders and contempt citations. All confidential sources are anonymous, but most anonymous sources are not confidential. An anonymous source won't see his or her name in the publication. The commitment to maintain a source's anonymity is serious and worth defending in the courts. But if you lose in the courts, you give up the name. A confidential source has a contractual relationship with a reporter and with the publication. That contract should be adhered to even if the courts hold against the reporter and publication and the reporter and publication are held in contempt—unless, of course, the source grants a waiver. There might be other exceptions, such as the source lying to the reporter or the reporter realizing that the grant of confidential source status could lead to war, kidnapping, and so on. But it is a contract that should be negotiated and adhered to. Given what a grant of confidentiality implies, reporters and their publishers should be reluctant to grant confidential source status to anyone except in the most important and most exceptional stories. Since we routinely litigated to protect anonymous and confidential sources, I believed the distinction would become relevant only if we were unsuccessful in the courts. That was a serious mistake. I would continue to make it in the months to come.

Putting Rove's and Libby's names in e-mails undermined Matt's commitment (as he understood it) to treat both men as confidential sources. In Matt's defense, he was primarily a political reporter, and political reporters don't expect legal repercussions from talking to their sources. Few such reporters instinctively think about subpoenas, contempt citations, and possible jail sentences when they are engaged in brief interviews, especially when there hasn't been a specific commitment to grant the source confidentiality. Getting Karl Rove to answer a query was a big deal, even for *Time*.

But experienced investigative reporters, covering national security and other sensitive subjects, know to keep their sources to themselves and never to put their names in e-mails. E-mails create a permanent record, subject to legal discovery. They create far more risks for the sender than do telephone calls.

Matt's e-mails went to senior news executives in Washington and New York. He didn't intend that they be widely disseminated. Neither he nor anyone else at *Time* stopped to think about how many people might have access to them. It was troubling to learn later that the identity of Matt's sources was also the subject of watercooler conversation among some fellow members of *Time*'s Washington bureau in the days following his interviews with Rove and Libby.

On May 21, 2004, Cooper received a subpoena ordering him to appear before the grand jury. Although Calabresi and Dickerson had shared the byline with Matt on the Time.com story, they weren't served since Fitzgerald had accepted our stipulation that they had not dealt with confidential sources on the Plame part of the story. Matt, however, was instructed to bring "all notes, tape recordings, e-mails, or other documents" relating to the website article and to a separate article that appeared in the *Time* magazine that was on the newsstands when Cooper's story appeared online. (In preparing the two articles, Cooper had sent more than fifty e-mails to his editors.) The magazine article, "A Question of Trust," prepared by eight *Time* staffers including Cooper, was part of the "Untruths and Consequences" cover package. The story had focused on the yellowcake saga, explaining how the sixteen-word sentence about Iraqi efforts to buy uranium in Africa ended up in the President's State of the Union speech. Referring to Tenet's July 11 statement, it had said, "In what looked like a command performance of political sacrifice, the head of the agency that expressed some of the strongest doubts about the charge took responsibility for the President's unsubstantiated claim." The story went on to ask, "Where else did the U.S. stretch evidence to generate public support for the war?"

The day the subpoenas were served, I met with Jim Kelly, *Time's* managing editor, and with Robin Bierstedt, Time Inc.'s deputy general counsel and the most senior lawyer responsible for cases involving the First Amendment, libel, and the use of anonymous sources. We were going to hash through what, if any, laws might have been broken.

Time had reported in October 2003 that Plame had worked abroad for the CIA through much of the 1990s. Plame, who posed as a private energy analyst, was a "NOC," *Time* wrote, "that is, a spy with nonofficial cover who worked overseas as a private individual with no apparent connection to the U.S. government." NOCs are harder to train, expensive to place, and are "among the government's most closely guarded secrets," *Time* said, because they can "remain undercover longer than conventional spooks" and can "go places and see people whom those under official cover cannot." She was not, however, a "deep-cover NOC," since the CIA hadn't created a complex cover story that reinvented her biography, making it more difficult for foreign governments to identify her as an agent.

Outing Plame was sleazy and shameless, and it blew her cover and her career. After Novak's column was published, officials with two foreign governments told *Time* their counterintelligence offices were checking whether she had worked in their countries and, if so, what she had done there. Plame would testify in March 2007 that she was a "covert" officer at the agency when her identity was revealed. Nonetheless, my reading of the Intelligence Identities Protection Act of 1982 and other laws meant to protect national security convinced me that no laws had been broken.

The 1982 act had been passed largely in response to the efforts of a former CIA agent, Philip Agee, to name thousands of undercover agents in books and newsletters that were published between 1975 and 1978.

Although Plame was clearly undercover, I didn't think she met the law's strict definition of "covert" at the time her identity was revealed. Among other things, the law requires that the "covert" agent "has within the last five years served outside the United States." Joe Wilson had recently published his book, *The Politics of Truth: Inside the Lies That Led to War and Betrayed My Wife's CIA Identity: A Diplomat's Memoir.* In it, Wilson said that Plame had returned to the United States in late 1997, more than five years before her identity was revealed in July of 2003. Overseas trips after returning to the United States to live would not meet the test for what constitutes "served." Moreover, Fred Rustmann, who had been Plame's boss for five years in the 1990s, speculated in an interview with *Time* that he thought that Plame's cover began to unravel when Wilson first asked her out, soon after her return to the United States. It unraveled further when she and Wilson, a high-profile diplomat, were married in April 1998.

Beyond that, the law required that the leak had come from a government official who had "authorized access" to classified information and had "intentionally" revealed it, even though the leaker knew that the government was "taking affirmative measures to conceal" the agent's identity. From what I had read, I thought it would be tough to prove that the CIA was taking such "affirmative measures" or that either Rove or Libby was acting with unlawful intent.

The law, which contains penalties of up to ten years' imprisonment and a $50,000 fine, is so difficult to enforce that only one person had been prosecuted in the decades since the act was passed. That was Sharon Scranage, a twenty-nine-year-old CIA operations support assistant in Ghana, who served eight months in prison after pleading guilty in 1985 to violating the law when she told her boyfriend, a cousin of Ghana's military ruler, the names of two agents.

I assumed Fitzgerald would also look at the Privacy Act, especially after Congressman Henry A. Waxman, a Democrat and the ranking minority member of the House Committee on Government Reform, had asked if the act had been violated. But the Privacy Act—which treats illegal disclosures of information about government employees as a misdemeanor subject to fines of up to $5,000 but no jail time—didn't seem to carry harsh enough penalties to merit the special counsel's attention.

There was, of course, the theoretical possibility that the leakers could be tried under the Espionage Act of 1917, which, as amended in 1950, provided penalties for the leaking of confidential information. But the statute was more concerned with spies than with leakers.

Kelly, Bierstedt, and I decided that Matt should resist the subpoena. There was nothing unusual in this—it was what we and other publications did routinely when confronted with prosecutors or plaintiffs using subpoenas to obtain information we didn't want to disclose. We also decided to hire Floyd Abrams to defend us.

Abrams, a partner in the New York firm of Cahill, Gordon & Reindel, was famous for serving as co-counsel to *The New York Times* in the Pentagon Papers case in the early 1970s, successfully defending the paper's right to publish classified material leaked to it by a disaffected Defense Department adviser, Daniel Ellsberg. Abrams had represented *Time* in the past, most notably in a decade-long and ultimately successful defense against a libel suit from the Church of Scientology. Although there was some grumbling about his fees, there was no quarrel with his results.

Bierstedt had recommended Abrams, and I had embraced her recommendation. Abrams had become the preeminent defender of press freedom in the decades since his triumph in the Pentagon Papers case, speaking and writing frequently on libel, free speech, and the protection of confidential sources. Fred Friendly, former president of CBS News, once said that Abrams "is to First Amendment rights what Clarence Darrow was to the rights of the accused." The late senator Daniel Patrick Moynihan called Abrams "the most significant First Amendment lawyer of our age."

He was well known for his appearances before the Supreme Court and for representing the media in such high-profile cases as Las Vegas singer Wayne Newton's libel suit against NBC. (In that case, NBC had reported that the Nevada Gaming Commission had granted Newton a license to run the casino at the Aladdin Hotel after he had provided false testimony to it. At the trial, Abrams was unable to overcome the city's obvious affection for Newton. "A taxi ride into the city required driving on Wayne Newton Boulevard," he wrote. "If a visitor was very lucky, his driver might tell him that his arrival date coincided with the celebration . . . of Wayne Newton Day." The jury found for Newton, and a judgment of more than $22 million was entered. A federal appellate court reversed that decision, and the Supreme Court declined to hear the case, leaving the reversal intact.)

Abrams had a solid, dedicated team working with him, and many members of the First Amendment bar had apprenticed at his knee. His quiet demeanor belied a tough, competitive streak. He thought reporters and publishers should resist any government effort to interfere with their work. His absolutism gave journalists confidence and comfort. I was among the many proud members of Floyd Abrams's fan club.

I had also admired Robin Bierstedt. During her two decades at Time Inc., she had developed a national reputation as one of the toughest, most passionate lawyers working on libel and First Amendment cases. Reporters elsewhere might feel corporate pressure to seek compromises with prosecutors and plaintiffs, but Bierstedt was known for her unyielding support for public service journalism.

I thought Time Inc. and Cooper should keep a relatively low profile, preferring to make our arguments in court and to avoid inflammatory statements and articles. Kelly would speak for Cooper and for *Time*. He and Bierstedt would keep me apprised of developments, and I would stay in the background. I saw no need to brief top management at Time Warner on the case, as neither *Time* nor Time Inc. had received subpoenas.

Three days after Cooper received his subpoena, Fitzgerald called Abrams to say he was willing to limit the subpoena to questions about Libby. Abrams was initially reluctant to have Matt ask Libby for a waiver of confidentiality. He reasoned that any contact might smack of coercion, putting undue pressure on a confidential source. He also argued, more persuasively, that such contact was premature. If we had a chance of getting the subpoena quashed by the federal district judge, why get involved in negotiations with the source? Bierstedt, Kelly, and I agreed.

Instead of contacting Libby or his lawyer, Abrams filed motions to resist Cooper's subpoena with the federal district court for the District of Columbia. Those motions argued that the grand jury's subpoenas violated a reporter's right to keep his sources confidential, a privilege that we said was embodied in the First Amendment, the common law, and the District of Columbia's shield law.

Cooper submitted an affidavit detailing his experience and the importance of confidential sources for much of his reporting. In it, he said:

> I have reported extensively for TIME's four million–plus readers about White House policy in Iraq, the chances of passage of major legislation such as Budget and Energy Bills, and the Clinton White House. This month I revealed to TIME's readers and the public, in a story that gained wide notice, that President Bush displays Saddam Hussein's personal pistol as a trophy in the White House. I would not have been able to report on any of these matters—or countless other newsworthy stories—without being able to promise confidentiality to my sources . . . Some of the most important journalism in American history has depended on confidential sources, such as the figure identified as 'Deep Throat' during the Watergate period. Without confidential sources, it would be virtually impossible to effectively investigate and report on current government issues, including government scandals. This would deprive the public of critical information.

Fitzgerald responded by filing an affidavit of his own, detailing his investigation and his need for Cooper's testimony. Invoking the need for grand jury secrecy, he refused to share his affidavit with Abrams. On July 20, the district court denied Cooper's request to review Fitzgerald's affidavit.

In early August, Fitzgerald raised the stakes. He subpoenaed Time Inc. His subpoena asked us to appear before the grand jury with all of Cooper's "notes, tape recordings, e-mails, or other documents" related to the online article and to "A Question of Trust," the article that had appeared in *Time*.

The Time Inc. subpoena changed the game and my role in it. It raised the possibility that Fitzgerald might want to issue subpoenas to anyone who had had custody of or had seen Matt's e-mails about Rove and Libby and the e-mail traffic they'd generated, both of which I considered corporate property. If held in contempt for withholding the materials, Matt might face jail and Time Inc. might face fines. Although I thought it unlikely that fines would be large enough to have much impact on Time Inc.'s or Time Warner's bottom line, I had an obligation to brief a number of corporate executives after receiving the subpoena.

In early August 2004 we began to revisit the idea of seeking a waiver from Libby. Matt had retained Richard Sauber, a Washington-based lawyer who worked for or was friendly with many of the city's prominent journalists. A *Washington Post* reporter, Glenn Kessler, had also received a subpoena. His lawyers negotiated an agreement with Fitzgerald under which Kessler provided testimony limited to his conversations with Libby in early July 2003. Kessler told Fitzgerald that Libby had not disclosed Plame's identity to him, but apparently wasn't asked broader questions about other information or other sources.

After several discussions in July and early August, Abrams and Bierstedt agreed that Matt could call Libby and ask for a waiver of confidentiality. Cooper made the call on August 5. He told Libby that if he was freed to testify, he would tell the grand jury that Libby hadn't identified Plame in their conversation. Libby told Matt that he was inclined to grant the waiver. He asked, however, that Abrams call his lawyer, Joseph A. Tate, to negotiate it. Abrams did so the following week.

Fitzgerald, however, wasn't sitting still while we were negotiating with Libby. Nor was Thomas F. Hogan, the district court judge who was hearing the case. Before we could get Libby's waiver, Hogan, the chief judge of the federal court for the District of Columbia and a Reagan appointee, held Cooper and Time Inc. in civil contempt for not complying with the subpoenas. On August 9, he ruled that Matt was to be jailed and Time Inc. was to be fined $1,000 a day. Hogan's ruling was all about the legal precedents governing our case. Inadvertently but inexorably, it prompted a return to what I had spent much of my life running away from.

5

A Journalist's Education

I was born to be a lawyer. My father was the senior partner in a twenty-man suburban-Philadelphia law firm that included six of my relatives. As a child I would sit for hours in his office, watching him dictate briefs and contracts, while playing with the toy cars and trucks he had bought to amuse me. As I crashed them into each other, he would explain negligence, contributory negligence, and "pain and suffering."

As a young teen, I was put in charge of the firm's "dead files," cataloging and storing the oppressively routine matters that filled the subbasement of the converted town house that served as his office. "Conshohocken Saving & Loan." "North Penn School Board." "Trusts & Estates (Misc.)." Only the divorce files, with allegations of adultery, alienation of affection, and third-party co-respondents, provided lurid details that could occasionally compete with the copies of *Playboy* I hid behind the file cabinets.

Although I played a secondary role on my prep school's newspaper, I was the president of Q.E.D. (*Quod Erat Demonstrandum*, Latin for "which was to be determined" or "demonstrated"), the school's championship debate team. When I spoke, I was told I sounded just like my father.

Journalism didn't matter until college. I spent my summers working for newspapers in Allentown, Pennsylvania, and Philadelphia. I learned the importance of accuracy. My first week in Allentown, I was nearly fired after writing an obituary for Mrs. Druckemiller—I had spelled it Drunkenmiller.

I was fascinated by the range of subjects a reporter could write about, and I loved the instant gratification that accompanied a by-lined story. I also saw the power of the press, to punish and to reward, fairly and unfairly, during a summer as a police reporter for *The Philadelphia Inquirer*. I often covered west Philadelphia and the Main Line suburbs, where the paper's owner, Walter Annenberg, lived. The night editor had given me a list of Annenberg's acquaintances, and I was told to keep it with me at all times, to make sure we never printed something bad about a friend or something favorable to one of the owner's many enemies. I once did some legwork for Harry Karafin, the *Inquirer*'s most feared investigative reporter. Karafin often broke stories with the help of anonymous police sources. He went to jail after he was convicted of extortion in 1968 for taking thousands of dollars from companies he promised not to write about. Walter Annenberg became a patriotic, philanthropic American, and he helped fund great schools of communications at the University of Pennsylvania and the University of Southern California. But his *Inquirer* was a terrible newspaper.

I also worked on the college paper at Haverford, editing it my senior year. My fellow editors on the *Haverford News* included John Carroll, who went on to be the editor of the *Los Angeles Times*, and Loren Ghiglione, who became the dean of the Medill journalism school at Northwestern.

It was also at Haverford—a Quaker college whose students were more likely to be conscientious objectors than to enlist for military service in Vietnam—that I first read and thought about passive resistance and civil disobedience, coming to appreciate its power when confronting unjust and arbitrary laws. I read everything from Gandhi to Thoreau to Bertrand Russell to the earliest writings of Howard Zinn. The *Inquirer* sent me to Cambridge, Maryland, during the summer of 1963 to cover civil rights sit-ins, and I spent time with representatives of the Student Nonviolent Coordinating Committee (SNCC).

I was confused about the law, about society, about journalism, and about myself. There had always been pressure to join the family law firm, but I had loved my early newspaper experiences. After college, I was accepted by Columbia Journalism School and the law school of the University of Pennsylvania. Acceding to family pressure, I went to law school, but I skipped many classes and, in a lame act of defiance, read six newspapers a day. I worked as a legislative assistant to Richard S. Schweiker, then a Republican congressman from my home county, between my first and second years at law school. I learned to draft bills, wrote speeches on arcane subjects such as Captive Nations Day, and, most enjoyably, got to know the reporters from the *Inquirer* and the Philadelphia *Evening Bulletin* who covered the congressman.

The next summer I worked as an intern for Anthony G. Amsterdam, Penn's superstar, a tenured law professor at twenty-nine, who was already considered one of America's foremost civil rights attorneys. In addition to teaching criminal and constitutional law, Amsterdam worked insane hours as an unpaid attorney for the American Civil Liberties Union and the NAACP Legal Defense Fund Inc. One week I went to work each day an hour earlier and left an hour later in the hope that I might be there before Amsterdam arrived or after he left. I concluded that he never left the office during that seven-day period.

As one of Amsterdam's assistants—a position I held through much of my third year in law school—I did research on civil rights and capital punishment, and I once drafted an appellate brief for one of his death-row clients. I was also a leader of the local chapter of the Law Students Civil Rights Research Council. When I graduated from law school, the only job offers I received were from the NAACP Legal Defense Fund Inc. and, of course, the family law firm.

The pressures to join my father's practice seemed overwhelming. But I had benefited from psychoanalysis while in law school, trying to deal with my conflicting feelings about life and work. Thus fortified, I was ready to flee the stifling, albeit loving, family embrace, leaving southeastern Pennsylvania and the law.

I passed the bar exams in Pennsylvania and the District of Columbia, only to join *The New York Times* in the summer of 1967 as a copyboy. It was a terrible job. While veteran reporters lived in fear of the legendary A. M. Rosenthal, who was then an assistant managing editor, I was being terrorized by Sammy Solovitz, the head of the copyboys. One of a number of sins could lead to instant dismissal: no whistling while walking around the copy desks; no touching lead type in the composing room, lest it lead to a walkout by the unionized typesetters.

One of my jobs was to go from Times Square across town at midnight to pick up the final edition of the *Daily News*, then headquartered at 220 East Forty-second Street. The night I learned I had passed my bar exams, I celebrated by drinking seven beers at the printers' bar behind the *News*'s presses, and, drunk, I returned to the *Times* with an early edition of the *News*, instead of the final everyone was waiting for. I was nearly fired. Dealing with trusts and estates in the family firm was beginning to look good.

After four months at the *Times*, however, I was hired into *The Wall Street Journal*'s Dallas bureau as a staff reporter. My law degree had more to do with the *Journal*'s hiring me than did my journalism experience. After joining the *Journal*, I became fascinated by business and business news. Every human emotion, aspiration, or foible could be found there.

Determined not to disappoint my new employers, I signed up for postgraduate courses in securities and commodities law at Southern Methodist University, hoping to make up for the classes I had skipped at Penn. I did so with a typical northern snob's approach to southern education. All I knew about SMU was that Doak Walker, Kyle Rote, and Don Meredith had played football there, and I assumed the night classes would burnish my résumé without much effort on my part.

I was wrong. My professor, Alan Bromberg, was tougher and smarter than most of my Haverford and Penn professors, and most of my classmates were practicing attorneys. After three years of engaging in Socratic dialogue and reading appellate decisions at Penn, I was ready to sit on the Supreme Court, but I couldn't draft a simple contract. I learned at SMU that a question need not be answered with another question. A typical assignment might require me to write a registration statement for a company planning a public offering or to draft a complaint in a civil case involving commodities fraud.

Although business was at the core of its coverage, the *Journal*'s readers valued and expected superb coverage of politics and important social issues. The *Journal* was also committed to tough exposés and to great storytelling. Unlike the *Times*, the *Journal* had no star or seniority system. It was a meritocracy where the youngest reporters could get and keep a big national story if they were good enough to cover it.

Shortly after joining the *Journal*, I was sent to Memphis to cover a march by striking garbage workers. It was led by the Reverend Martin Luther King Jr. I was the last reporter to interview him before he was assassinated, and I wrote about his death and its aftermath in Memphis—one of the biggest stories of 1968. I also covered oil and gas, the pipeline industry, and a couple of big securities fraud trials.

I had my lapses. I was sent to rural New Mexico to write about life on a hippie commune, the Hog Farm, which was run by Hugh

Romney, better known to generations of freaks everywhere as Wavy Gravy. The assignment was supposed to last a week. I stayed nearly a month, embracing "free love," grass, peyote, and other hallucinogens. But I realized that news was my one true addiction, and I returned to the *Journal* determined to excel.

I was transferred to Detroit in 1970, where I covered the Big Three automakers and the United Auto Workers. In 1971 I was sent to the *Journal*'s Los Angeles bureau. I covered Las Vegas, where I wrote about mobsters, Howard Hughes, and the Mormons who guarded him, as well as the West Coast aerospace industry and cocaine-snorting music moguls in Hollywood.

I became comfortable socializing with my sources, including many CEOs. Many of my best stories came from people I had befriended. While writing a profile of Ross Perot in Dallas, I babysat his children on a couple of occasions. Lee Iacocca and I began a thirty-five-year friendship the night he realized I was dating his daughter's French teacher—the kid was flunking French. While covering the GM autoworkers' strike, I befriended an assembly worker who had come to Detroit to serve on the UAW's strike committee. He had left his wife and seven children at home. I drank beer and ate pizza with him and his nineteen-year-old girlfriend several nights a week, gaining twenty-five pounds while the strike dragged on.

There is an active debate among journalists about the wisdom of befriending sources. My best sources tended to be people I knew and had spent time with. But there is also the risk of getting too close to sources, losing perspective, even coming to act like the sources rather than like a reporter. Watergate, after all, was broken by Bob Woodward and Carl Bernstein, two young reporters without sources, while experienced beat reporters, relying on White House and Republican sources, were caught flat-footed. As the Plame episode developed, *Time* itself would be embarrassed by a reporter who had become too close to a source.

A few of my colleagues at the *Journal* criticized me for "hanging out with the people we cover." But as Eldrin Bell, the former Atlanta police chief, famously replied, when asked why he hung out at a bar frequented by coke dealers and other riffraff, "You don't look for crooks in church." There is always danger in getting too close to your sources. But some of the best journalists I knew, such as the *Post*'s Ben Bradlee or the *Journal*'s Al Hunt, had been able to befriend their sources without compromising their standards.

There was always the possibility that a relationship would be shredded. I had developed a good social relationship in the 1980s with James Robinson, then CEO of American Express Co., and his wife, Linda Gosden Robinson, a powerful public relations executive in New York. But we stopped speaking to each other in 1990 after the *Journal* ran a story whose editing I had supervised about the ways in which American Express had used anti-Semitic publications around the world to smear Edmond Safra, a former chairman of American Express Bank. I enjoyed my encounters with sources, but I assumed they knew our socializing was part of my job and theirs too.

My closest friends included social activists, labor organizers, antiwar activists, and political dissidents. Finally able to disassociate law and family, I also, inevitably, made close friends with lawyers wherever I worked. In Memphis, the experience I'd gained with civil rights cases while working for Anthony Amsterdam led me to Marvin Ratner, a lawyer with strong ties to the sanitation workers and to the city's large black community. In Detroit, the lawyers at the UAW, General Motors, and Ford became my best sources. Bill Gould, a labor law professor at Wayne State who went on to head the National Labor Relations Board, befriended me. In Las Vegas, Oscar Goodman, an old friend from summer camp, college, and law school, was building a reputation as the nation's leading wiretap lawyer while representing Mafia bosses across the country. (Goodman is now the city's improbable, irrepressible mayor.) In Los Angeles, I was friendly with Geoffrey Cowan. He went on to become the dean of the USC Annenberg School for Communication after a career in government and teaching communications law at UCLA.

I also began what became a lifelong friendship with Michael R. Mitchell, a brilliant securities lawyer who nonetheless spent most of his time bringing police brutality cases on behalf of indigent plaintiffs. We regularly finished the day at the same Malibu dive, the Raft, where over glasses of scotch we spent hours debating the best and worst of journalism and the law, discussing my stories and his cases. I resisted Mitchell's offer to join his practice; and except for a few years working as a partner in Johnnie Cochran's criminal law firm, he has remained a solo practitioner and one of my closest friends and confidants.

Instead of joining Mitchell, I moved on to Asia, where I worked from 1973 until 1978, first as the *Journal*'s Tokyo bureau chief and then as *The Asian Wall Street Journal*'s first managing editor. Dick Rabinowitz and the lawyers at his firm, Anderson, Mori & Rabinowitz, explained the intricacies of foreign investment in Japan, while in Hong Kong some of my best friends were at Coudert Brothers, representing corporations that were trying to crack the China market.

I returned to Los Angeles in 1978 and worked there for two years as an executive editor of *Forbes* before rejoining the *Journal* in New York as its national editor in 1980. I was sent to Brussels in late 1981, where I became *The Wall Street Journal Europe*'s first editor and publisher, responsible for the paper's business and balance sheets as well as its journalism.

From 1983 through 1992 I was in New York as the *Journal*'s managing editor and then its executive editor, the top editorial positions at the paper. After resigning in 1992, I started *Smart Money*, a personal-finance magazine for the *Journal*'s parent, Dow Jones & Co., and

Hearst Corp., and I formed a partnership designed to invest in and operate media companies. The partnership was a failure, in part because the CEOs of two of the three limited partners—Martin Davis of Paramount Communications and Barry Diller, then head of QVC—were at war with each other. (My third partner was billionaire investor Richard Rainwater.) I also stumbled because twenty-five years of covering business hadn't prepared me for the real world, with all of its complexities and subtleties. I, nonetheless, came to agree with the maxim that failure teaches more than success.

Anyone who is honest about his or her professional success will acknowledge that it is far better to be lucky than smart. Yes, hard work is important when the opportunities come. But my own career is much more Forrest Gump than Horatio Alger.

I got that internship in Allentown because the paper's managing editor, an Ursinus College graduate, mistakenly thought I went there instead of Haverford. (I had grown up in Collegeville, Pennsylvania, where Ursinus is based.) The *Journal* hired me on the recommendation of a high school acquaintance who was working there. After being in Memphis the day King was assassinated, I was subsequently transferred to Detroit in 1970 to cover a quiet year of labor negotiations. Turmoil ensued after Walter Reuther, founder of the United Auto Workers, was killed in a plane crash. The resulting strike was the longest in automotive history and gave me the chance to cover the best business story of 1970. I had never worked in Southeast Asia, but in April 1975, I was the only *Journal* reporter able to get into Saigon. I arrived on April 24, three days after President Nguyen Van Thieu resigned, and I was airlifted out of the country on an Air Force C-141 on April 30, the day Duong Van Minh surrendered. Many, many reporters would have looked good if handed that story.

My luck continued as I moved to news management. Peter Kann, the *Journal*'s Pulitzer Prize–winning Southeast Asia correspondent, had been asked to start an Asian edition in 1976. The New York executive running the project wanted to send the paper's Cleveland bureau chief to Hong Kong to work as the paper's managing editor under Peter. But Kann, who didn't know me well, insisted he needed someone who had covered business in Japan to complement his own strength in Southeast Asia. I got the job, and the close friendship with Kann led to all my success at the *Journal* over the next sixteen years as he rose to CEO at Dow Jones & Co., the paper's parent.

Then, in 1994, as I was discussing my busted business partnership with bankruptcy lawyers, Gerald M. Levin called from Time Warner Inc. to ask if I had any interest in being Time Inc.'s editor in chief. Levin, Time Warner's brilliant but quixotic CEO, and I had both gone to Haverford and the law school at Penn, but we didn't overlap at either school. We did meet, however, at a Haverford board meeting in 1986, and when I left the *Journal* in 1992, he was the first person to whom I pitched my business proposal. Although Jerry rejected it, that meeting was the first of several over the next couple of years that led me to the best job in journalism when, in late 1994, Levin confounded his colleagues by naming me Time Inc.'s fifth editor in chief—the first person from outside the company to hold the top editorial position. I held that job for eleven years, stepping down in December 2005.

At Time Inc., I supervised the editors at our various magazines, and I made a point of reading—prior to publication—as many stories as possible in our weeklies and our business titles. I tried, however, to avoid second-guessing the managing editors responsible for each of our titles. I had come to believe, from my first management job in the 1970s, that the more I could delegate, the more I would get to do. I preferred being known for the reporters and editors who worked for me and for the quality journalism they produced. Although I would typically spend thirty to forty hours a week reading stories before publication, I rarely questioned the editors' judgments and I rarely interfered with the coverage.

In my eleven years as editor in chief, I killed only one *Time* cover, a story about a walking tour of Jerusalem that was scheduled to run the week the U.S. Supreme Court was to decide whether George W. Bush or Al Gore would be our forty-third president. Instead, at my insistence, *Time* published a cover on the court.

Although I read stories before they were published in the magazines, I rarely reviewed stories before publication if they were written solely for the online editions. We weren't yet at the point where online stories received the same scrutiny as did stories appearing in print editions. In the years since 2003, that has obviously been changing.

I rarely heard about problems with a story after publication unless litigation ensued. The primary responsibility for the words and pictures in each magazine rested with that title's managing editor. I wish I had focused on the Plame episode much earlier, but given the way I worked with our managing editors, my involvement was limited until mid-2004, when Time Inc. was served with its first subpoena.

In addition to working closely with managing editors, I was responsible for hiring and firing them. I replaced the top editors at six of our eight most important magazines during my first three years in the job. *Time* and *Fortune* experienced strong revivals under Walter Isaacson and John Huey respectively, and *In Style* and *People* both benefited from Martha Nelson's inspired leadership.

Most editors have limited exposure to the business side of their publications. During the launch of the *Journal*'s European edition, I served as the paper's editor and publisher. I also worked on business issues with Don Logan, Time Inc.'s CEO from 1994 through 2002, including strategic planning and mergers and acquisitions. I was responsible for the company's international and online businesses between 1996 and 1998. Don is the smartest business executive I

ever worked with or for. A plainspoken native of rural Alabama, he has a gentle demeanor that hides a brilliant mind. Don is happiest talking about Auburn's football team and bass fishing. You have to dig to learn about his master's degree in mathematics and that he worked as a computer programmer for NASA before going into the magazine business. Don was a great, patient teacher, who managed to be a boss and a partner at the same time.

Publishing is a business. Editors should acknowledge the role they should play in assuring a publication's profitability. If we aren't profitable, we won't have funds to invest in improving coverage. I enjoyed learning about marketing and explaining our editorial mission to advertisers and readers. Unlike most editors, I thought the business challenges made the editing job more exciting.

The story, of course, always comes first. I prided myself on the tough stories that the *Journal* and Time Inc. published on my watch. At the *Journal*, that coverage included exposés of insider trading on Wall Street and aggressive coverage of politics and the Iran-contra scandal in Washington. At Time Inc., our magazines ran tough, compelling stories on politics, foreign policy, sports, business, and the world of celebrity and entertainment. None of those stories was tougher than the ones we wrote about Time Warner.

It was *Sports Illustrated*, for example, that quoted John Rocker, a pitcher for the Atlanta Braves, a team owned by Time Warner, saying he would never play for a New York team because he didn't want to ride a subway "next to some queer with AIDS." *Entertainment Weekly* routinely wrote critical reviews of company movies and once described the culture at one Time Warner studio as "*Caligula* meets *Animal House.*"

I was most proud of *Fortune*'s and *Time*'s coverage of Time Warner's disastrous merger with AOL and of AOL's devious practices before, during, and after the merger. The coverage was especially tough on Jerry Levin, whose commitment to editorial independence and integrity was such that he never complained about our stories.

These stories brought me in contact with many First Amendment and securities lawyers. In the process, I became familiar with libel, privacy, and insider-trading cases and laws. But before the Plame episode, I had never dealt with a case involving confidential sources and a grand jury.

Publications can and do make mistakes, and those mistakes can destroy a publication's credibility unless editors are willing to acknowledge them. On occasion, that has meant settling out of court with plaintiffs if the mistakes were serious enough.

Soon after I became the *Journal*'s managing editor, the Securities and Exchange Commission's chief of enforcement called to tell me that one of the paper's reporters, Foster Winans, was about to be charged with selling the contents of his "Heard on the Street" column to traders in advance of publication. I decided the *Journal*'s credibility was at stake. We had to investigate ourselves as rigorously as we would investigate important crimes at other companies. Working over a weekend with more than a dozen reporters and editors, we published an exhaustive front-page profile of Winans and his scam. After it appeared, Donald A. Macdonald, the top advertising executive at Dow Jones, accosted me. He complained bitterly about my willingness "to wash our dirty laundry in public." I threw him out of my office. Although new to my job, I knew that Warren Phillips, Dow Jones's CEO, and Peter Kann, then the *Journal*'s publisher, would support me—and they did.

At the *Journal* I worked closely with an extraordinary libel lawyer, Robert D. Sack. Sack had worked at Patterson, Belknap (Time Warner CEO Dick Parsons's old firm) before moving to Gibson, Dunn & Crutcher, one of America's largest firms. Sack acted like a lawyer, but he thought like an editor. Following his advice, I settled a libel suit for hundreds of thousands of dollars after realizing that one of our front-page stories had unfairly damaged the reputations of two Department of Justice lawyers. Our story had asserted that they had improperly pressured a prisoner to testify against the Mafia. I hated settling, in part because I understood that the plaintiffs' lawyer would seek new cases to bring against us. He did just that, filing a lawsuit on behalf of Ramada Inns following a story about skimming at one of its casinos. This time I thought our story was right, and with the help of Robert Warren, one of Gibson, Dunn's top litigators, we won the case after a three-month trial in Wilmington, Delaware.

Time Inc., like Dow Jones, was one of a handful of media companies that had made important case law, defending its publications from litigation. In 1967 the Supreme Court ruled in its favor in an important free speech case, *Time Inc. v. Hill*, defeating Richard Nixon, then a private lawyer, who argued the case for the plaintiff.

In 1977, well after Hedley Donovan had succeeded Henry R. Luce as Time Inc.'s editor in chief, Synanon filed a $77 million libel suit against *Time*. The magazine had asserted that the once respected program for alcohol and drug addicts in California had degenerated into a "kooky cult" that mandated divorces, remarriages, and vasectomies for many of its adherents. Synanon had also developed a menacing reputation when two of its members were convicted of attempted murder by putting a rattlesnake in the mailbox of a lawyer who had opposed the organization. It harassed Donovan, calling him a "murderer." After many of its members picketed the Time and Life Building in New York, some Time Inc. executives wore bulletproof vests to a stockholders meeting. Two years later the suit was dismissed by a California superior court.

By the time I arrived, however, many of Time Inc.'s lawyers seemed tired, and they performed erratically. They also had a limited view of their jobs. The lawyers who read our stories seemed to be concerned only with libel. If they thought a story was unfair or lacked balance but was not libelous, they rarely raised any concerns.

The legal department was still traumatized by a nasty libel case that had been tried in 1985. Israel's General Ariel Sharon had sued *Time*, claiming damages of $50 million, after the magazine alleged that Sharon, while serving as Israel's defense minister, bore "indirect" responsibility for the Lebanese Christian militia's 1982 massacre of hundreds of Palestinians in Beirut. The jury found *Time* had "negligently and even carelessly" defamed Sharon, but after five days of deliberation, it concluded there would be no recovery because the story was not published with malice or reckless disregard for the truth. Although the magazine paid no damages, its reputation for accuracy was tarnished.

The lengthy, expensive battle between *Time* and the Church of Scientology also seemed to have taken its toll.

Soon after I became editor in chief, *Fortune* magazine published a story saying that John Gutfreund, the former CEO of Salomon Inc., had been barred from working in the securities industry. The story was wrong. Gutfreund had settled a charge of failure "reasonably to supervise" in 1992 and had agreed not to become the CEO of a securities firm without SEC approval. But he was never suspended nor barred from working in the securities industry, and when the story was published, he was actively advising foreign and domestic clients from a company he had set up in New York.

Gutfreund's suit asked for nonspecific damages "including an amount sufficient to purchase full-page retractions in major business and general-interest newspapers and periodicals worldwide." We calculated that demand would cost more than $1 million, and Time Inc.'s general counsel told me that he thought we should negotiate a financial settlement.

I refused to do so. I knew Gutfreund from my days at the *Journal* and had always thought him honorable and reasonable. I called him to ask for a personal meeting. He agreed but asked that his attorney join us. At the meeting, I acknowledged our mistake but told him the proper response was a prominent correction in *Fortune*, not a financial settlement. If he insisted on litigating, I said, we would spend whatever it would take to defend ourselves. He was, after all, a public figure, and I didn't think he could prevail, since there was no proof of malice. Gutfreund agreed and we gave prominent display to a correction and apology in *Fortune*. I thought the outcome fair and obviously superior to what our general counsel was prepared to agree to. But I heard later that the Time Inc. lawyers thought I was doing their job and resented it.

A few years later *Fortune* was again sued for libel, this time in a British court, by David and Simon Reuben, two businessmen whose efforts to build an aluminum empire in the former Soviet Union had been chronicled by the magazine. The brothers complained that the *Fortune* article had suggested they had been complicit in murders at aluminum plants in the former Soviet Union. The article hadn't done so, but it had suggested that law enforcement agencies in many nations were investigating possible money laundering by the brothers and were primed to "redouble efforts to finish them off." *Fortune's* prediction was wrong. Prosecutors in Germany and elsewhere ended their investigations without bringing a case against the brothers.

Our lawyers wanted to try the case, but I feared a lengthy, expensive trial in an unfriendly forum. (In British courts, the defendants typically need to prove the truth of an article. In the United States plaintiffs need to prove its falsehood.) Instead, after my yearlong negotiation with Howard Rubenstein, the Reubens' New York–based public relations representative, the brothers dropped their suit in return for a thousand-word "Update and Clarification" in *Fortune*. The article acknowledged that they hadn't been indicted and stipulated that *Fortune* never intended to accuse them of sanctioning murders. This time many of Time Inc.'s lawyers seemed disappointed that I had managed to avoid a trial, even though the article was innocuous and we paid no damages.

I don't tell these tales to denigrate the Time Inc. legal department but to illustrate how much time I spent with legal problems as editor in chief. The legal department and I weren't always in disagreement. I admired Bierstedt's libel work. I also worked well with Robert McCarthy, a hard-nosed advocate who headed the department for a few years, as well as his successor, John Redpath, who came to Time Inc. from HBO, another division of Time Warner. Both could be aggressive in defending us, but they also knew when we had to settle.

Time Inc.'s lawyers and I agreed, for example, that *Sports Illustrated* should settle one suit, even though I thought our story was an example of outstanding journalism that was legally defensible. *Sports Illustrated* had written a well-documented story in 1999, detailing how child molesters infiltrate youth sports leagues. Our hope was that the story would encourage parents to work harder to minimize the risks posed to children. Several players and two assistant coaches on a California Little League team, however, sued the magazine for invasion of privacy. They claimed that publication of their team photograph in conjunction with the story created the impression that they were either victims of or participants in the actions of their head coach, Norman Watson, who was subsequently convicted of thirty-nine lewd acts with children. Neither the article nor the caption accompanying the picture said anything of the sort, and neither named any child who had been victimized by Watson. We became convinced while preparing for the trial, however, that a jury was likely to find for the children and against us and that the damages could be massive. We settled out of court in 2003.

6

Branzburg's Long Shadow

Judy Garland was out of work in the mid-1950s, and the *New York Herald Tribune* wondered why. Marie Torre, a columnist for the paper, quoted a "spokesman" for CBS saying, "I wouldn't be surprised if it's because she thinks she's terribly fat." Garland sued for defamation and deposed three CBS executives whom she thought might have been responsible for the quote. After they all denied making the statement, Garland's lawyer sought to force Torre to reveal her source. Her refusal to do so led to a decision that severely limited the scope of the First Amendment.

Torre argued that the First Amendment protections of freedom of the press allowed her to protect her source, but the trial judge disagreed, holding her in criminal contempt. Torre also lost on appeal when Judge Potter Stewart, shortly before being named to the Supreme Court, held that freedom of the press is not "absolute" and that in this case the court's need to learn the truth was more important than Torre's right to protect her source. The Supreme Court refused to hear the case, and Torre was ordered to serve ten days in jail. The trial judge showed his sympathy for Torre, calling her "the Joan of Arc of her profession" before sentencing her.

Judy Garland's weight controlled the right of reporters to protect their unnamed sources for almost two decades until a far more important case, *Branzburg v. Hayes*, was decided by the Supreme Court in 1972. In that case, the court held that society's interest in law enforcement outweighed a reporter's need to protect confidential sources. Journalists, like all other citizens, were compelled to testify before a grand jury, the court ruled.

Although the Pentagon Papers and Watergate were the cases that captured the public's imagination in the 1970s, making heroes of anonymous and confidential sources, it was *Branzburg v. Hayes* that established far more important and lasting precedents. And it was *Branzburg* that Judge Hogan cited when he held Cooper and Time Inc. in contempt.

In *Branzburg*, the Supreme Court dealt with four different cases involving journalists and grand jury investigations. Two of the cases grew out of stories about the sale and manufacture of illegal drugs written by Paul Branzburg, a reporter at the *Louisville Courier-Journal*. A third case involved a television reporter, Paul Pappas, who had covered plans for protests by the Black Panthers in Massachusetts. All three cases resulted in contempt orders that had been upheld by appellate courts.

The fourth case, also involving coverage of the Black Panthers, had led to a different result in a federal court for the Northern District of California and in the Ninth Circuit Court of Appeals. In that case, Earl Caldwell, a reporter for *The New York Times*, succeeded in getting the district court to limit his testimony to what had appeared in print while permitting him to withhold "confidential associations, sources of information received, developed or maintained by him as a professional journalist." When Caldwell still refused to testify, he was held in contempt, but the Ninth Circuit reversed that order, holding that compelling his testimony would "suppress vital First Amendment freedoms" by "driving a wedge of distrust and silence between the news media and the militants." Instead, the Ninth Circuit, which had a reputation for being far friendlier to the press than any other Circuit Court of Appeals, held that the government must show "a compelling need" before a witness could be required to testify before the grand jury.

In a 5–4 decision, the Supreme Court upheld the contempt holdings against Branzburg and Pappas and reversed the Ninth Circuit's decision in the Caldwell case. Writing for the majority, Justice Byron R. White began with a blunt ruling against the press: "The issue in these cases is whether requiring newsmen to appear and testify before state or federal grand juries abridges the freedom of speech and press guaranteed by the First Amendment. We hold that it does not."

White agreed that gathering and publishing news is protected by the First Amendment. "Without some protection for seeking out the news, freedom of the press could be eviscerated," he wrote. Nonetheless, he quickly concluded that society's interest in law enforcement far outweighed any burden that might result from journalists testifying before a grand jury. The majority held that the long-standing principle that "the public has a right to every man's testimony" was especially applicable to grand jury proceedings and that there was insufficient evidence to support the belief that forcing journalists to testify about their confidential sources would present an undue burden on their newsgathering.

The majority opinion held that the First Amendment gave no protection to journalists' confidential sources. A journalist could be compelled to name a source, to testify as to what the source had said, and to produce documents provided by the source. If sources were engaged in criminal activity, "their desire to escape prosecution . . . while understandable, is hardly deserving of constitutional protection." The court also thought innocent sources that had confidential information about others' crimes should trust public officials and grand juries as much as they trusted journalists.

Among the four dissenters, Justice William O. Douglas took an absolute position. Assuming the journalist is not a criminal himself, Douglas argued, "The First Amendment protects him against an appearance before the grand jury, and, if he is involved in a crime, the Fifth Amendment stands as a barrier."

Potter Stewart was less strident but was sympathetic to the "critical role of an independent press in a free society" and to society's interest in the "free and full flow of information to the public." He insisted that "the longstanding rule making every person's evidence available to the grand jury is not absolute," citing the protections against compelled disclosures provided by the Fourth Amendment (search and seizure) and the Fifth Amendment (due process and self-incrimination).

Stewart, extending the line of reasoning he had proposed in Judy Garland's case, proposed a three-part test to balance the needs of the grand jury and those of journalists: "I would hold that the government must (1) show that there is probable cause to believe that the newsman has information that is clearly relevant to a specific probable violation of law; (2) demonstrate that the information sought cannot be obtained by alternative means less destructive of First Amendment rights; and (3) demonstrate a compelling and overriding interest in the information."

Despite the closeness of the vote, the *Branzburg* case would have been far less controversial had Justice Lewis F. Powell, who voted with the majority, not written a concurring opinion that seemed to support Justice Stewart's balancing test. Powell's confusing opinion, just three paragraphs long, insisted that White's majority opinion "does not hold that newsmen, subpoenaed to testify before a grand jury, are without constitutional rights with respect to the gathering of news or in safeguarding their sources." He then added, *"The asserted claim to privilege should be judged on its facts by the striking of a proper balance between freedom of the press and the obligation of all citizens to give relevant testimony with respect to criminal conduct."* Most important, Powell said the balancing should be done *"on a case-by-case basis."* (Italics added.)

Powell's opinion was inconsistent with his vote, so much so that three years after *Branzburg*, Justice Stewart wrote, "The Court rejected the [reporters'] claims by a vote of five to four, or, considering Mr. Justice Powell's concurring opinion, perhaps by a vote of four and a half to four and a half."

The differing opinions in *Branzburg* had led to thirty-three years of debate and divergent lower-court rulings in the years before we received the special counsel's subpoenas. Relying largely on Powell's ambivalence, Abrams and James C. Goodale, then general counsel for *The New York Times*, were among a small group of lawyers who had successfully carved out exceptions to *Branzburg*. Some courts recognized a First Amendment privilege in criminal cases, while others asserted a common law privilege based on precedents growing out of case law.

Goodale, Abrams, and other First Amendment lawyers had done such a good job that I had rarely worried about sourcing questions in my years as a reporter and editor. If we received a subpoena seeking information about our sources, I relied on our lawyers to get it quashed.

Judge Richard Posner, a conservative, articulate, and influential member of the U.S. Court of Appeals for the Seventh Circuit, was one of those who agreed that despite *Branzburg*, many cases had concluded that there is a reporter's privilege. Posner was determined to halt the erosion of the Supreme Court's majority opinion in *Branzburg*, and in 2003, he got his chance in a Seventh Circuit case, *McKevitt v. Pallasch*.

Michael McKevitt was being prosecuted in Ireland for directing terrorism. He asked a federal district court in Illinois for an order requiring journalists to produce tape recordings of the prosecution's key witness, David Rupert, whom McKevitt wanted to interrogate. The district court ordered the journalists, who were working on a biography of Rupert, to make their tapes available to McKevitt. The journalists appealed that ruling to a three-judge appellate court, whose members included Posner.

Writing for the majority, Posner reviewed the many cases that had relied on Powell's concurrence to limit the scope of *Branzburg* and questioned the logic of their reasoning. Instead, he relied on Justice White's majority opinion in *Branzburg* and affirmed the district court decision.

In our case Judge Hogan echoed Judge Posner's opinion in *McKevitt*. On July 20, 2004, Hogan held that *Branzburg* required him to rule that society's interest in law enforcement outweighed a reporter's need to protect confidential sources, and that journalists, like all other citizens, were compelled to testify before a grand jury.

The pace quickened after Hogan's opinion was announced. Within hours, Fitzgerald served a subpoena on *The Washington Post's* Walter Pincus, asking for testimony about a source for his coverage of Wilson and Plame. The *Post* initially said it would resist the subpoena, but Pincus subsequently provided limited testimony, without a waiver from his source, after the source revealed himself to Fitzgerald.

A few days later Fitzgerald served subpoenas on *New York Times* reporter Judith Miller and on the *Times* itself. These subpoenas were a surprise. Miller, a Pulitzer Prize–winning reporter, had written extensively about the suspected existence of weapons of mass destruction in Iraq. She was known to have good government sources, and her stories had reflected the Bush administration's positions on Iraq. But she had written nothing about Valerie Plame or Joseph Wilson. That fact was of no relevance, however, to Fitzgerald. Miller had information he thought the grand jury should hear, and he was right in thinking that the courts wouldn't distinguish between a reporter whose stories had been published and one who hadn't written anything.

The *Times*'s subpoena was dropped after the paper's lawyers told Fitzgerald that it had none of the documents the grand jury had asked for. But the paper did retain Floyd Abrams to represent Miller, and she refused to comply with the subpoena.

We weren't initially concerned about a possible conflict. Cooper, after all, had obtained a waiver of confidentiality from Libby and had agreed to give Fitzgerald a deposition. We presumed the contempt orders against Matt and Time Inc. would be withdrawn after his deposition. Moreover, to the degree that Cooper's and Miller's cases seemed to raise the same constitutional issues, Abrams and Bierstedt agreed it would be more efficient to have Abrams represent Miller, as well as Cooper and Time Inc.

Fitzgerald deposed Cooper in Abrams's Washington office. Cooper told the special counsel about his conversation with Libby and repeated under oath that Libby had never mentioned Plame's name to him. Hogan lifted his contempt orders against us.

But our hope that Matt's deposition would put the matter behind us was dashed on August 31, 2004, when Fitzgerald told Abrams that Matt's testimony had revealed that he had other sources. Fitzgerald insisted that he needed additional testimony from Cooper and that he would still need all of Time Inc.'s records.

I was puzzled. NBC's Tim Russert had agreed to be interviewed under oath by Fitzgerald just before Hogan's findings against us were announced. An NBC statement said that Russert "was not required to appear before the grand jury and was not asked questions that would have required him to disclose information provided to him in confidence." Why had Fitzgerald let Russert off the hook while he was still demanding additional testimony from Cooper?

Abrams said he was disappointed that Matt's testimony hadn't put an end to the matter, but he insisted that Fitzgerald had never promised that Matt's deposition would end the grand jury's interest in him and us.

In his deposition, Russert did acknowledge that Libby had "initiated" a telephone call to him in early July of 2003. The network said that Russert didn't know Plame's name or her role at the CIA until he read Novak's July 14 column.

NBC said that Russert was "not a recipient of the leak" and that Russert "did not provide that information" about Plame to Libby. The NBC statement was confusing. I had expected Russert's testimony to focus on what Libby had told him, not on what he had told Libby. At the time, the statement made no sense.

Adding insult to injury, *New York Times* columnist William Safire contrasted *Time* and Time Inc. with the *Times* and Judith Miller, writing that he wouldn't want to be represented by a "weak-kneed Time Inc. lawyer." Safire, of course, didn't realize that the *Times* was paying Abrams to represent Miller while he continued to represent Cooper and Time Inc.

We puzzled over Robert Novak, whose story had first mentioned Plame. I presumed that Novak had been subpoenaed and had testified, but neither he nor Fitzgerald would comment. Novak had said he had two sources, and *The Washington Post* had reported that members of the administration had called a half-dozen reporters in an effort to discredit Plame's husband, Wilson. I had initially assumed that Novak's and Cooper's sources were the same. But there were recurring rumors that one of Novak's sources was at the State Department, either Deputy Secretary of State Richard L. Armitage or Marc Grossman, the undersecretary of state. Neither Armitage nor Grossman, however, had been hawks on the Iraq war, so it was hard to see why they would want to undermine Wilson, who had spent his entire career at the State Department and had been well regarded there.

Although we believed that Cooper's testifying about the interview would be to Libby's benefit, since Libby hadn't mentioned Plame by name, we couldn't say that about his conversation with his other source, Karl Rove. Rove hadn't mentioned her by name either, but he did reveal that Wilson's wife worked at the CIA. (With that information any good reporter could quickly learn her name.)

In a conference call on September 10, Cooper asked Abrams, Bierstedt, and Kelly whether he should call Rove to see if he could get another waiver from a source. Abrams and Bierstedt again insisted that any call to Rove or his lawyer would be coercive. As such, they said, Cooper would be violating his pledge of confidentiality, presumably because a refusal by Rove to grant the waiver might be alleged to be obstruction of justice.

So we agreed to resist Fitzgerald's second request, and on September 13, Cooper and Time Inc. were again served with subpoenas. The new subpoenas were more focused than the earlier ones, asking specifically for any material reflecting conversations between Cooper and "official source(s) prior to July 14, 2003," concerning Wilson, his trip to Niger, Plame, "and/or any affiliation between Valerie Wilson Plame and the CIA."

Judge Hogan denied our motions to quash the subpoenas on October 7, and on the same day he held Miller in civil contempt for her refusal to testify. A week later, Hogan reinstated the orders holding Cooper and Time Inc. in civil contempt. The judge consolidated Miller's case with ours, granting her and Cooper bail. He stayed Time Inc.'s fines, pending our appeal of his decision. Judge Hogan's ruling led me to seek the October 20 meeting with Parsons and the group of corporate executives and lawyers.

. . .

Two days later Abrams filed his brief with the U.S. Court of Appeals for the District of Columbia, appealing Judge Hogan's orders. It argued that the First Amendment and common law rules of evidence give journalists the right to keep their sources confidential. It further asserted that Judge Hogan had erred in allowing Fitzgerald to keep secret the evidence that had been presented to the grand jury because, in doing so, he was denying Cooper, Miller, and their publications a constitutional right to due process. Given the workings of the grand jury and the facts of our case, however, I thought it would be difficult to get the appeals court to rule that grand jury secrecy could be breached.

I also thought the argument that Fitzgerald had failed to comply with Department of Justice guidelines for issuing subpoenas to journalists was a stretch. The DOJ guidelines instruct the department's lawyers that they should pursue reporters' confidential sources only as a last resort and never as a first option. Over the years, those guidelines have been codified, and although they didn't cover the actions of special counsels, they provided some basis for arguing, by analogy, that if Fitzgerald had been appointed because the attorney general had a conflict, he should be governed by the DOJ's rules. All true, but what the argument failed to acknowledge was that there were only two persons Fitzgerald could question, Matt and his source. If the source wasn't talking, Matt was the special counsel's "last resort."

I was also concerned by the brief's strident, inflexible tone. The argument focused on reporters' First Amendment protections. It also tried to argue that Powell's confusing concurring opinion was controlling in *Branzburg* instead of White's majority opinion. Abrams's argument began by stating that forcing Cooper and Miller to reveal their sources would diminish the public's access to information of "grave national concern" from confidential sources. "Under these circumstances, one would have thought that at the very least, that the First Amendment would have some role to play in determining whether such a disturbing societal price must be paid in the interests of furthering the Special Counsel's leak investigation." The brief went on to complain that "the district court, acting contrary to the significant weight of authority, saw no role for the First Amendment at all." It was as if Abrams was resigned to losing in the court of appeals, leaving it all to the Supreme Court, which would first have to agree to accept a petition for review and then overturn *Branzburg*.

When the court of appeals heard Abrams's oral argument on December 8, Judge David B. Sentelle, perhaps reacting as I had to the tone of Abrams's brief, was especially rough on him, repeatedly asking how our case was different from *Branzburg*. Abrams's efforts to answer only inflamed Judge Sentelle, who finally said, "I take it that you do not have a material difference between this case and *Branzburg* or you would have answered my question on one of the first three, four, or five opportunities."

In an article about the oral argument in the next day's *New York Times*, Adam Liptak noted that even Judge David S. Tatel, one of the country's most press-friendly appellate judges, "was impatient with Mr. Abrams's contention" that a protection he had sought for journalists should be "absolute."

The three-judge panel affirmed Judge Hogan's rulings on February 15, 2005, agreeing that Cooper and Miller must testify before the grand jury and that Time Inc. must turn over the e-mails in our possession. All three judges held that the Supreme Court's refusal in *Branzburg* to find protection for confidential sources in the First Amendment was absolute in cases where reporters were called before a grand jury and that only the Supreme Court could reverse itself. We asked the entire court of appeals to rehear our case on March 21, 2005, but that request was quickly denied.

It was clear what we had to do. We would ask the Supreme Court to hear the case. As I had told Parsons in October 2004, if the court denied our petition, or accepted it and then ruled against us, I assumed that Matt Cooper would go to jail and we would pay any fines imposed on us. I kept telling myself that civil contempt isn't a judicial determination of wrongdoing. It is an effort to coerce us to give up sources. Refusing to comply with a contempt order was noble and consistent with more than two hundred years of honorable journalistic practice.

7

Abrams v. Olson

Before we filed our Supreme Court petition, I had to find new counsel. We had to separate ourselves from Floyd Abrams, Judith Miller, and *The New York Times*.

I realized that our cases and our causes were different. I worried that Abrams was predisposed to favor the interests of the New York Times Co. over those of Time Inc. and Matt Cooper. Although he had done work for Time Inc. in the past, Abrams's history was deeper and longer with the *Times*, going back to *Branzburg* and the Pentagon Papers. His caseload included several other cases in which he was representing *Times* reporters. I had also realized that his legal philosophy was much closer to that of Arthur O. Sulzberger Jr.—chairman of the New York Times Co. and publisher of the *Times*—than to my own.

Initially, I had not fully appreciated the significance of Time Inc. being held in contempt while the New York Times Co. was not. In our case, Abrams had a corporation as well as an individual to represent. In addition to protecting Matt, I was responsible for the livelihood of all the people who had access to his e-mails, not to mention the rest of Time Inc.'s twelve thousand employees. I blamed myself for not addressing the conflict question in August 2004, when Abrams took on Miller's case while continuing to represent us.

Abrams and his staff were handling several complicated cases. He was representing Miller and *Times* reporter Philip Shenon in another case involving Fitzgerald (in his role as a U.S. attorney). Shenon had written in 2002 about FBI raids on Muslim charities in Illinois that were suspected of terrorist ties. Fitzgerald had sought interviews and phone records from him and Miller in an effort to determine who had leaked news of the raids to Shenon.

Abrams had also agreed to defend two other *Times* reporters in 2005, James Risen and Jeff Gerth. They had received subpoenas in a privacy suit that had been brought against the government by Wen Ho Lee, a nuclear scientist who claimed that the government had leaked damaging, inaccurate information about him to the reporters.

In his early years as a First Amendment lawyer, Abrams had a reputation for putting his clients' interests—winning cases—ahead of making law. But now I thought he had become too much the constitutional lawyer, more focused on overturning *Branzburg* than on pragmatic ways in which we might fashion a compromise with Fitzgerald that could keep Cooper out of jail while getting our contempt orders lifted.

Although I recognized that we would have to rely on judicial theory if we were to get the Supreme Court to hear our case and overturn *Branzburg*, my primary goals from the outset were less lofty—to get the subpoenas dropped, to keep Matt out of jail, and to avoid a contempt citation. The more I reviewed Abrams's work—especially in comparison with that of the criminal lawyers who had represented NBC's Tim Russert and *The Washington Post*'s Glen Kessler—the more I was disappointed with his performance.

I asked myself whether Abrams might have contested the legitimacy of the special counsel's investigation, on the grounds that no law had been broken in disclosing Valerie Plame's identity and her relationship to her husband, Joseph Wilson. I was also bothered by his continued resistance to speaking to Karl Rove's attorney about getting a waiver from Rove so Cooper could testify before the grand jury. From the transcript, Abrams's argument before the court of appeals seemed unfocused. Fairly or not, I was worried that he was spread thin—distracted by his other cases and his desire to publicize his autobiography, which was set for publication a month before our Supreme Court petition was due.

I had known Sulzberger for many years and had admired his passion for the best, most aggressive public-service journalism. But his morale and his newspaper's reputation had been badly damaged by reporter Jayson Blair's fabrications in scores of *Times* stories. The Blair scandal had prompted an insurrection in the *Times's* newsroom. In the face of withering criticism of his handpicked editor, Sulzberger had dumped Howell Raines in June 2003, the month before Novak and Cooper first wrote about Wilson and Plame.

I worried that Sulzberger, consciously or unconsciously, saw strident, uncompromising defiance of the courts as a way to redeem his and his paper's reputations, regaining the glory days of the Pentagon Papers with Abrams. I had met with Sulzberger shortly before the court of appeals affirmed Judge Hogan's opinions. He seemed energized by the case. The New York Times Co. and Time Inc. both had long, distinguished histories as defenders of editorial independence. But I came away from our meeting realizing he was much more focused on the court of public opinion than on the courts of law.

Sulzberger and Judith Miller had appeared on NBC's *Today* show October 8, 2004. In an interview with co-host Matt Lauer, Miller had questioned our strategy in seeking a waiver from Libby. Sulzberger made it clear that he expected Miller to go to jail if we couldn't overcome Hogan's contempt citations in the courts.

That same month Sulzberger and Russell T. Lewis, then the

New York Times Co.'s president and CEO, had coauthored an article the *Times* ran on its op-ed page calling for a federal shield law to protect reporters and their sources. When I met with Sulzberger, he discussed ways to lobby for it and he pushed for us to coordinate our public statements and to do joint press conferences. He also pulled out a button that said FREE JUDY, FREE MATT, FREE PRESS. He wanted to distribute at least ten thousand of them to employees at the *Times* and at Time Inc. We agreed about the need for a shield law, but I worried that distributing the buttons and lobbying for the shield law might inflame the courts without increasing public support for our case.

Although we were ready to spend millions of dollars on litigation, I had to ask whether this strange case was the one on which we wanted to draw the line by ignoring a contempt order. Abrams and Sulzberger thought we should, but I was increasingly coming to think we should not.

I knew that firing the nation's most famous First Amendment lawyer just as we were beginning to prepare our Supreme Court petition might not go unnoticed among journalists and attorneys, many of whom worshipped Abrams. I wasn't sure how to proceed.

Ideally, I would have gone to my old friend Bob Sack. But he had left his libel law practice at Gibson, Dunn in 1998 to accept an appointment to the Second Circuit Court of Appeals in New York. As a federal judge, he was precluded ethically from speaking to me about our case.

Bierstedt was undeniably the smartest First Amendment lawyer at Time Inc., but I thought she and Abrams were too much in sync for her to give me objective advice. With few other obvious options, I decided to meet with Paul Cappuccio, Time Warner's general counsel. It says a lot about the way Time Warner operates that the corporation's general counsel had been uninvolved in our case. Each of Time Warner's divisions operates with a great deal of autonomy, so much so that Time Inc.'s general counsel reported to an executive vice president in the division instead of to Cappuccio.

Although we didn't know each other well and had little in common, the decision to meet with Cappuccio paid huge dividends in the weeks and months to come. The son of a working-class family from West Peabody, Massachusetts, Cappuccio had graduated from Georgetown and Harvard Law School. His nickname, Pooch, notwithstanding, Cappuccio was a brilliant and tenacious lawyer who had clerked for two Supreme Court justices, Antonin Scalia and Anthony M. Kennedy, before going to the Justice Department, where he quickly became a key deputy to Attorney General William Barr and worked closely with Solicitor General Kenneth Starr.

Cappuccio prided himself on his conservative beliefs and his strong connections with the lawyers who came to Washington to participate in the "Reagan Revolution." In *Storming the Court*, a book about how a group of liberal Yale law students challenged the White House to gain political asylum for Haitian refugees trapped at Guantánamo Bay, the author, Brandt Goldstein, paid Cappuccio grudging respect: "At Harvard Law School, nothing had irked him more than liberals holding forth about the plight of the underprivileged as if they were bringing down Truth from the Mount." Calling him "one of the Justice Department's rising stars," who was "boisterous, unkempt, and very, very smart," Goldstein also recognized Cappuccio's pragmatic side and his ability to negotiate a deal.

After three years at Justice, Cappuccio left in 1993 to become a partner in the Washington office of Kirkland & Ellis, where he worked until 1999. He then became America Online's general counsel. Of all the AOL executives who'd landed prominent positions after the company merged with Time Warner, only Cappuccio had survived to become one of Parsons's trusted lieutenants.

Although our political positions were often at odds, I loved the way Cappuccio's mind worked. He understood why Abrams's continued representation was troubling, and in a matter of minutes we agreed to drop Abrams's firm, replacing it with Gibson, Dunn, the firm I had come to know so well in the years Sack was there.

Cappuccio had only one reason for preferring Gibson, Dunn—Ted Olson, a partner in the firm's Washington office with an unmatched record of victories in Supreme Court cases. Olson had been the U.S. solicitor general between 2001 and 2004 and served as Ronald Reagan's principal legal adviser in the 1980s. (His wife, Barbara Olson, had been a passenger on one of the planes that had been hijacked on September 11, 2001, and died when it crashed into the Pentagon.) His conservative beliefs, like Cappuccio's, didn't get in the way of his pragmatism. Over his career, Olson had argued more than forty cases before the Supreme Court, including *Bush v. Gore*, which determined the 2000 presidential election. Of the twenty-three cases argued and decided while he was solicitor general, Olson had won twenty of them. *Times* columnist William Safire correctly called Olson his generation's "most persuasive advocate" before the Supreme Court and "the most effective Solicitor General" in decades.

Olson also possessed superb credentials as a First Amendment lawyer, having represented the *Los Angeles Times* for many years before moving to Washington from California in 1980. Olson was so committed to the defense of journalists that he had insisted over the years that Gibson, Dunn wouldn't represent plaintiffs in libel cases against journalists and media companies. Despite his strong Republican credentials, Olson had also defended Tim Phelps, a reporter for *Newsday*, after the Senate hired a special prosecutor to investigate leaks during the 1991 confirmation hearings for Supreme Court nominee Clarence Thomas. Phelps was among the first to report that law professor Anita Hill had accused Thomas of sexual harassment.

I hadn't met Olson, so in March 2005, Cappuccio, John Redpath,

Time Inc.'s general counsel, and I went to his Washington office. Within minutes of our meeting, I realized what had been missing. Olson was Abrams's equal on First Amendment theory, but he also showed his mastery of criminal law, criminal procedure, and the workings of special counsels. Olson's work for Presidents Reagan and Bush gave him an intimate understanding of the Supreme Court's more conservative members, and he was a master tactician. Moreover, one of his partners, Ted Boutrous, had filed important friend-of-the-court briefs on behalf of dozens of news organizations with Judge Hogan and with the Court of Appeals. Those briefs had prompted Judge Tatel to write his opinion focusing on a common law privilege. Another partner, Miguel Estrada, provided insight into Fitzgerald's thinking, having worked with him in the U.S. attorney's office in Manhattan.

Olson was willing to represent us, but he made it clear at the outset that it was late in the game and our chances of getting the Supreme Court to review our case were slim. The court typically accepts only 1 percent of the seventy-five hundred petitions it receives annually. The three-judge court of appeals had been unanimous in its affirmation of Judge Hogan's order. Olson explained that Supreme Court rules severely limited his ability to make arguments that hadn't been made before Judge Hogan and the appellate court. I had wondered, for example, whether we should have made more of the fact that the cases decided by *Branzburg* involved drugs and violent anarchists and had nothing to do with protecting government sources. But Bierstedt and Abrams had been uncomfortable raising this issue in the lower-court arguments and briefs—presumably because they didn't want the courts basing privilege on the pedigree of the source—and it wasn't easy for us to raise it at this late date.

Even so, Olson gave us some reason for hope. He began by writing down the names of the nine Supreme Court justices on a sheet of yellow legal paper. He made clear that each of the justices came to every case with a set of preconceptions and prejudices. "The Court won't hear our case unless four justices vote to accept our petition," he said, "so we need to craft arguments designed to play to the interests of individual justices." He then laid out the different arguments he would make, noting which justice would be most likely to respond to each argument.

Olson's pragmatic approach was refreshing, but we didn't have much time or much ability to develop new arguments in our petition. In an effort to distinguish our case from *Branzburg*, our petition stressed how the law had changed since the Court's 1972 ruling. In 1975, for example, Congress passed a rule governing the use of evidence in trials. Known as Rule 501, it authorized the courts to define privileges permitting confidentiality by interpreting "common law principles . . . in the light of reason and experience." In the years following adoption of the rule, the courts recognized many privileges, including one between spouses, one between psychotherapists and their patients, and one involving clergy and penitents.

In our own case, although all three appellate judges said *Branzburg* precluded a First Amendment defense, the panel couldn't agree on whether rules of evidence enacted post-*Branzburg* created a reporter's privilege under federal common law. Judge Sentelle, a Reagan appointee, said *Branzburg* rejected any possibility of a First Amendment or common law privilege. Judge Karen L. Henderson, appointed by President George W. Bush, thought there might be a common law privilege but that the special counsel's affidavit "overcomes any hurdle, however high, a federal common-law reporter's privilege may erect." Judge Tatel, a Clinton appointee often thought sympathetic to the press, enunciated a broader formula for keeping reporters' sources confidential, but he, too, determined that the formula didn't cover Miller or Cooper. We argued that "the differing conclusions of the three panel members reflect the confusion in the lower courts."

Among the cases establishing new privileges, the 1996 Supreme Court ruling in *Jaffee v. Redmond*, establishing a psychotherapist-patient privilege, seemed the most favorable for us. Our petition noted that in *Jaffee*, the court had ruled that the privilege applied to social workers if the privilege is "widely recognized by the States"; if the "proposed privilege serves significant public and private interests"; and if those interests outweighed the "the burden on truth-seeking that might be imposed by the privilege."

Although most states had not recognized a privilege for journalists and their sources when *Branzburg* was decided in 1972, by 2005 forty-nine states had recognized a privilege. Eighteen of those states had done so through judicial rulings, but thirty-one states and the District of Columbia had enacted shield laws giving journalists different measures of protection. The refusal to recognize a federal common-law reporter's privilege, we argued, would nullify these state law protections.

We also thought we might be able to convince the Supreme Court that we were entitled under the Constitution's due-process clause to know why Fitzgerald required Cooper's testimony and his e-mails to other *Time* staffers. Appellate judge Tatel's concurring opinion included eight pages explaining how the special counsel, in "voluminous classified filings," had demonstrated that the information he sought from the reporters "is both critical and unobtainable from any other source." But those eight pages were redacted, or left blank, in Tatel's opinion. Instead, all three appellate judges agreed that Miller and Cooper had no constitutional right to see the special counsel's evidence in support of his need for their testimony. Moreover, if there were any such right, it was outweighed by the government's interest in grand jury secrecy.

Those arguments made up the bulk of our petition for Supreme Court review. We also tried to remind the justices that the public is the primary beneficiary of the free flow of information and that protecting confidential sources is a way of protecting the public's rights, not just the rights of journalists. We buttressed our petition with amicus (friend-of-the-court) briefs from the Magazine Publishers Association and the American Society of Newspaper Editors.

I was surprised to learn the attorneys general of thirty-four states and the District of Columbia filed a separate petition arguing that the law had become so confused that the states needed the Supreme Court to revisit *Branzburg*. Their brief said, "The lack of a federal reporter's privilege undermines the legislative and judicial determinations of the states," and argued that changes in state laws since *Branzburg* "make the issue ripe for decision by this Court." The group of attorneys general, led by W. A. Drew Edmondson, of Oklahoma, noted the many state shield laws in effect and concluded:

> The consensus among the States on the reporter's privilege issue is as universal as the federal courts of appeals decisions on the subject are inconsistent, uncertain and irreconcilable. For example, the Eleventh Circuit holds that the privilege exists in both criminal and civil cases, the Ninth Circuit applies the privilege in the civil and criminal trial contexts, but not in the grand jury context, and the Seventh Circuit concludes that there is no privilege at all. These vagaries in the application of the federal privilege corrode the protection the States have conferred upon their citizens and newsgatherers.

While eschewing the buttons that Sulzberger had wanted to distribute, we also designed a tightly focused public relations campaign to get the attention of those justices most likely to reject our petition. Ted Olson wrote a persuasive article for *The Wall Street Journal*'s conservative editorial page. In it, he said:

> However imperfect the process may sometimes be, we have learned that a robust and inquisitive press is a potent check against abusive governmental power. And the press often

cannot perform that service without being able to promise confidentiality to some sources. Those sources would not talk, and the public might never learn vital information, if reporters could be forced to disclose to the very government they are investigating the names of persons providing them with the information that government wishes to conceal.

I wrote a full-page letter to readers that appeared in *Time* and *Fortune*, explaining why we were seeking Supreme Court review, and arguing that "the issues at stake are crucial to our ability to report the news and inform the public." Miguel Estrada and I met with Rupert Murdoch and many of his key lieutenants from the Fox Network and the *New York Post*, who agreed to support the petition. Many other newspapers editorialized in our favor.

Abrams's brief, submitted on behalf of Judith Miller, inevitably made many of the same points as ours did, since it is difficult to raise issues before the Supreme Court that weren't litigated in the district court and considered by the court of appeals. I was nonetheless convinced we had improved our position significantly by retaining Olson and Gibson, Dunn.

We filed our petition on May 10, 2005. I was satisfied that we had filed the best possible brief, the friend-of-the-court brief from the state attorneys general was especially strong, our public relations campaign had gone well, and the Supreme Court's justices might savor the opportunity to respond to arguments from Olson and Abrams in the same case.

Still, I recalled Olson's warning at our first meeting that the odds were strongly against the court's agreeing to hear our case. After submitting our petition, I focused on what we might do should the court refuse to hear our case.

8

The Pentagon Papers and Watergate

The Role of Time Inc.'s Editor-in-Chief" is an evolving document, first written by Hedley Donovan in 1978. Donovan was Time Inc.'s second editor in chief, following founder Henry Luce. His original version stipulated that Time Inc.'s board of directors had final responsibility for the editorial quality of Time Inc. publications and exercised that responsibility through its appointment of the editor in chief. Although it was true that the board could fire the editor in chief, he declared, the board exercised no meaningful oversight over what the editor in chief chose to publish. Donovan's successors Henry Grunwald and Jason McManus each rewrote the document as Time Inc. expanded, ultimately becoming part of Time Warner Inc. in 1990.

(Luce and Donovan built the world's largest magazine company, but it never comprised more than a half dozen magazines. By the time I stepped down as editor in chief at the end of 2005, the division had more than 150 domestic and international titles with annual revenues of about $5 billion; it employed thirty-three hundred journalists, and its annual editorial expenses totaled hundreds of millions of dollars.)

As Time Inc.'s fifth editor in chief, I reported to the board of

Time Warner Inc. until Time Warner completed its acquisition of the Turner Broadcasting System, including CNN, in January 1997. Time Inc.'s CEO, Don Logan, and I then agreed that it didn't make sense for me to report to the board while CNN's top editorial executive reported to the head of TBS. Besides, I felt safer reporting to Logan than to the Time Warner board, which included many members who had been angered by stories about them and their companies that had appeared in the *Journal, Fortune,* and other publications during the years they had reported to me.

I rewrote "The Role of Time Inc.'s Editor-in-Chief" in 1997 to reflect the new reporting structure and to reassert Time Inc.'s commitment to editorial independence. I stated that our publications are "expected to provide unbiased coverage of the myriad interests of advertisers and of Time Warner itself. Editorial independence is essential so that the Editor-in-Chief can produce publications that advance the public interest while delivering a superior return on investment."

I noted, "The Editor-in-Chief shall report to the chief executive of Time Inc. on all business and financial matters." I purposely omitted anything that indicated to whom I reported on editorial matters. (In my own mind, I reported to the ghost of Henry Luce on editorial matters. His will included his wish that Time Inc. "operate in the public interest as well as the interest of the shareholder.") Instead, I inserted two sentences: "The board and the chief executive hold the Editor-in-Chief of Time Inc. accountable for the editorial quality and integrity of the company's magazines. To this end, they are committed to upholding the Editor-in-Chief's unique level of editorial independence."

Logan, Time Warner CEO Jerry Levin, and the Time Warner board all signed off on the document. I always took the position that any legal issues growing out of our coverage were the responsibility of the editor in chief, and that position was never questioned. I know of no other editor whose independence is so clearly defined.

. . .

There is another evolving document at Time Inc.: the Editorial Guidelines for reporters and editors working at the company's magazines. Those guidelines had always recognized the importance of confidential sources, but they were badly in need of updating when Robin Bierstedt began to rewrite them for me in early 2003. The old guidelines, for example, still had a section on "Carbon Files." Bierstedt began her work months before Matt Cooper wrote his piece on Valerie Plame for Time.com, but we weren't ready to publish them until June of 2004, shortly after Matt received his first subpoena from the special counsel.

The new guidelines recognized the importance of confidential sources and the risks for journalists in granting confidentiality to a source, especially in criminal cases involving a grand jury. As I had reminded Dick Parsons at our October 2004 meeting, the guidelines warn reporters that there may be occasions in which the only way to keep a promise of confidentiality to a source is to serve a jail term for contempt of court. They reiterated our policy of not revealing the identity of a confidential source, even if a journalist is questioned about the identity of the source in litigation.

The new guidelines were good—not unlike the guidelines at other quality publishing companies. But they weren't as precise as they should have been. As editor in chief, I should have worked more closely with Bierstedt on the revisions, but the guidelines were competing with innumerable other responsibilities. I had, of course, read and signed off on her proposed changes, but since I had rarely thought about confidential sources before the Plame episode, I missed important nuances. I viewed her work primarily as an exercise in updating, to reflect changes in technology and reporting practices. My failure to involve myself more in the revisions was another mistake that came back to haunt me.

. . .

Our guidelines reflected a long history of publishers resisting prosecutors' efforts to gain information from anonymous and confidential sources. I understood that nonjournalists might not always agree with this line of reasoning, and I knew that defiance of contempt citations was often unpopular. But I also believed that the First Amendment's references to "freedom of speech" and "freedom of the press" protected the press in ways that were different from the practice in most other countries.

Thomas Carlyle, writing in 1841, quoted Edmund Burke saying that there were three estates in Parliament (presumably the Crown, the Lords, and the Commons), "but in the Reporters' Gallery yonder, there sat a Fourth Estate more important than they all." Although William Safire's *New Political Dictionary* states, "Diligent research has failed to turn up the phrase in anything Burke said or wrote," Justice Stewart and others have accepted Carlyle's reference to Burke. Carlyle himself wrote in his 1837 treatise on the French Revolution about "A Fourth Estate of Able Editors" that kept watch on the church, the nobles, and the bourgeoisie.

Many landmark Supreme Court cases have enshrined the freedom of the press. In *New York Times v. Sullivan*, the court held in 1964 that there had to be a showing of "actual malice" in libel cases involving public figures. Writing for the majority, Justice William J. Brennan Jr. held that debate on public issues "should be uninhibited, robust and wide open." (In an interview, Justice Antonin Scalia told me that given the chance, he would probably vote to reverse *New York Times v. Sullivan*.)

The ability to ignore court orders has, of course, always been a more complicated issue. But the willingness of American journalists to defy government efforts to learn their sources predates the Revolution. In November 1734, John Peter Zenger, a New York publisher, refused to name the anonymous authors who criticized colonial governor William Cosby. Cosby jailed Zenger, then had him tried for seditious libel. Acting as the lawyer for Zenger, Andrew Hamilton persuaded the jury that Zenger's ability to keep the names of Cosby's critics confidential was "in the cause of liberty," and the jury acquitted him in 1735.

The First Amendment itself grew out of the Federalist Papers, many of which were written by Alexander Hamilton, John Jay, and James Madison, using the pseudonym Publius. Anonymity was thought important for debate and worthy of protection well before freedom of the press was enshrined in the Bill of Rights.

Nonetheless, many state courts as well as the U.S. Senate, beginning in the nineteenth century, were willing to jail reporters who refused to identify their sources. In 1848, the Senate confined John Nugent, a reporter for the *New York Herald*, in the Capitol for a month after he refused to name the source of a leak about the Treaty of Guadalupe Hidalgo, which ended the Mexican War. In the late nineteenth century and throughout the first half of the twentieth century, state courts in California, Georgia, Florida, New York, and elsewhere held journalists in contempt for refusing to identify sources in criminal cases. In most instances, the journalists refused to name the sources, choosing instead to go to jail.

Paradoxically, none of the defendants in *Branzburg* was ever jailed. Paul Branzburg had left the *Louisville Courier-Journal* to work for the *Detroit Free Press* before the Supreme Court ruled on his case, and Michigan's governor refused to extradite him back to Kentucky to serve a six-month sentence. The U.S. attorney in San Francisco said that the grand jury that had investigated the Black Panthers had lapsed, thus voiding Caldwell's subpoena. The prosecutors in the Pappas case also dropped their case against him following the court's decision.

In the years between *Branzburg* and our case, the Reporters

Committee for Freedom of the Press (RCFP) identified at least thirty-five cases in which reporters were jailed or fined after refusing to name their sources. Some were trivial—fines of $1 a day or $100 to $500 total—but others were severe. William Farr, a reporter for the *Los Angeles Herald-Examiner*, was jailed for forty-six days around the time of *Branzburg*. The longest sentence was served by Vanessa Leggett, a book researcher, who served 168 days after refusing to name her sources to a federal grand jury investigating a murder.

It is worth noting that during the same period, a few reporters and publishers revealed the names of confidential sources and turned over their notes after the courts ordered them to do so. None, however, worked at a publication as large and prestigious as *Time*.

The decisions that interested me the most involved cases where the government sought to compel behavior and the press sought to defy relevant statutes and decisions. I saw analogies between our case and cases involving prior restraint—that is, disputes illustrating tensions between a government wanting to suppress information and the press being able to tell the public what it knows. Our case involved a different kind of government compulsion, but the result was the same. If we weren't able to keep our sources confidential, we wouldn't be able to publish what we knew.

My study of prior restraint cases inevitably led me to *Near v. Minnesota*, a 1931 Supreme Court case that overturned a gag law Minnesota had enacted four years earlier to suppress some of the state's more notorious scandal sheets.

Jay Near, a reporter and publisher described as "anti-Catholic, anti-Semitic, antiblack and antilabor" in *Minnesota Rag*, Fred W. Friendly's riveting account of the case, had written about backroom politics and shakedowns of businesses, using offensive language that probably libeled several public officials, including County Attorney Floyd Olson. Olson filed a complaint against Near's publication, the *Saturday Press*, calling it a "malicious, scandalous, and defamatory publication." His complaint asked that Minnesota's Public Nuisance Law be invoked and that "said nuisance be abated." The trial judge issued a temporary restraining order that prohibited publication of the *Saturday Press*, effectively putting it out of business.

Despite support for Near from Robert McCormick, the powerful publisher of the *Chicago Tribune*, and from the American Civil Liberties Union, the Minnesota Supreme Court affirmed the lower court ruling. The U.S. Supreme Court agreed to hear the case after McCormick, who paid for much of Near's defense, persuaded the American Newspaper Publishers Association and *The New York Times* to join him and the ACLU in supporting Near.

The Supreme Court, in a 5–4 decision, overturned the Minnesota state courts. In his majority opinion, Chief Justice Charles Evans Hughes quoted James Madison, who had said, "Some degree of abuse is inseparable from the proper use of everything, and in no instance is this more true than in that of the press." Madison had added, "It is better to leave a few of its noxious branches to their luxuriant growth, than, by pruning them away, to injure the vigour of those yielding the proper fruits."

Hughes did note that protection from prior restraint isn't absolute, asserting, "When a nation is at war many things that might be said in time of peace are such a hindrance to its effort that their utterance will not be endured so long as men fight." But he stated that in Near's case, this limitation was clearly not applicable.

Not until 1971, in the Pentagon Papers case, did the Supreme Court confront the right of the press to publish when national security issues were involved. Four years earlier, the Pentagon under Defense

Secretary Robert S. McNamara had ordered a full examination of America's involvement in the Vietnam War. More than three dozen experts worked on the report for over a year. The result was more than seven thousand pages of documents and analysis gathered in forty-seven volumes, showing how four administrations had escalated America's military commitment to South Vietnam.

When the report was delivered to McNamara's successor, Clark M. Clifford, in early 1969, it carried a Top Secret classification. But a former Defense Department consultant, Daniel Ellsberg, had access to one of fifteen copies of the report while working at the Rand Corporation. Disillusioned with the conduct of the war, Ellsberg turned over major parts of the report to Neil Sheehan, a reporter for *The New York Times*, and later to *The Washington Post*.

The *Times* began publishing its lengthy report on the Pentagon Papers on June 13, 1971. The next night, John N. Mitchell, President Nixon's attorney general, demanded that the *Times* cease publication. Mitchell insisted that in publishing classified material the *Times* had violated the Espionage Act and that continued publication of the Pentagon Papers would result in "irreparable injury" to the country.

The *Times*'s outside counsel, Lord, Day & Lord, had warned the paper against publishing, but some of the paper's top editors and James Goodale, then the *Times*'s general counsel, had persuaded publisher Arthur O. Sulzberger to publish the papers. Lord, Day & Lord refused to represent the *Times* after hearing that Mitchell and the Justice Department would seek to halt publication. Goodale then retained Floyd Abrams and Yale law professor Alexander M. Bickel to represent the newspaper. (Abrams and Bickel were working at the time on a "friend of the court" petition for the *Times* in the *Branzburg* case.)

Relying on Chief Justice Hughes's opinion in *Near*, in which he opined that rules against prior restraint wouldn't apply during wartime, the Justice Department obtained a temporary injunction against the *Times*, and, later, *The Washington Post*. A federal district court in New York ruled for the *Times* and against the Justice Department.

Judge Murray Gurfein's opinion made him an instant hero to the press. Gurfein, newly appointed by President Nixon, said, "Any system of prior restraints of expression comes to this Court bearing a heavy presumption against its constitutional validity." Gurfein concluded that the government had not met that burden. His decision was reversed, however, by the Court of Appeals for the Second Circuit. Meanwhile, a district court and the Court of Appeals for the District of Columbia Circuit followed Judge Gurfein's logic and ruled in the *Post*'s favor.

The *Post*'s outside counsel, as well as Fritz Beebe, a lawyer who was chairman of the Washington Post Co., had opposed publishing the Pentagon Papers. Moreover, the company was about to go public with a $35 million stock offering. As the *Post*'s executive editor, Ben Bradlee, explained in his autobiography, *A Good Life*, "Under terms of this offering, the *Post* was liable for a substantial claim by the underwriters if some disaster or catastrophe occurred. No one wanted to say whether an injunction, or possible subsequent criminal prosecution, qualified as a catastrophe. Just as no one wanted to mention the fact that any company convicted of a felony could not own television licenses, a fact which added another $100 million to the stakes." (The *Post*'s ownership of its television stations, then worth in excess of $100 million, was subject to review by the Federal Communications Commission, which places some restrictions on ownership of newspapers and television stations by the same company, and the licenses might well be revoked if the company was convicted of a felony.)

But Bradlee persuaded the *Post*'s owner, Katharine Graham, that the *Post* should publish its version of the Pentagon Papers story. Before speaking with Graham, Bradlee sought and received support for publishing from a close Graham confidant, famed attorney Edward Bennett Williams.

The Supreme Court, recognizing the importance of the case, expedited the appeals process and heard arguments on June 26, 1971. Among the papers submitted by the *Times* before the case was argued was an eighteen-page affidavit by Max Frankel, then the *Times*'s Washington bureau chief. It is the best explanation of the symbiotic relationship between the press and government sources I have read.

Frankel says he "wrote it late one night in a feverish effort to educate our own lawyers after Bickel and others taking our case into court the next day gave me the impression that they nonetheless judged us guilty of a terrible act. I realized that they, like so many judges in my experience, had no sense of the nature of military and diplomatic reporting throughout the Cold War. With the benefit of service in Moscow, Havana, and Washington, I thought I'd better give them a quick course. And when they read it, they added paragraph numbers, had me sign it, and sent it along to the district, appeals, and finally Supreme Court."

Frankel explained how "a small and specialized corps of reporters and a few hundred American officials regularly make use of so-called classified, secret, and top secret information and documentation. It is a cooperative, competitive, antagonistic, and arcane relationship." It wasn't news to Frankel that "presidents make 'secret' decisions only to reveal them for the purposes of frightening an adversary nation, wooing a friendly electorate, protecting their reputations." Similarly, he added, "The military services conduct 'secret' research in weaponry only to reveal it for the purpose of enhancing their budgets, appearing superior or inferior to a foreign army, gaining the vote of a congressman or the favor of a contractor."

He then cited examples from his own career in which Presidents

Kennedy and Johnson, Secretary of State Dean Rusk, and other officials had used him as a conduit to get a message to the public, despite its "secret" classification.

On June 30, 1971, one of the last days of its term, and only seventeen days after the *Times's* first story appeared, the Supreme Court ruled in a 6–3 decision that the *Times* and the *Post* could continue to publish the Pentagon Papers. Perhaps reflecting the speed with which the Supreme Court ruled, there was no majority opinion. Instead, the six judges in the majority filed five concurring opinions.

New York Times Co. v. United States was a landmark case. In his 2005 autobiography, *Speaking Freely*, Abrams noted, "The effect of publication on the press was substantial." He cited Fred Friendly's belief that the decision "stiffened the spines of all journalists." He also quoted Benno Schmidt Jr., then a professor at Columbia University Law School, who noted that the Papers "signaled the passing of a period when newspapers could be expected to play by tacit rules in treating matters that Government leaders deem confidential."

For Bradlee and *The Washington Post*, the decision to publish the Pentagon Papers "crystallized for editors and reporters everywhere how independent and determined and confident of its purpose" his paper had become. It was "a paper that stands up to charges of treason, a paper that holds firm in the face of charges from the president, the Supreme Court, the Attorney General . . . A paper that holds its head high, committed unshakably to principle."

I found much in the Pentagon Papers case that was comforting. But upon close study, it was clear that the *Post's* and the *Times's* willingness to defy the law had its limits.

Confidentiality wasn't the issue I had assumed it would be, in part because the Justice Department never demanded in court that the *Times* or the *Post* reveal Ellsberg as each paper's source. Instead,

Ellsberg, who had initially gone underground to avoid arrest, publicly surrendered to the U.S. attorney's office June 28, two days before the Supreme Court decision.

Moreover, when it came to court orders, the *Times*, to my surprise, was the model of compliance. In a bylined story that began on the *Times*'s front page as the case went before the Supreme Court, Frankel revealed that the paper "would abide by the final decision of the court." That meant that the *Times* would cease publication of the Pentagon Papers if the Supreme Court ruled against it.

Abrams's book notes that the *Times* had agreed to obey restraining orders from the lower courts as well. Recalling the argument over what the *Times* would do, Abrams quoted Bickel as saying, "What we are all about, the reason we are here, is to vindicate the rule of law."

In an even more telling paragraph, Abrams speculated in his memoir about the possible consequences had the *Times* been ordered to turn over its copy of the Pentagon Papers to the Justice Department:

Had the court ordered the *Times* to turn over the Pentagon Papers, covered as they were with Ellsberg's fingerprints, the paper almost certainly would have refused. The *Times* would, I believe, have concluded that it had no other choice, given its promise of confidentiality to him. Had the order been disobeyed, the court could have sanctioned the *Times* severely, possibly limiting its ability to defend itself in the action. Had there been sanctions, the nature of the case as it reached the Supreme Court would have been entirely different, with the *Times* accused of arrogantly viewing itself as entitled not only to make national security determinations contrary to those of the Department of Defense but to ignore binding court orders. While the Supreme Court might let the *Times* decide what to print, it would never allow the newspaper to decide which court orders to obey.

(In researching this book, I encountered a final irony: Contrary to Abrams's assertion, Ellsberg wasn't a confidential source. Ellsberg and Mike Mitchell had worked together at Rand Corporation, and after seeing an early draft, Mitchell asked Ellsberg about the ground rules surrounding his delivery of the papers to Sheehan. Ellsberg replied that the FBI knew, from interviews with his then wife and her stepmother, that he possessed a copy of the Pentagon Papers. "I knew I would almost surely be indicted," Ellsberg replied, "and I believed I would be convicted and spend the rest of my life in prison. So it's wrong to suppose that I demanded confidentiality from Sheehan, though I preferred not to be identified publicly." Ellsberg was subsequently indicted on twelve felony charges, but the charges were dropped after it was disclosed that G. Gordon Liddy and E. Howard Hunt, members of Nixon's notorious "White House Plumbers" unit, had broken into Ellsberg's psychiatrist's office in September 1971.)

There is, of course, a difference between ignoring an order involving prior restraint and ignoring a court's finding in a civil contempt case. But the professed willingness of the *Times* to adhere to a Supreme Court ruling made me wonder if any other large, publicly held media company had defied the Supreme Court. My research turned up none that had.

"Watergate" is the news story of my lifetime. It demonstrated the power of the press to triumph over a corrupt government. I shared Justice Potter Stewart's view that it showed "the established American press" performing "precisely the function it was intended to perform by those who wrote the First Amendment of our Constitution."

Many publications, including *Time*, published fine stories about the scandal, but *The Washington Post* owned the story from June 1972, when it first reported that five men had broken into the Democratic National Committee's headquarters in the Watergate office-apartment complex, to Nixon's resignation in August 1974.

The exploits of the *Post*'s most dogged reporters, Bob Woodward and Carl Bernstein, as well as the courage of Ben Bradlee and Katharine Graham in resisting government pressure, have been chronicled in books—most notably Woodward and Bernstein's own, *All the President's Men*, and memorialized in Alan J. Pakula's movie, starring Robert Redford, Dustin Hoffman, and Jason Robards.

The *Post*'s coverage was a remarkable example of public service journalism—journalism that won the Pulitzer Prize in 1973. It was also journalism that couldn't have been done without heavy reliance on confidential sources, most notably Mark Felt, the top FBI official code-named Deep Throat, who became Woodward's most celebrated source. Woodward honored his commitment to conceal Felt's identity for more than thirty years. Only after Felt's lawyer named Felt as Woodward's source in 2005 in *Vanity Fair* did Woodward, grudgingly, acknowledge his identity.

But in the 1970s the Nixon administration did what it could to intimidate the *Post*. Attorney General John Mitchell, responding to a late-night call from Bernstein seeking confirmation for one damaging story, thundered, "Katie Graham's gonna get her tit caught in a big fat wringer if that's published." Nixon himself wrote a memo demanding that his press secretary, Ron Ziegler, "under no circumstances is to see anybody from the *Washington Post* and no one on the White House staff is to see anybody from the *Washington Post* or return any calls to them."

More ominously, the White House began to orchestrate challenges to the renewal of the television licenses that Bradlee had worried about during the Pentagon Papers case. "Of all the threats to the company during Watergate," Graham wrote in her autobiography,

Personal History, "the attempts to undermine our credibility, the petty slights, and the favoring of the competition—the most effective were the challenges to the licenses of our two Florida television stations. There were three separate challenges in Jacksonville and one in Miami, all of which—not coincidentally—were filed between December 29, 1972, and January 2, 1973," she wrote, "leading us to the easy conclusion that the four petitions must have been orchestrated." The licenses were ultimately renewed.

But while the *Post*'s coverage of Watergate confirmed the value of an independent press and the importance of confidential sources, it provided little guidance as I considered what I should do if the Supreme Court ruled against us and upheld the demand for Cooper's e-mails.

Bernstein, Woodward, and Bradlee have made much over the years of a subpoena that Bernstein received in February 1973, requiring him to produce extensive notes and files used in the *Post*'s coverage of Watergate. Bradlee is quoted in Graham's autobiography assuring Bernstein and Woodward that the *Post* would fight the subpoenas, adding, "And if the Judge wants to send anyone to jail, he's going to have to send Mrs. Graham. And, my God, the lady says she'll go! Then the Judge can have that on his conscience. Can't you see the pictures of her limousine pulling up to the Women's Detention Center and out gets our gal, going to jail to uphold the First Amendment? That's a picture that would run in every newspaper in the world. There might be a revolution."

It was stirring stuff, and it came to be known as the Gray-Haired Widow Defense, after the *Post* used it again a couple of years later, when lawyers for Vice President Spiro Agnew tried, unsuccessfully, to subpoena notes of reporters covering a criminal investigation he was facing.

But what was lost in the telling and retelling of the *Post*'s subpoenas was that they were issued in civil cases involving plaintiffs, not prosecutors. As such, I thought them largely irrelevant to my considerations of what Time Inc. should do in the face of the Supreme Court's decision in *Branzburg*. Neither Archibald Cox, the Watergate special prosecutor, nor Judge John J. Sirica ever sought to drag the *Post*, its editors, or its reporters before a grand jury in an effort to learn the names of its confidential sources.

Moreover, Bernstein wasn't alone in receiving a subpoena. *Time, The New York Times*, and others also received subpoenas, all from the Republicans' Committee to Re-elect the President in a countersuit against the Democrats following the Republican break-in at the DNC headquarters. All of them were thrown out by the trial judge.

It was surprising to learn that *The Washington Post* and *The New York Times* both asserted ownership of the notes and files the Republicans were seeking. I thought their position offered firm precedent for my belief that we, and not Matt Cooper, owned his e-mails to other *Time* staffers in Washington and New York. I was surprised that the *Times* was now asserting that it had no ownership of or control over Judith Miller's notes—that they belonged to her personally.

Although it was never considered by the full Supreme Court, the case that seemed closest to our own also involved *The New York Times* and one of its reporters, Myron Farber. Both were held in civil and criminal contempt by a New Jersey state judge in 1978 after Farber refused to turn over his notes or identify his sources in a murder case. Farber was initially fined $2,000 and sentenced to the county jail until he complied with the court's order. He was then to serve an additional six months for criminal contempt. The New York Times Co. was fined $100,000 for criminal contempt, and $5,000 a day in fines for civil contempt for every day that elapsed until Farber complied with the trial judge's order.

The story began in the mid-1960s at the Riverdell Hospital, an osteopathic facility in Oradell, New Jersey, where a number of patients died under mysterious circumstances. Rumors spread that Dr. Mario E. Jascalevich, an immigrant from Argentina, had poisoned them with curare, a powerful muscle relaxant. The Bergen County prosecutor launched an investigation but dropped it without bringing indictments.

A decade later the *Times* put Farber on the story after an editor on the metro desk received a letter from an acquaintance asking the paper to investigate the still unsolved deaths at the hospital. The letter didn't name the hospital or doctors that might be involved, but charged that the chief surgeon at a hospital had murdered dozens of patients. Farber spent months investigating the story. He identified the hospital and the doctor, and in January 1976 the *Times* published two lengthy articles about the case. The articles didn't name Jascalevich but identified the suspect as Doctor X, and they revealed that curare had been found in his locker at the hospital in the 1960s. The *Times* stories prompted saturation coverage in local media, and the doctor's name became public after a few days. Soon after that the prosecutor then in office called a grand jury to review the case. This time Jascalevich was indicted on five counts of murder.

Jascalevich's lawyer, Raymond Brown, subpoenaed all Farber's notes, an office full of documents. Although Farber had used confidential sources, he and the paper insisted that he had no information that would establish Jascalevich's innocence or guilt. Since the notes weren't relevant to the case, Farber and the *Times* argued that he wasn't bound to turn them over to defense counsel. Abe Rosenthal, then the paper's executive editor, insisted that the subpoena should be fought as "a matter of principle."

New Jersey had a shield law in effect at the time that offered extensive protections to journalists and their confidential sources.

Nevertheless, the judge ruled that the defendant's Sixth Amendment guarantee of a fair trial was more important than Farber's privilege under the shield law, and that he should turn over his notes.

Farber and the *Times* asked several U.S. Supreme Court justices to intervene as the case worked its way through the New Jersey courts, but none agreed to do so. The New Jersey Supreme Court affirmed the trial judge's findings of contempt. Farber served forty days in jail but was later pardoned by Governor Brendan Byrne, who also returned $101,000 of the $286,000 in fines that the *Times* had paid.

The case is troubling on many fronts. Farber's stories were definitely in the public interest, but it is not clear that his sources (whoever they were) fit the definition of whistle-blowers deserving confidential status. Farber's book on the subject, *"Somebody Is Lying,"* is maddening. He insisted that he must keep his sources and his notes confidential but then made clear that his most important sources were known to Jascalevich's lawyer. If, as he also insisted, his notes weren't relevant to the trial, were they worth protecting? Perhaps, but Farber gives no indication why that should be so.

Under such circumstances, it is hard not to sympathize with a judge who wants to gather all the facts in the case and to be sure that a murder suspect is given every opportunity to defend himself. Bergen County Court Judge William J. Arnold may have made a number of rulings against Farber and the *Times* that seemed arbitrary and capricious—for example, the subpoena was much too broad—but the judge did seem to recognize the problem and, to avert a fishing expedition, offered to review Farber's notes and the names of his sources in his chambers before deciding whether they needed to be made available to the defense. Farber and the *Times* rejected that offer.

The *Times* did propose to turn over a small file of its own, in an effort to get the contempt citations against it lifted. Its file, however, related primarily to the paper's initial involvement in the story, and the paper insisted that it could not and would not force Farber to give up his notes. Testifying on behalf of the *Times*, Katharine Darrow, a company lawyer, explained that when a reporter receives a subpoena, the paper gives the reporter "all ownership interest" in the notes "and leaves all decisions as to the disposition of the notes to the reporter." That, as Farber explained in his book, was a longstanding policy of the paper. I didn't understand how notes could be the property of the paper one day and the property of the reporter the next. Instead, I believe that any employee's work product belongs to the publisher.

The *Times* appealed the case to the New Jersey Supreme Court, saying the notes and sources should have been protected by the state's shield law or, in the alternative, despite *Branzburg*, by the First Amendment. The state Supreme Court affirmed the lower court judgments.

While Farber was in jail, the case went to trial. Jascalevich's lawyer argued that the patients all died of natural causes, that his client was a victim of a conspiracy between the prosecutor and envious colleagues at the hospital, and that Farber was a "greedy and ambitious" reporter who had received a substantial advance to write a book about the case. At the conclusion of the trial, the judge directed that Jascalevich be acquitted on two counts of murder, finding that the prosecutor had failed to prove there was curare in the bodies. After three hours of deliberation, the jury acquitted the doctor on the other three counts.

Many news organizations supported the *Times*'s arguments, and following the trial, the New Jersey legislature further strengthened its shield law, making it one of the strongest in the nation. I also respect Farber and the *Times*'s arguments, but I'm unsure whether I would have done the same thing under the circumstances. The trial judge's efforts to balance the needs of a free press and a fair trial strike me as reasonable. This didn't strike me as a case where it made sense to argue that the right to keep sources confidential was absolute.

In addition, with Jascalevich under indictment and the passage of more than a decade between the deaths, the publication of the articles, and the trial, I don't understand why Farber's sources would continue to fear exposure, especially if they weren't important to the case. There is no indication that Farber sought a waiver from any of them.

Even though the Sixth Amendment to the Constitution guaranteed Jascalevich a speedy trial, I thought that in this case it was wrong for New Jersey's courts to jail Farber and fine the *Times* before all their appeals were exhausted. It was the defendant, after all, who was seeking to compel Farber's testimony. As a result, Farber was in and out of jail before the U.S. Supreme Court had a chance to consider review of his case. If nothing else, I was grateful that Judge Hogan and Special Counsel Fitzgerald had agreed to stay imposition of our penalties until we had a chance to petition the Supreme Court. In any case, it was clear that whatever Farber's relationship might be with his sources, it was different from the facts that I was facing.

9

Are Journalists Above the Law?

Can publicly held corporations engage in civil disobedience? The answer is a very qualified yes. The risks are great when a publisher chooses to resist a finding of civil contempt and even greater should the corporation be held in criminal contempt. No one is above the law and that includes publishers. The rare exception must be limited to the important story that serves the public interest, a story that couldn't have been written without a confidential source whose livelihood, reputation, or life would be endangered if his or her identity was exposed. Prior to publication, the reporter, a top editor at the publication, and the confidential source must all be certain that confidentiality has, in fact, been granted, and they must agree to the conditions, if any, under which it might be waived.

I did not come to this restrictive position, with all its attendant caveats and fire escapes, easily. Nor, it turned out, did our case fit within the standards I am advocating. Only from my efforts to sort out the consequences of a denial of our petition to the Supreme Court was I able to understand the significance of the question and the need for a carefully considered answer.

I began by asking what individuals can and cannot do. Individuals, including reporters and editors, can engage in civil disobedience, knowing we must be prepared to live with the consequences of our actions. If a reporter and an editor are the only ones who know the reporter's sources, they can discuss whether the sources are truly *confidential*, as the term is used by the courts and should be used by journalists and their publishers. If they are, the reporter and the editor should be able to choose jail and fines as an alternative to compliance with contempt citations. Any editor who insists on knowing the name of a reporter's source should be willing to join that reporter in jail.

A landmark law-review article written in 1971 (the year before *Branzburg*) by Vince Blasi, then a law professor at the University of Michigan, found that most journalists have mixed feelings about their relationships with confidential sources. While willing to go to jail to protect the identities of their own sources, most journalists accept that the journalist's privilege to keep sources confidential isn't absolute. Blasi and others cite examples, such as information about enemy troop movements or about a kidnapped child, where revealing the names of confidential sources might be appropriate. Blasi found in his study that "most reporters simply do not know how they would react in these troubling situations that involve conflicting obligations to society and to sources."

In a few notable cases, journalists have decided, without court pressure, to name sources who thought the reporters had agreed to protect them. In 1984, Milton Coleman, a *Washington Post* reporter, included Jesse Jackson's references to Jews as "Hymies" and to New York as "Hymietown" in an article that discussed Jackson's run for the presidency and his conflict with some American Jews on domestic and foreign policy issues. Jackson had used the derogatory words in a conversation with Coleman, a black journalist, after saying, "Let's talk black," which, Coleman wrote, is a "phrase that Jackson often uses to talk on what reporters call 'background.'" Coleman wrote that he thought Jackson's use of the offensive words was "germane." But what Jackson said was clearly not for publication. I thought Coleman had crossed the line and betrayed his source without justification.

Three years later, in 1987, Marine colonel Oliver North accused members of Congress of leaking classified information about the 1985 apprehension of Arab terrorists who had murdered an elderly Jewish man, Leon Klinghoffer, by tossing him and his wheelchair over the side of the cruise ship *Achille Lauro*. *Newsweek*'s Jonathan Alter knew that North himself had leaked that information to another *Newsweek* reporter, expecting confidentiality. Alter decided that in doing so "North was using confidentiality as a weapon." So Alter identified North as the leaker in *Newsweek*, implying that North had waived his right to confidentiality by lying.

Investigative reporter Seymour Hersh objected, "You can't eat off a source's plate and then later say you don't like the food." But Michael Gartner, then the editor of the *Louisville Courier-Journal*, told *Time*, "In this instance, where the source publicly accuses someone else of leaking a story for devious purposes, it's incumbent upon you [as the recipient of the leak] to set the record straight."

Our situation, however, was very different from that of the *Post* or *Newsweek*. The relatively large number of people with access to Matt's e-mails and to the name of Matt's source made it no longer a matter of individual conscience.

If Special Counsel Fitzgerald truly wanted the identity of Matt's sources, he needed only to subpoena dozens of *Time* and Time Inc. employees. It would be tempting, of course, to call his bluff and let him issue dozens of subpoenas. But everything I had learned about Fitzgerald told me he wouldn't be intimidated by the prospect of the negative publicity that issuing subpoenas to innocent IT staffers would call forth. I saw no way we could ask journalists and nonjournalists who weren't involved in the story to risk punishment to protect the identity of Matt's source.

The prospect of heavy fines, in contrast, didn't bother me. Judge Hogan had imposed a fine of $1,000 a day on Time Inc. when he first held us in contempt, and I presumed he would increase the fine substantially if we received an adverse decision from the Supreme Court. My guess was that fines wouldn't exceed $100,000 a day. That was the amount a federal judge had levied against IBM in the early 1970s when the company refused to give the Department of Justice documents it demanded in an antitrust case. IBM's revenues and earnings at the time were about the same as Time Inc.'s were in 2005. A daily fine of $100,000 would be significant, but with annual revenues of more than $5 billion and operating income of about $1.2 billion, I thought Time Inc. could handle the fines. Besides, we were a division of Time Warner Inc., which had annual revenues exceeding $40 billion. I joked that no fine could intimidate Time Warner, a company that had taken a write-down of more than $100 billion in 2002 following its disastrous merger with AOL. More seriously, our lawyers suggested if the fines were much larger than what I had estimated, we could contest them in court, arguing that their size violated our constitutional right to due process.

I also figured that a judge's fine, no matter how large, was unlikely to affect any large media company's stock. Investors in media companies should recognize that a news organization's reputation for public service journalism, integrity, and for protecting its sources brings readers, advertisers, and profits to the publisher. Investors should also recognize that an occasional story might lead to a libel verdict, a judge's fine, or some editor launching a program that offends people who then boycott the company. I assumed these possibilities were already built into Time Warner's stock price. Besides, such events are nonrecurring and therefore relatively unimportant, no matter how much short-term pain they might cause.

What did begin to bother me was a more philosophical and less pragmatic question. How, I asked, could we, as journalists, criticize others who ignored the courts if we did so ourselves? One night, unable to sleep, I called my lawyer friend Mike Mitchell around 3 a.m. Knowing it was midnight in Los Angeles, where he lives, I assumed he would be awake, scotch in hand, doing some late-night reading.

He was succinct. "Read *Youngstown v. Sawyer*. If presidents cannot ignore the Supreme Court, how can you?" In 1952, President Harry S. Truman had ordered his secretary of commerce to seize and operate most of the nation's steel mills in an effort to avert a nationwide steel strike. The steel companies sued to overturn the seizures. Lawyers for the commerce secretary, Charles Sawyer, had argued that the Korean War had created a national emergency and that the need for steel to make weapons, ships, and aircraft justified Truman's efforts to avert a strike. The Supreme Court, however, ruled 6–3 that Truman lacked the statutory authority to seize the mills. Instead, the court held that only Congress had the power to authorize "governmental seizures of property as a method of preventing work stoppages and settling labor disputes." In the face of the court's ruling, Truman backed down.

I then spoke to Ted Olson. Until mid-June, all our conversations had focused on our legal and public relations efforts to get the Supreme Court to hear our case. But when I asked about our continuing to ignore the contempt order if the top court rejected our plea, his answer was similar to Mitchell's. He reminded me that President Nixon had resisted turning over his tapes to the Watergate special prosecutor, Archibald Cox, until the Supreme Court ruled 8–0 against him. Nixon then turned over the tapes and resigned.

Olson also told me of a dilemma he had faced arising out of his service to the Reagan administration. An independent counsel had been named to investigate whether Olson had misled a House Judiciary Committee subcommittee during testimony about President Reagan's claim of executive privilege over Justice Department and Environmental Protection Agency documents. The independent counsel had subpoenaed some documents from Olson and his attorneys, and Olson had used the occasion to challenge the constitutionality of the independent counsel statute by refusing to produce the documents. The trial judge held Olson in contempt but the court of appeals for the District of Columbia backed Olson, finding the independent counsel law unconstitutional. That decision was then overturned by the Supreme Court in a 7–1 decision. "I thought I had no choice but to testify once the Supreme Court had ruled," he said. The independent counsel ultimately found that Olson had not misled Congress.

These decisions led me to think about more recent instances where public officials had bowed to the rule of law. Florida governor Jeb Bush would clearly have preferred to win favor with his supporters by sending state troopers into Terri Schiavo's room to keep doctors from removing her feeding tube, but he backed down when the courts told him he lacked the power to do so.

In Alabama, Roy Moore, the chief of the state's supreme court, after much protest, ultimately agreed not to put a copy of the Ten Commandments in the state courthouse after the U.S. Supreme Court ruled against him. Moore's threat to ignore the U.S. Supreme Court prompted *The New York Times* editorial page to demand that that Moore adhere to the "Rule of Law."

I realized that all of these cases involved public officials who had sworn that they would uphold the law and that journalists made no such commitment. But if investigating lawbreakers is an important part of our commitment to public service, how can we morally thumb our noses at the law every time we get a decision that displeases us?

Justice Potter Stewart, in an oft-quoted law review article, wrote in 1975 that that the press was designed to operate as a "Fourth Estate," able to check the excesses and abuses of the Congress, the executive branch, and the courts themselves. Stewart also argued that while every citizen was given the right of free speech under the First Amendment, the reference to freedom of the press "extends protection to an institution. The publishing business is, in short, the only organized private business that is given explicit constitutional protection."

The First Amendment protects the press's right to investigate, expose, and criticize government. But it also holds us to a standard closer to that of public officials when we engage in journalism that is designed to serve the public interest. Since I believe no journalistic privilege should be absolute, we should apply a balancing test of our own before deciding whether and when to defy a court order.

Another troubling point was nagging at me. Neither Rove nor Libby fit the classic profile of someone deserving confidential-source status—a "whistle-blower" who was jeopardizing his livelihood, his reputation, even his life, to provide valuable information to the press and expose wrongdoing. Rove and Libby were instead working to undermine a whistle-blower, Joe Wilson, by naming his wife, Valerie Plame, as a CIA operative. That might not be reason to remove confidential status that had been granted, but it did argue against granting it in the first place.

Occam's razor is an ancient piece of logic that holds one should embrace the simpler course of action when evaluating two equally valid alternatives. It was a maxim I would have to overcome as I moved toward a decision.

The arguments for refusing to name our source or hand over notes, despite an adverse Supreme Court ruling, were simple and straightforward: Matt Cooper thought Rove was a confidential source, therefore we couldn't compromise his identity. To do otherwise would undermine our integrity and credibility. It would also make sources far less likely to trust us in the future.

The arguments for Matt's agreeing to testify and for our turning over our notes to the special counsel were more convoluted. The leak of Plame's identity seemed like politics as usual. We hadn't thought the story important enough to put in our magazine. Rove wasn't a whistle-blower.

Fitzgerald had, nonetheless, insisted that Matt's testimony and his e-mails were critical to his investigation—an investigation that involved important matters of national security. It was difficult to disprove these contentions since the rules assuring grand jury secrecy kept us from knowing exactly what he was looking for. The Supreme Court's ruling in *Branzburg* has left journalists and their confidential sources with little protection if hauled before a grand jury.

And yet, Cooper had given "confidential" status to his source. Or had he?

10

Rove's Ground Rules

A s a reporter and an editor, I had distinguished between "anonymous sources," whose names we wouldn't use in a story, and "confidential sources," whose identity we might decide to protect even after litigating and losing. In fact, I had made exactly that distinction in an all-but-forgotten memo to the staff of *The Wall Street Journal* while I was its managing editor in 1986.

I was comfortable with reporters granting anonymity to their sources, but I thought a pledge of confidentiality required more thought and more review, since it could conceivably lead to jail for the reporter and substantial fines for the publisher.

Since reporters were supposed to be trying to get their sources to go on the record whenever possible, it seemed axiomatic that the source had to ask for confidentiality. A reporter couldn't make a source "confidential" without the source's agreement.

A review of Matt's e-mails made clear that Rove had stipulated he was speaking on "deep background" (what Matt had called "super secret background"), but there was no indication that he had demanded the confidentiality that Matt had unilaterally and, therefore, improperly granted him. By my reasoning, Rove was an anonymous source at best. In their hurried conversation, Rove had not asked and Matt had not promised that, if their conversation ever became part of a criminal legal matter, Matt would go to jail to protect Rove's identity.

That was my "tipping point"—the reason that finally changed my mind. Rove wasn't a confidential source and hadn't asked to be one.

So, why had I gone along for more than a year with Matt's insistence, and that of *Time's* editors and lawyers, that Rove was a confidential source? Instinct and practice made me think that as editor in chief I should back the decisions of the managing editors to whom I had delegated so much authority and to their journalists. If Matt Cooper, his bureau chief, his managing editor, and our in-house First Amendment lawyer all viewed Rove as a confidential source, it would take special circumstances for me to overrule them. The Supreme Court's refusal to hear our case was the first such circumstance I had encountered. It was hard to think of a second reason to do so.

Recognizing the consequences of my decision, I began to test my thinking with a small group of lawyers, editors, and friends. Bierstedt clearly favored our remaining in contempt—Cooper going to jail and our paying fines—if the Supreme Court refused to hear our case. Sam Klagsbrun, the psychotherapist I had been seeing weekly for five years, was adamant. A promise was a promise and I couldn't go back on it. Klagsbrun, an ethicist as well as a physician, was one of three physicians who had sued to overturn New York's ban on assisted suicide in the 1990s, taking their case to the Supreme Court, where they lost, 9–0.

I called one of my personal lawyers, Barbara Robinson, a partner at Debevoise & Plimpton and a former president of the New York City Bar Association. She conferred with two of her partners, James Goodale, the former general counsel to the New York Times Co., and Mary Jo White, a former U.S. attorney for the Southern District of New York in Manhattan. The next day she told me there was a split decision. "Goodale is stunned that you are thinking about turning over Cooper's notes. White insists you should have turned over the notes when you received the subpoena."

Mike Mitchell put me in touch with Joel M. Gora, associate dean of Brooklyn Law School, and we spent an hour discussing the choices. Gora, an expert on and a strong supporter of the "reporters' privilege," had worked on the ACLU's "friend of the court" petition to the Supreme Court in 1972, supporting Caldwell in the *Branzburg* case. Gora saw the obvious downside to our turning over Matt's notes, but he concluded, grudgingly, that a publisher couldn't ignore a Supreme Court ruling. Ira M. Millstein, an expert on corporate governance and a senior partner of the major New York law firm Weil, Gotshal & Manges, told me that corporations cannot engage in civil disobedience and that while Matt might choose to go to jail to protect his source, I should turn over the notes if our petition failed.

I solicited opinions from academics and several editors I admired at other publications, including John Carroll, then the top editor at the *Los Angeles Times* and one of my oldest friends in journalism. John and I had frequently discussed our respective careers over the four decades since we worked together on the *Haverford News*. He was stunned. He couldn't imagine that I would even consider turning over Matt's notes. It wasn't a lengthy conversation, since I understood his arguments. (None of the lawyers or editors with whom I discussed the case was told Rove's identity.)

I valued the feedback from my fellow editors, but their thinking was precisely where mine was before I had begun to apply legal reasoning to a journalistic problem. Their arguments were similar to the ones I had made to Parsons in the fall of 2004. Moreover, they worried that journalists—especially at smaller, less profitable publications—would see their independence undermined if I caved in and turned over the e-mails. That was reason enough not to do it.

Time's Jim Kelly, who was about to go to Italy on a long-planned vacation, clearly agreed with Bierstedt and the editors in and outside Time Inc. I had spoken to. He was against turning over the e-mails. I told him I would track him down if the court ruled against us and I decided to comply with the court order.

John Huey, my deputy for four years and my closest friend in journalism since we first met at the *Journal* in 1980, was also about to go on vacation. I had deliberately kept Huey in the dark about the evolution of my thinking. Although it hadn't been announced, we had planned an orderly succession at the end of 2005. I knew this decision would be my legacy, and keeping John out of my deliberations would ensure that he could succeed me free of the baggage I was accumulating. While I wrestled with the Plame case, John continued to supervise our weeklies and our business publications—a full-time job.

Matt Cooper and I met in my office on Tuesday, June 14. I thought he had handled the pressures of the case with intelligence and integrity from the time he had received the special counsel's first subpoena. He too had begun to question Abrams's guidance—he was especially bothered that in meetings Abrams continually confused Libby and Rove—and he was relying more heavily on Richard Sauber, whom he had retained the previous August. (Listening to Abrams make an argument in a contempt hearing before Judge Hogan in October 2004, Cooper had written *Je Suis Fucked* in his notebook.) At this meeting, I first told Matt that I was leaning toward turning over the notes if the Supreme Court refused to accept our petition.

Matt had thought about the issues, and I could sense his ambivalence. Sauber had told Matt that as a matter of law, he should agree to testify if the Supreme Court refused to take our petition. But he also told Matt that the decision was one of conscience as much as law. Matt made it clear he had no interest in naming his source or in testifying before the grand jury. But he understood that refusing to testify wouldn't make much sense if I had already revealed Rove's name by turning over the e-mails between him and his editors. We agreed to talk again after hearing from the Supreme Court.

Later in the week I met with Cappuccio for the first time since we had gone to Washington to engage Olson and Gibson, Dunn. After receiving his assurance that our conversation would stay between us, I briefed him on my thinking. He thought we should be asking Rove for a waiver, but assuming we weren't willing to do so, he agreed that we should turn over our notes if the Supreme Court refused to hear our case.

By the weekend I had become completely comfortable with my decision. There had been no *Eureka!* moment. My thinking had evolved over the prior two months, but only then did I admit to myself that it was no longer in question.

I had a conference call the next Monday, June 20, with Ted Olson and his partners Miguel Estrada in Washington and Ted Boutrous in Los Angeles. I told them of my decision. Olson and Estrada leaned toward my position. Although Boutrous, who had the most active First Amendment practice among the lawyers, said little, there was little doubt that he disagreed. Boutrous urged me to read law professor Alexander Bickel's brilliant treatise *The Morality of Consent*. It argued that the First Amendment could be interpreted to cover a reporter's privilege or right to keep sources confidential. But, referring to *Branzburg*, Bickel expressed his "regret" that the Supreme Court had rejected that position. He did not suggest ignoring it.

Before we could discuss the pros and cons of any decision, however, Estrada interrupted with some disturbing news. He had heard from Fitzgerald's office that Fitzgerald would ask Judge Hogan to lift the stay on Matt's incarceration and our fines immediately if the Supreme Court refused to hear our petition. More ominously,

Fitzgerald had made it clear that he would push Hogan to add bigger fines and criminal contempt citations if we didn't turn over our notes and the name of our confidential source.

I asked Gibson, Dunn for a memo explaining criminal contempt. I got one back a few days later. While a court's civil contempt power is fundamentally coercive, the memo explained, the criminal contempt power is "purely punitive and meant only to vindicate the court's authority." Although it rarely happens, I learned that judges have the power to impose criminal contempt and "summary punishment," imprisoning a defendant for up to six months without a trial. In 2004, for example, Jim Taricani, a reporter with WJAR-TV, an NBC affiliate in Providence, Rhode Island, refused to identify the confidential source who had given him a videotape in a bribery case. After a $1,000-a-day fine had been enforced for about forty-five days for civil contempt, the court charged Taricani with criminal contempt and sentenced him to six months of home confinement. The actual sentence was lifted after four months.

Although a refusal might result in my being held in criminal contempt, the memo suggested it was extremely unlikely that any officers of Time Warner could similarly be held or that a judge could levy fines against the parent corporation. The editorial independence established in "The Role of Time Inc.'s Editor-in-Chief" created a corporate veil, the memo said, sparing other executives from responsibility for my acts. For the same reason my fear was allayed that a criminal contempt conviction could threaten Time Warner's cable division or other operations that depended on government licenses.

But Olson and several lawyers specializing in corporate governance warned that criminal contempt proceedings against Time Inc. could force Time Warner to disclose the proceedings to shareholders, and that the corporation's board might ask why Time Inc.'s management was not complying with the court's orders. Others went further, stating that no corporate officer of a public company could defy a finding of criminal contempt without gaining a formal resolution approving that defiance from the company's board of directors.

None of the lawyers thought a board of any publicly held company would approve such a resolution, especially since it was unlikely their liability insurance would protect them if shareholder suits were to follow. Ira Millstein, a lawyer specializing in issues of corporate governance, provided a telling hypothetical: "Suppose a division of General Electric decided to continue polluting the Hudson after being held in criminal contempt. Can you imagine the GE board approving that decision?"

Although the words I had written about "The Role of Time Inc.'s Editor-in-Chief" might protect the corporation from damages in a criminal contempt case, my own editorial independence, and that of my successors, would be severely compromised if I had to seek permission for anything from the corporate board. Under such circumstances, turning over our notes to the special counsel appeared to be far less damaging to our editorial independence than asking the board for permission to defy the courts.

All of this, of course, was hypothetical, since I had already determined that we would turn over our notes if the Supreme Court refused to hear our petition in the civil contempt case. Nonetheless, it was important—for me and, as would soon become clear, for journalists everywhere—to understand the likely consequences of continued defiance if the court ruled against us.

As the week progressed, we learned that the Supreme Court would announce its decision on our petition on Monday, June 27. I met with John Redpath and Robin Bierstedt and told them what I had decided. I called Matt Cooper, as well as Jim Kelly, who was now in

Italy, and John Huey, who was in the Caribbean, to keep them informed. I didn't tell anyone outside Time Inc.—although I thought it slim, there was still a chance the court would grant our petition—but, in a brief telephone call, I told Arthur Sulzberger of the *Times* that I was talking with our lawyers about the possibility of turning over our notes if our petition was unsuccessful.

On Monday the decision came down. As I had feared for months and had come to think inevitable, the Supreme Court announced that it had refused to hear Time's petition or that of Judith Miller. The only surprise in the brief ruling was the announcement that Justice Stephen G. Breyer, whom we had counted on to support our petition, had recused himself without explanation. Although the court's deliberations weren't made public, Judge Hogan later told a group of reporters that he had heard that not one of the Supreme Court's nine justices wanted to hear our case.

11

Complying with the Courts

I was ready to give Fitzgerald the notes right away. But Boutrous argued for holding off until we had a better sense of what Judge Hogan would do following the Supreme Court's refusal to hear our case. Although Hogan had agreed to every one of Fitzgerald's arguments, his asides from the bench recognized that the Constitution had created a clash between competing values, and he had indicated some sympathy for our plight.

The day after the Supreme Court turned us down, we announced our view that there were grounds for the judge to reconsider his contempt findings because Fitzgerald's focus appeared to have shifted. We had come to believe that the special counsel was no longer looking for possible violations of the Intelligence Identities Protection Act by those who had exposed Plame. Instead, everything we were hearing suggested Fitzgerald was now focusing on possible charges of perjury by witnesses making false and misleading statements to FBI investigators or to the grand jury. Where once it had seemed that Fitzgerald wanted Matt's notes to prove that Rove and Libby had leaked intelligence secrets, he now seemed to want them to prove that they had somehow perjured themselves under oath before federal investigators and the grand jury.

We prepared a memorandum urging the judge to find that if national security was no longer an issue, the basis for the subpoenas had lapsed. Our memorandum quoted from legislative history. It showed that the law that had initially prompted Fitzgerald's investigation had been narrowly drawn to "exclude the possibility that casual discussion, political debate, the journalistic pursuit of a story on intelligence, or the disclosure of illegality or impropriety in government will be chilled by enactment of the bill." We argued that subpoenas issued to prove a perjury charge chilled our reporting in just that way. We also quoted one of the bill's authors, Angelo M. Codevilla, who had written that it was "nonsense" to assert that the identification of Plame was a criminal violation.

We met in Judge Hogan's court two days after the Supreme Court's ruling. It was the first time I had seen Fitzgerald. He was right out of central casting—a modern Jimmy Stewart—the dedicated, brilliant public servant, tall, imposing, unfailingly polite, and laser-focused on the issues. Fitzgerald asked the judge to begin his deliberations with Time Inc. "I can't figure out how Time could make contempt lawful," he said. "If the court order is final, then Time has to turn over the documents. I don't know how under any set of circumstances a corporate board could meet and agree to break the law."

Fitzgerald then suggested that if Time Inc. produced documents, including Cooper's notes, "I think that might be a material fact that might aid the rest of Mr. Cooper's situation." I thought Fitzgerald meant that if we turned over our notes, he might not ask Cooper to testify, but he quickly dispelled that notion, saying only that if we were to comply, "that may sway Mr. Cooper to follow the court's order" as well.

Boutrous and Matt Cooper's attorney, Richard Sauber, asked for a short delay to consider what we should do, but Abrams and Robert S. Bennett, a Washington lawyer who had recently joined Judith Miller's defense team, made it clear that Miller would refuse to testify before the grand jury. When Judge Hogan again mentioned the "clash of values" presented by our case, Fitzgerald replied, "We need to step back and realize this case is not about a whistle-blower. This case is about potential retaliation against a whistle-blower."

Hogan ordered all of us to return for a final hearing on July 6, but in doing so, he made it clear that he would side with Fitzgerald and that he had lost patience with Time Inc. "The time has come," he said, quoting the walrus in Lewis Carroll's *Through the Looking-Glass*. He added, again quoting Carroll, that he thought our behavior had become "curiouser and curiouser." Hogan warned that if we didn't turn over our notes, his penalty would involve "a very large sum," in accordance with the company's size and net income.

After the hearing, I told Cooper that I would turn over the notes the next day. That night I called Parsons with the same news. The next morning I made the following announcement to Time Inc.'s twelve thousand employees:

> The First Amendment guarantees freedom of the press, including the right to gather information of interest to the public and, where necessary, to protect the confidentiality of sources.
>
> Time Inc. believes in that guarantee. That is why we have supported from the outset the efforts of *Time* magazine reporter Matt Cooper in resisting the Special Counsel's attempts to obtain information regarding Mr. Cooper's confidential sources. Time Inc. and Mr. Cooper have fought this case all the way from the district court to the Supreme Court of the United States.
>
> In this particular case, where national security and the role of a grand jury have been at issue, the Supreme Court chose to let stand the district court's order requiring Time Inc. and Mr. Cooper to comply with the Special Counsel's subpoenas.

It did so after the United States Court of Appeals for the District of Columbia affirmed that order.

In declining to review the important issues presented by this case, we believe that the Supreme Court has limited press freedom in ways that will have a chilling effect on our work and that may damage the free flow of information that is so necessary in a democratic society. It may also encourage excesses by overzealous prosecutors.

It is unfortunate that the Supreme Court has left uncertain what protections the First Amendment and the federal common law provide journalists and their confidential sources.

It is also worth noting that many foreign governments, including China, Venezuela, and Cameroon, to name a few, refer to U.S. contempt rulings when seeking to justify their own restrictive press laws.

Despite these concerns, Time Inc. shall deliver the subpoenaed records to the Special Counsel in accordance with its duties under the law. The same Constitution that protects the freedom of the press requires obedience to final decisions of the courts and respect for their rulings and judgments. That Time Inc. strongly disagrees with the courts provides no immunity. The innumerable Supreme Court decisions in which even Presidents have followed orders with which they strongly disagreed, evidences that our nation lives by the rule of law and that none of us is above it.

We believe that our decision to provide the Special Prosecutor with the subpoenaed records obviates the need for Matt Cooper to testify and certainly removes any justification for incarceration.

Time Inc.'s decision doesn't represent a change in our philosophy, nor does it reflect a departure from our belief in the need for confidential sources. It does reflect a response to a profound departure from the practice of federal prosecutors when this case is compared with other landmark cases involving confidentiality over the past 30 years. Since the days of Attorney General John Mitchell, the Justice Department has sought confidential sources from reporters as a last resort, not as an easy option. Neither Archibald Cox, the Watergate Special Prosecutor, nor Judge John Sirica sought to force the *Washington Post* or its reporters to reveal the identity of "Deep Throat," the prized confidential source.

Although we shall comply with the order to turn over the subpoenaed records, we shall continue to support the protection of confidential sources. We do so with the knowledge that forty-nine states and the District of Columbia now recognize some form of protection for confidential sources, and that legislation is now pending in Congress to enact a federal shield law for confidential sources.

Olson and I had worked on the statement in the week before it was issued. It was a difficult balancing act. Since Cooper's testimony was still up in the air, I didn't want to undercut him by arguing Rove wasn't a confidential source. And as much as I thought it important to make the Rule of Law argument, it was equally important to make clear that we remained committed to the use of confidential sources when we could. Recognizing the ambivalence that a careful reader would discern, I deliberately left vague whether there might be other cases where the public interest was such that we would defy the Supreme Court.

"Pearlstine has hung his own staff of many hundreds of reporters and many dozens of editors out to dry," Steve Lovelady, a former managing editor at *The Philadelphia Inquirer*, wrote on the *Columbia*

Journalism Review website. Lovelady, whom I had worked with at the *Journal* and, again, at Time Inc., added that I had "joined that select handful of people who know with assurance precisely how the first sentence of his obituary is going to read."

An hour after receiving our statement, Arthur Sulzberger Jr. released a statement on behalf of the *Times*, saying, "We are deeply disappointed by Time Inc.'s decision to deliver the subpoenaed records." Sulzberger added that the *Times* "faced similar pressures in 1978 when both our reporter Myron Farber and the *Times* Company were held in contempt of court for refusing to provide the names of confidential sources. Mr. Farber served 40 days in jail and we were forced to pay significant fines." Sulzberger also said, "Our focus is now on our own reporter, Judith Miller, and in supporting her during this difficult time."

My decision was the lead story in the next day's *Times*, and it also made the front pages of *The Washington Post*, the *Los Angeles Times*, and many other large daily newspapers. *The New York Times* ran nearly a page of coverage inside its front section, including a lengthy profile of me. It focused on my determination to make the decision myself and on the deliberations leading up to it. The story of my decision led the evening news on NBC and was prominently featured on the other broadcast networks and cable channels.

Although support from many other journalists would eventually emerge, most of the next-day commentary from writers and editors was critical. The late David Halberstam, a former *Times* reporter who wrote *The Powers That Be*, a 1979 book on Time Inc. and other large media companies, called the decision "very disturbing." He and others worried that the decision reflected larger corporate concerns. "It is a strange company and it is really part of an entertainment complex," Halberstam told the *Times*. "The journalism part is smaller and smaller. There is a great question out there: is this a journalistic or an entertainment company?"

Newspaper editorials in Denver, San Francisco, Portland (Oregon), and elsewhere denounced my decision. *The Salt Lake Tribune* in Salt Lake City said the decision was "in contempt of Henry Luce, the fearless founder of *Time* and *Life*," leaving a "stain of corporate cowardice." David Kidwell, a columnist in *The Miami Herald*, asked "where blacks and women would be today if journalists like *Time* magazine's Editor-in-Chief were the custodian of their convictions." Steve Breen's editorial-page cartoon in *The San Diego Union-Tribune* had a caricature of me on a cover of *Time*, proclaiming me "Wimp of the Year."

12

Matt Cooper Testifies

All the while, as I was pondering the Plame episode and the First Amendment, I had become a newlywed. I had married Jane Boon, a scientist and engineer whom I had met and had been living with for more than a year. Jane is different from any other woman I had known. A Canadian with three degrees from American universities, including a doctorate in industrial engineering, Jane had spent a decade in Cambridge, Massachusetts, far removed from the self-absorption of big-city journalism. Although she had been a sympathetic and supportive listener as I obsessed over the Plame episode, she was skeptical when I told her my decision would lead the nightly news and be on the front page of every big metro daily. We had married in the middle of April, but the pressure of the case had forced us to postpone our honeymoon. Now, with the decision behind me, we began a four-day vacation in Big Sur.

But there was no escaping the case. Among the calls and e-mails awaiting our arrival was one from a senior *Time* editor, saying he had "similarly had a problem with the notion that journalists are above the law," so "I admire your argument and your courage." Less than ten hours later, this same editor sent his edited draft of a one-page story for publication in the issue closing that weekend. It was far from admiring. The draft was accompanied by a note from him, telling me, "You figure prominently in it, but I said to myself that if we weren't *Time*, and we were writing about the issue, that's just how it would be." I have no explanation for the abrupt turnaround.

It was a close call whether I should have seen drafts of the story. I understood the story better than anyone else working on it, and as Time Inc.'s editor in chief, I read every story in *Time* prior to publication. I thought the typical *Time* reader would assume I would read a story about *Time* and me. But as a story's subject, I would typically have had no involvement with its editing. I had worked hard over the prior decade to reassert the editorial independence of Time Inc.'s publications, especially when it came to covering ourselves and our parent, Time Warner.

The editors working on the story, however, were having trouble reaching the two most logical final readers, John Huey and Jim Kelly. Huey was without his computer or access to a reliable phone in the Caribbean. Kelly, who was in Italy, was uncharacteristically out of reach. So the story came to me.

The story wasn't terrible. Under the headline "When to Give Up a Source," it properly included criticisms from Lucy Dalglish, executive director of the Reporters Committee for Freedom of the Press, and Tom Rosenstiel, director of the Project for Excellence in Journalism. Bill Saporito, the story's writer, also raised thoughtful concerns of his own about the decision. But there were no quotes from anyone who agreed with me, even though every other major publication that had covered the story had found defenders of my decision.

I was reluctant to go back to the editor who had sent me the draft, or to Saporito, the writer, with my criticism. I did, however, reach Steve Koepp, *Time*'s deputy managing editor, and finally, Kelly. After reading the draft, they agreed that Saporito should insert a quote that supported my decision. He found one from Jay Rosen, chairman of New York University's journalism department, that had run in *The Wall Street Journal*. This final draft also quoted Newton Minow, the former chairman of the Federal Communications Commission, who also supported the decision. None of the critical quotes were deleted and the tone of Saporito's draft remained the same.

The rest of the weekend was given over to interviews with reporters from other publications. At one point Jane called me from a hot tub outside our suite and asked if I cared to join her. I did. While in the tub, I took three calls on a mobile phone. "I went to bed with an editor and I woke up with a lawyer," Jane said. It was not a compliment.

Matt Cooper and Judith Miller had a far more difficult Independence Day weekend. Although we had hoped that turning over the notes would lead Fitzgerald to drop the contempt citation against Cooper, Fitzgerald maintained that he still needed Matt's testimony, presumably to authenticate the notes. Some of Matt's friends, among them Steven Waldman, editor of Beliefnet.com and a former editor at *U.S. News & World Report*, encouraged him to testify. Waldman sent Cooper an e-mail, first reported in the *Times*, asking, "Do you go to jail to protect the confidentiality of a source whose name has been revealed, and not by you but by someone else?" Waldman also told Cooper to think about his family as he wrestled with his decision.

Matt was concerned about the impact that his absence would have on his five-year-old son. He spoke of his ambivalence to many friends, calling himself a "tower of Jell-O" to more than one of them. Matt's wife, Mandy, however, argued that his professional credibility would be destroyed should he testify instead of going to jail. By the end of the weekend, Matt was with Mandy, determined not to testify.

Matt's position again changed on the morning of Wednesday, July 6. His lawyer, Dick Sauber, described what happened on the

Legal Times website: "What changed is that I'm flying back on the red-eye Tuesday night, on the night of July 5, directly from Anchorage to Chicago," where he would change planes for Washington. At O'Hare Airport, Sauber bought a copy of Wednesday's *Wall Street Journal* and read a comment from Robert Luskin, Karl Rove's lawyer, acknowledging that Rove had spoken with Cooper. Sauber said he inferred from Luskin's comment that Rove had never asked for confidentiality. Sauber said he called Matt and said, "Read this article. It changes everything."

The *Journal* article quoted Luskin as saying that Rove "didn't disclose Valerie Plame's identification to anyone." Luskin added that Rove hadn't asked any reporter to treat him as a confidential source in the Plame case, "so if Matt Cooper is going to jail to protect a source, it's not Karl he's protecting."

A flurry of signed notes and phone calls confirmed what the *Journal* had reported: as far as Luskin was concerned, Rove hadn't sought confidentiality. With that information, Cooper told Judge Hogan he would testify because "a short time ago, in somewhat dramatic fashion," he had received an "express, personal consent from my source."

Luskin, however, said that he was surprised by Cooper's claim that he had received a new waiver. Instead, Luskin told the *Times*'s Adam Liptak that he had only reaffirmed the blanket waiver, in response to a request from Mr. Fitzgerald, that all White House employees had been told to give. In any case, "Karl was not afraid of what Cooper is going to say and is clearly trying to be fully candid with the prosecutor," Luskin said.

If Rove had said a week earlier that he had no problem with Matt's testifying, the contempt citation against Time Inc. would also have been dropped. Then again, if I hadn't turned over the notes, would Rove have really said he had no problem with Matt testifying?

. . .

With Matt agreeing to testify, the focus quickly shifted from him to the *Times*'s Judith Miller. Although she had never written a story about Joseph Wilson or Valerie Plame, she was known for her many sources within the Bush administration, especially among the hawks on the Iraq war. Fitzgerald was seeking testimony about one of those sources.

Miller and the *Times* would become the story for the next several months. Miller continued to defy orders to testify and gave an impassioned speech at a hearing on July 6 justifying her decision. "If journalists cannot be trusted to guarantee their [sources'] confidentiality, then journalists cannot function and there cannot be a free press," she said. Referring to her government sources, she added that many "will not talk to reporters if we cannot be trusted to protect their identity. The risks are too great. The government is too powerful and the country is too polarized."

Miller rejected the blanket waivers that Bush had imposed on White House employees because "waivers demanded by a superior as a condition of employment are not voluntary. They are coercive and should they become common practice, and I fear they are, they will be yet another means by wrongdoers in government to silence people who want to report facts of public import to journalists or to express views that differ from the official orthodoxy."

Miller said she was "gratified that The New York Times understands the importance of such pledges of confidentiality, and I am deeply grateful to my paper and to its publisher [Sulzberger] in particular" for supporting her decision not to testify. She concluded, "In this case I cannot break my word just to stay out of jail. The right of civil disobedience based on personal conscience is fundamental to our system and honored throughout our history."

The *Times* and Robert Bennett, a criminal lawyer whom Miller had retained to augment Abrams, were clearly hoping to portray her as a martyr defending investigative reporting as the highest level of public service. Bennett noted that "Judith Miller committed no crime. Judith Miller never even wrote an article." He added that "perhaps more important," Miller "served with the most sensitive units in Iraq. She was embedded. She was trusted by our government to maintain confidentiality and secrets. She got top-secret clearances and she swore she would not breach the confidences that were shared with her." But Bennett said he was perplexed because "another part of the government is saying she has to go to jail because she's maintaining confidentiality." Bennett also insisted that sending Miller to jail "will not coerce her" to reveal her sources.

Fitzgerald was equally forceful, telling the packed courtroom, "The law says that a jury is entitled to every man's evidence," and that neither Miller nor anyone in government can promise confidentiality when the law doesn't allow it. He added that the "public does have to know that there is a check on governmental power called a grand jury. The public does need to know that we are doing the honest best to get to the bottom of whether crimes were committed and by whom, and we can't have that all thrown out because one person wants to hold on to a promise that can't be made."

Fitzgerald said we cannot have "journalists given a power that no one in the executive branch through the attorney general, the FBI director, and the head of the CIA" has. He argued the merits of coercion through fines and the prospect of jail time. "People change their mind," he said. "We saw here today that a source reached out to Mr. Cooper and asked him to testify. How do we know the same wouldn't happen to Ms. Miller?"

Fitzgerald also urged Judge Hogan to consider holding Miller and the *Times* in criminal contempt. "It is particularly important in this case where Miller and *The New York Times* appear to have confused Miller's *ability* to commit contempt with a legal *right* to do so.

A clear indication that the Court views defiance of its Order as criminal behavior, as opposed to conduct which can be condoned, may have a positive effect," he wrote.

Judge Hogan insisted, "It is Miss Miller's decision" to refuse to testify. "She has the keys to her release within herself." He added, "We are not above the law. Miss Miller feels otherwise. She has claimed the prerogative of deciding for herself what information the grand jury is entitled to hear," and he noted that her "publisher now backs her up in that regard in a criminal investigation."

Hogan then said he would "require the confinement of Miss Miller . . . until such time as she testifies or until the grand jury expires, which is in approximately four months." Hogan ordered that Miller be jailed at the conclusion of the hearing. She was immediately taken to the Alexandria (Virginia) Detention Center, where she remained for the next eighty-five days.

Bill Keller, the *Times's* executive editor, called Miller's jailing "a chilling conclusion to an utterly confounding case." Arthur Sulzberger Jr., the publisher, said that his company "will do all that we can to ensure Judy's safety and continue to fight for the principles that led her to make a most difficult and honorable choice."

The next day the *Times* printed a lengthy editorial—nearly two thousand words running over two columns—entitled "Judith Miller Goes to Jail." It said that *Time* had "decided, over Mr. Cooper's protests, to release documents demanded by the judge that revealed his confidential sources. We were deeply disappointed by that action." The editorial added, "We do not see how a newspaper, magazine or television station can support a reporter's decision to protect confidential sources even if the potential price is lost liberty, and then hand over the notes or documents that make the reporter's sacrifice meaningless . . . No journalist's promise will be worth much if the employer that stands behind him or her is prepared to undercut such a vow of secrecy."

The editorial, despite its length, was far more interesting for what it omitted than for what it discussed. There was no mention, for example, that Time Inc. had been held in contempt while the New York Times Co. had not been. It therefore made no effort to distinguish between an individual's and a public company's right to engage in civil disobedience—one of the important distinctions that had been at the heart of my decision to hand over the notes.

It also discussed the First Amendment without ever mentioning the Supreme Court's *Branzburg* decision. It argued that Miller was "surrendering her liberty in defense of a greater liberty, granted to a free press by the founding fathers so journalists can work on behalf of the public without fear of regulation or retaliation from any branch of government."

Although the editorial acknowledged that "press freedoms are not absolute," it seemed to conclude that the press, and only the press, could determine when the confidentiality privilege could be exercised. "These limits cannot be dictated by the whim of a branch of government," it said, concluding that "the founders warned against any attempt to have the government set limits on a free press, under any circumstances."

It was as if the Supreme Court had never addressed the issues Miller, Cooper, and Time Inc. had had to face. That the Court had dealt with and disagreed with every important point in the editorial was of no consequence to *The New York Times* and its editorial writers. Nor, apparently, was the *Times's* own pledge in the Pentagon Papers case that it would cease publication of the papers if the Supreme Court ruled that publication was against the law. The editorial writers may have been unaware of this analogy. Or they may have found it inconvenient.

13

Dealing with the Fallout

On July 11, Jim Kelly, John Huey, and I had lunch in the capital with more than a dozen members of *Time*'s Washington bureau. With Judith Miller in jail and Matt Cooper due to testify two days later, we expected a tense reception and we got it. Members of the bureau felt they had been blindsided by my decision. Over sandwiches in the bureau's conference room, several reporters showed us e-mails from sources saying they would never speak to anyone working for *Time* again. Karen Tumulty, one of the bureau's most senior and most respected journalists, had told the *Times*, "We're very worried about what kind of signal this sends," since "confidentiality is the lubricant of journalism." Matt Cooper repeated that my decision had been made over his objections, but he said he understood the reasons for it.

As I had feared, the distinction I had made between anonymous and confidential sources didn't wash. The journalistic culture in Washington is different. "When I pick up the phone, call a source, and agree to do an interview on background, I assume everything in it is confidential," one reporter said. Many also argued that sources assumed the same thing even if the word *confidential* was never uttered.

Besides explaining why I had chosen to turn over the notes—and emphasizing the distinction between anonymous and confidential sources—I insisted that we remained committed to investigative stories using confidential sources. Two such recent stories had been written in Washington: an investigation into the interrogation of a prisoner held in Guantánamo Bay, and a story about the Nuclear Regulatory Commission's failure to prepare civilian nuclear plants for a terrorist attack. A third story, a profile of a suicide bomber in Iraq, had been prepared by the Baghdad bureau. "I approved all three stories, knowing we might have to defend each of them," I said.

The bureau's journalists were unimpressed. Michael Weisskopf, a *Time* senior correspondent and a genuine hero to his fellow journalists, was among the angriest staffers at the lunch. Weisskopf, who had had a distinguished career at *The Washington Post* before coming to *Time*, had gone to Baghdad to work on *Time*'s Person of the Year cover story about the American soldier. While he was accompanying a routine patrol, a grenade had landed in the back of his Humvee. Weisskopf had grabbed it, and while he was trying to throw it away, the grenade exploded, resulting in the loss of his hand.

Huey was asked during the lunch what he would have done in my shoes. He stopped short of an outright endorsement of my decision.

When asked point-blank by an angry Karen Tumulty whether he would have made the same choice, he said he didn't know. He said he was convinced that I had reached a principled decision and was not influenced by any corporate pressure, and for those reasons he was supporting me—but not happily. (Since then, he has said publicly that if he had known everything he knows now, he would have seen no other choice.) "That's a cop-out!" Weisskopf replied, adding that those challenges made it all the more important that we hold tightly to our journalistic principles. Quiet descended over the room, and the meeting ended a few minutes later with an agreement that Michael Duffy, then *Time*'s Washington bureau chief, would work with me to come up with new editorial guidelines for handling information and for treating confidential sources.

Jim, John, and I returned to New York for a dinner that evening with about twenty of *Time*'s most senior editors, writers, and columnists. There, the proposition that every conversation with a source that is not explicitly on the record should be considered confidential was taken to its most absurd conclusion by the magazine's senior political columnist, Joe Klein.

Klein spoke about his coverage of the Michael Dukakis presidential campaign for *New York* magazine in 1988. As he was about to board the campaign plane, Dukakis came up to him and asked, "Off the record, how am I doing?" Klein told us that he would keep his answer "confidential to my death." I told him later that I thought it more likely that he had dined out on the exchange the next night. "Perhaps," he agreed, "but I would never disclose the information in response to a subpoena from anyone." The banality of the exchange notwithstanding, Klein was arguing that his answer must be kept confidential, since he, not Dukakis, was the confidential source. At least Joe is consistent in his willingness to keep information off the record. His novel *Primary Colors* was written under the pseudonym Anonymous.

Matt Cooper testified before the grand jury for more than two hours on July 13. Outside the courtroom, Cooper said little. Rove's identity was old news because *Newsweek* had obtained and published a facsimile copy of Matt's e-mail identifying Rove as his source.

Cooper kept the rest of his story for the next issue of *Time*. Under federal law, prosecutors and grand jurors are sworn to secrecy, but those who testify can discuss what they said. I had asked Matt to write an account of his testimony for us even though Fitzgerald had asked him not to disclose any of his testimony.

Matt told the grand jury that before Rove ended their brief conversation he said, "I have already said too much," indicating that he may have realized that he had overstepped his bounds in the interview. Matt wrote that Fitzgerald, in his questioning, was especially interested in whether Matt had ever called Rove to speak about welfare reform. The previous day, Rove's lawyer, Robert Luskin, had told reporters that Matt had sought an interview about welfare reform in July 2003 but had then switched topics to ask about Wilson's column. Cooper wrote that he might have left a message with Rove's office expressing an interest in welfare reform but that he had no record or recollection that it was discussed when they actually spoke on July 13, 2003. Cooper wrote that he concluded that Rove might have testified otherwise.

Cooper also explained that his reference to "double super secret background" in his e-mail to editors naming Rove as his source was not "a journalistic term of art" but a reference to the film *Animal House*, in which John Belushi's wild Delta House fraternity is placed on "double secret probation." Cooper said the use of "super" was his own addition and that in fact Rove had told him the conversation was on "deep background." Cooper then wrote that he took that term "to mean that I can use the material but not quote it, and that I must keep the identity of my source confidential."

The same issue included a column by Joe Klein, which began with a lengthy denunciation of my decision to hand over our notes. Klein argued that anytime someone in Washington asked for protection, "a blood oath has been signed, no matter how scurrilous or trivial the information involved."

After more meetings with larger groups of Time Inc. journalists, I sensed some of the anger dissipating, even though there remained ample disagreement with my decision. Outside the Time and Life

Building, however, the attacks seemed to gain intensity, and in some cases, they were intensely personal.

There was also considerable support, albeit often from journalists working outside the New York–Washington corridor. The divergent opinions reflected the battles that had raged within my own mind, as well as profound differences about the Bush administration and the war in Iraq. Although it sometimes felt as though I were undergoing an appendectomy without anesthetic, every story and every encounter fascinated me.

Soon after Judith Miller went to jail, the Tribeca Film Institute, whose board I sat on, sponsored a screening of Alan Pakula's *All the President's Men*. I was in Washington and unable to attend. But Ben Bradlee, Carl Bernstein, and Bob Woodward all participated in a panel discussion following the film. Bernstein spoke of his own subpoena and Katharine Graham's willingness to hide his notes—the Gray-Haired Widow Defense. "That's quite a difference from what we've seen in the last few weeks," Bernstein added. He failed, of course, to distinguish between his subpoena, served in a civil suit and thrown out by a district judge, and a contempt citation the Supreme Court had left in place. Bradlee said, "I don't know why the *Time* lawyers didn't fight that some more."

In a subsequent article in *Vanity Fair*, Bernstein repeated the comparison between Katharine Graham's willingness to take legal custody of his notes and my own decision. He also raised what came to be the central argument of my most vociferous critics—that "Pearlstine's actions suggested that he had a responsibility to protect the profits and corporate interests of Time Warner first—and journalistic principle second."

Once it was clear that Karl Rove was Matt's source, some of the commentators who had initially opposed my decision now argued that *Time*'s greater sin was protecting Rove in the first place.

Michael Wolff, a *Vanity Fair* columnist, appeared with me on one panel where he went so far as to argue that our refusal to name Rove had prolonged the war in Iraq and so was responsible for the deaths of thousands of American soldiers.

Most of the criticism, however, followed Bernstein's line. *The New York Observer*, a small but influential weekly that obsesses over coverage of the media, put two articles on the front page of its July 11 issue under the headline "The Norman Evasion." The subhead was "Time Inc. Editor Pearlstine's Halfway Solution Doesn't Stop Media Giant's Journalistic Slide; His Dusty Law Degree May Have Failed Him." The piece was written by Robert Sam Anson, a former *Time* correspondent who saw my decision as part of a slide from quality journalism to an emphasis on corporate profits that he claimed had begun more than thirty years earlier.

Anson argued that I had forgotten what real editors stand for. As for Time Inc., he wrote, the company first went astray in 1973, six years after Luce's death, when it bought a forest-products firm. The descent continued through the launch and acquisition of profitable but undistinguished magazines and accelerated after Time Inc. merged with Warner Bros. to form Time Warner. My own sordid decline followed the decision to replace Floyd Abrams as our counsel with Ted Olson, whom Anson dismissed as "more accustomed to pummeling the press than protecting it."

At year's end *Fast Company*, a business magazine, had me as number two on its list of top ten Cowards of the Year, asking, "Is Time Inc. a journalistic institution or the maidservant to an entertainment behemoth, Time Warner? Pearlstine gave us the answer when he turned over *Time* reporter Matt Cooper's notes to the prosecutor investigating the CIA-agent outing." Only Microsoft's CEO, Steve Ballmer, finished ahead of me on the magazine's Cowards list, for waffling on antidiscrimination legislation supported by gay-rights proponents in Washington State.

Graydon Carter, *Vanity Fair*'s editor and another *Time* alumnus, made a similar point in his monthly Editor's Letter, claiming that, unlike leading newspapers and magazines in the days of Watergate and the Pentagon Papers, most major news businesses now are "minor cogs in the machinery of far-flung entertainment complexes that often rely on federal permission to complete their extensive growth plans." Obviously seeking to compare Time Warner with *Vanity Fair*'s parent company, Advance Publications, Inc., which is owned by the Newhouse family, he opined that people who own media assets, "which in a democracy virtually amount to public trusts, should realize that standing up for principles of those assets—journalists' being allowed to protect their sources, for one—is not just a cost of doing business. In the long run, it is good business."

Shortly after the appearance of Carter's Editor's Letter, however, Newhouse's Cleveland newspaper, *The Plain Dealer*, announced that it was withholding two stories "of profound importance." The paper's editor, Douglas Clifton, said that the public interest would have been served by running the stories, but their publication would "almost certainly lead to a leak investigation and the ultimate choice: talk or go to jail. Because talking isn't an option and jail is too high a price to pay, these two stories will go untold for now." Carter never did write about this self-censorship within his own company.

Cokie Roberts and Steven V. Roberts took a similar tack in their syndicated column, but, unlike Carter, they attacked Time Inc. and the Newhouse chain of newspapers for Clifton's decision. In a column that ran under the headline "Profits Taking Precedence over Principles," they wrote, "While the *Times* is a publicly traded company, it is controlled by the Sulzberger family, and publisher Arthur Sulzberger Jr. did not have to consult anybody else in backing Miller." In contrast, they said that *Time* and *The Plain Dealer* are both "deeply beholden" to their parent company's "public stockholders."

They went on, "Media conglomerates can cause conflicts of interest. On the day that Time-Warner [*sic*] merged with AOL, a reporter for *Fortune* (a Time publication) received a call telling him to abandon his profile of AOL boss Steve Case. The message: 'We just bought you.'"

Cokie Roberts is a senior correspondent at National Public Radio, and before that she was chief congressional analyst for ABC News in Washington. Her husband worked for more than thirty years at *The New York Times* and *U.S. News & World Report* in Washington and elsewhere. An analysis of their piece is worth the detour, since it reveals so much about why journalism's credibility is in decline.

The Newhouse chain is owned by Advance Publications. Advance is privately held and has no "public stockholders," as the Robertses claimed. The alleged conflict of interest they referred to, using *Fortune* as an example, was equally off the mark. Howard Kurtz had written a column in *The Washington Post* quoting *Fortune* staffer Marc Gunther about the call he'd received from a member of the AOL public relations department. Neither Cokie nor Steve Roberts ever called Gunther to discuss the call.

When I asked Gunther about the call from the AOL publicist, he wrote that he did receive a call in January 2000—the day the agreement to merge was announced, not, as the Robertses wrote, the day the two companies merged (that would come a year later). Gunther said he had been working on a profile of Steve Case and that he was scheduled to interview Case that day. The publicist did indeed say, "We just bought you," but Gunther says the purpose of the call "was to make sure I'd heard and would get to the news conference in New York that day." Gunther's profile of Case did run in *Fortune*. "Of course, there was no interference," Gunther says.

Frank Rich, one of the Sunday columnists for *The New York Times*, wrote:

At *Time,* Norman Pearlstine—a member of the Committee to Protect Journalists, no less—described his decision to turn over Matt Cooper's files to the feds as his own, made on the merits and without consulting any higher-ups at Time Warner. That's no doubt the truth, but a corporate mentality needn't be imposed by direct fiat; it's a virus that metastasizes in the bureaucratic bloodstream. I doubt anyone ever orders an editor to promote a schlocky Warner Brothers movie either. (*Entertainment Weekly* did two covers in one month on [the Warner Bros. picture] *The Matrix Reloaded.*)

Time Warner seems to have far too much money on the table in Washington to exercise absolute editorial freedom when covering the government; at this moment it's awaiting an F.C.C. review of its joint acquisition of the bankrupt cable company Adelphia. "Is this a journalistic company or an entertainment company?" David Halberstam asked after the Pearlstine decision. We have the answer now. What high-level source would risk talking to *Time* about government corruption after this cave-in? What top investigative reporter would choose to work there?

I understood why many reporters and editors might disagree with my decision. How could I have called it the most difficult decision I had ever made as a journalist without expecting disagreement, including disagreement from role models and editors I had admired? Abe Rosenthal (who had served as executive editor of the *Times* for seventeen years and who was most responsible for its continued greatness), Bradlee, and Gene Roberts (the legendary editor of *The Philadelphia Inquirer*) all made it clear they thought I was wrong.

I had clearly failed in my efforts to get the pundits to focus on the issues I had been confronting. Nor had they understood the level of independence I had at Time Inc., or the limited financial impact any action I might take would have on its parent, Time Warner Inc.

We had often criticized our parent corporation and the company's other divisions. I had done an in-depth content analysis of *Entertainment Weekly*'s coverage of Warner Bros. and New Line, Time Warner's two studios, in the years since I became editor in chief. It was easy to see that the magazine was as tough on them as it was on other companies' studios. The executives I knew at Warner and New Line insisted we were tougher.

Fortune had also published several stories critical of Steve Case, AOL, and Time Warner, beginning in the first month following the announcement of the merger and continuing through Case's resignation as chairman of the merged company. To cite one memorable example, writing in February 2000, Carol Loomis dismissed the merged company's earnings projections for the years following completion of the merger with the famous kicker "It will be like pushing a boulder up an alp."

My presence on the board of the Committee to Protect Journalists also provoked a minidrama in the foundation's boardroom. CPJ is an important organization that was founded in 1981 to promote "press freedom worldwide by defending the rights of journalists to report the news without fear of reprisal." It was created by a group of foreign correspondents "in response to the often brutal treatment of their foreign colleagues by authoritarian governments and other enemies of independent journalism." Significantly, CPJ accepts no government funding.

I had chaired one of CPJ's annual dinners in New York in the 1990s, where four especially courageous foreign journalists were honored. Working with Tom Brokaw, the evening's master of ceremonies, we raised more than $1 million for CPJ. I was happy to join its board in 2004.

I had seen how the organization had benefited local journalists working in countries with repressive regimes and little press freedom in my years supervising coverage of international news. CPJ became more important to me after *Time's* Baghdad manager, an Iraqi, was murdered, and Michael Weisskopf lost one hand and was nearly killed by a grenade. Soon after I joined the board, David Laventhol, the former chairman of CPJ and publisher of the *Los Angeles Times*, asked if I would chair CPJ's twenty-fifth anniversary dinner in the fall of 2006. I readily agreed, even though the goal was to raise $2.5 million, much more than the dinner typically raised.

After I announced my decision to cooperate with the grand jury, James Goodale, the *Times's* former general counsel, launched a personal campaign to force my resignation from the CPJ board. Goodale told several board members he thought my decision "disgraceful."

Although most of CPJ's efforts were directed toward mistreatment of foreign journalists, nothing precluded it from expressing concerns about Judith Miller's jailing or any other government interference with journalism in the United States. I had applauded statements by CPJ's executive director expressing concern after the Supreme Court refused to hear our case and, again, after Miller was jailed. I was thinking of CPJ when I wrote that many foreign governments justify their own restrictive press laws whenever they see the United States enforcing contempt rulings against our journalists.

Goodale, who had served on CPJ's board for many years, found little support for his effort to force my resignation. But my decision was questioned at the board's September 2005 meeting. After one board member, author Kati Marton, asked me for an explanation, I spoke for about ten minutes. As I was speaking, I could see

Goodale's face reddening. When I finished, he exploded, calling my decision "dreadful," contrasting it with what the *Times* had done in the 1978 Farber case. He then said that limiting the impact of *Branzburg* had become his life's work, and he accused me of sabotaging it.

I left the meeting thinking that the discussion was similar to many of the public and private discussions I had been having lately, and that Goodale's diatribe would fade from memory. But during the board's October meeting, Paul Steiger, my successor as the *The Wall Street Journal*'s managing editor and Laventhol's successor as CPJ chairman, asked if we could go into executive session. I then learned that some members of the board had questioned my serving as chairman of the 2006 dinner. Although I thought no more than five or six of CPJ's thirty-five board members believed I should step down as the dinner's chair, I decided to do so to avoid making the event a referendum on my decision. I remain an active member of the CPJ board.

14

Welcome Support

With Judith Miller in jail and our notes in the hands of the special prosecutor, it was easy to see why so many people thought I was on the wrong side of history. I was heartened, though, by some important expressions of support.

I have always been wary of flattery from people whose paychecks I sign. But one note from Don Bartlett and Jim Steele cheered me, since for more than three decades, at *Time* and before that at *The Philadelphia Inquirer*, they had been among the best, toughest, and most honest investigative reporters working anywhere, with multiple Pulitzer Prizes, National Magazine Awards, and Polk Awards to prove it. They wrote:

> We think that turning over the subpoenaed records—after exhausting all possible legal remedies—will go a long way to dispelling the perception that journalists feel they are entitled to special treatment not accorded to ordinary citizens. It's an arrogant attitude that has contributed greatly to public resentment toward the news media. For those of us who believe deeply in the premise that there is one law for everyone, and

that all people should be treated equally, your decision was entirely proper.

Bartlett and Steele pride themselves on doing complex investigations that rely on documents, and they don't use confidential sources.

One of the first and strongest public statements in my defense came from Walter Isaacson, a former *Time* managing editor, who had briefly served as Time Inc.'s editorial director, my deputy, before going to Atlanta as chairman of CNN. Isaacson had moved on to become the head of the Aspen Institute, but he still commanded huge respect within *Time*. The day after the story broke, he told *The Wall Street Journal*, "It is very bad the way the court ruled and it is going to hurt the vibrancy of journalism, but that doesn't mean you can defy the final decision of the courts. Norm was vigorous in pursuing it to the Supreme Court. It is necessary not to put yourself above the law."

Hugh Sidey, a legendary bureau chief and reporter who had covered ten U.S. presidents during his fifty-one years at *Life* and *Time*, visited me in my office shortly before his death in November 2005. He brought copies of several speeches Henry Luce had given in which Time Inc.'s founder had argued for the importance of Rule of Law and insisted that Luce would have agreed with my decision.

Alex Jones, director of the Joan Shorenstein Center on the Press, Politics and Public Policy at Harvard University, told the *Los Angeles Times* that we had "pushed the issue to the limit, further than it's been pushed in years, and the judge finally said, 'OK, you've reached the end. Now you have to obey the law.'"

Michael Kinsley, who had written for *Time* for years and founded the *Slate* website, wrote a notable column in the *Los Angeles Times*, where he was then in charge of the editorial and op-ed pages. Kinsley, also trained as a lawyer, is one of America's most thoughtful liberal commentators. He accompanied his piece with a note saying, "Most of my colleagues at the *Times*, including the ed-

itorial board and the editor himself, disagree with what I say here."
The column, which also ran in *The Washington Post* and many other
papers, made some original and important points.

"For all the grand talk about the First Amendment," Kinsley
wrote, "this isn't about the press's right to publish information. It is
about a right to keep information secret." Kinsley added, "The
biggest problem in the way of a compromise is that journalists who
share the philosophy of *The New York Times* assert the right to decide unilaterally."

Kinsley concluded, "*The New York Times* is an influential newspaper owned by a large corporation. It is claiming an exemption from
one of the normal duties of citizenship. It has hired some of America's best lawyers to pursue this claim through every available avenue.
And then, when the claim has been rejected, it encourages its employees to defy the courts and break the law. If that is civil disobedience, then almost any law anyone does not care for is up for grabs."

Jacob Weisberg, Kinsley's successor as editor of *Slate*, agreed with
my decision but said it "doesn't go far enough." Instead, Weisberg argued that journalists who knew the identity of Plame's leakers
should share them with the public because discovery and publication
of the truth is more important than protecting a confidence. "Talking to a source 'on background' cannot be an offer of blanket immunity in all circumstances," Weisberg said. "In the Plame case, the
crime under investigation consists in speaking to reporters."

Steve Chapman, a *Chicago Tribune* columnist, wrote, "The editor-
in-chief of Time Inc. made news the other day by offering to do
what most of us take for granted: Obey the law. It's about time."

Gregg Easterbrook, an occasional contributor to *Time*, wrote to
the Letters Forum on *Romenesko*, a popular journalism website, that
he thought my conclusion that corporations must obey the law
should be "noncontroversial." Yet, he said, "response to Pearlstine's
decision could be headlined, BIG CORPORATION OBEYS

LAW, JOURNALISTS OUTRAGED." Easterbrook concluded, "Had Pearlstine in effect declared that the press is above the law, long-term harm to public respect for journalism might have been greater than whatever harm (possibly none) is caused by revealing one source after a long, determined, expensive attempt to avoid doing so."

15

Judith Miller—In and Out of Jail

Judith Miller went to jail believing she hadn't received a waiver from her source, that the maximum length of her sentence would be less than four months, and that Arthur Sulzberger would never turn on her.

After spending most of the summer in jail, Miller was released on September 29, 2005. The circumstances of her release were baffling, and to this day they haven't fully been explained. But it became clear that more was going on—or less—than a stand on principle.

I learned in early September that Miller, relying on attorney Robert Bennett instead of Floyd Abrams, had begun to negotiate her release from jail. The decision to negotiate came a few days after a tense meeting in late August between Miller and her lawyers in the Alexandria Detention Center's library. Sulzberger and George Freeman, an in-house lawyer at the New York Times Co., had encouraged Miller to believe that Hogan wouldn't keep her in jail beyond October 28, the date Fitzgerald's grand jury was due to expire. But Bennett told Miller and the other lawyers in attendance that he thought it far more likely that Fitzgerald would try to keep her in jail for a longer period. He might do so by calling a new grand jury that could run another eighteen months, or by asking Judge Hogan to hold her in criminal contempt. A new grand jury could prompt new contempt citations, and if Hogan agreed, Miller could theoretically be held without a trial until April 2007, or longer. Bennett reasoned that letting Miller out of jail without getting her testimony would weaken Fitzgerald's ability to force other witnesses to testify. Miller's husband, Jason Epstein, had also been arguing that it was time for Miller to negotiate her release. At the end of the meeting, Miller authorized Bennett to begin the negotiations with Libby's lawyer, Joseph A. Tate, and with Fitzgerald.

I didn't know Miller well, but I had read and admired her early work at the *Times*, especially her reports from Cairo in the 1980s. Her father, Bill Miller, was a well-known figure in the entertainment industry. He owned the Riviera, a nightclub in Fort Lee, New Jersey, that featured Frank Sinatra, Lena Horne, and other top acts, before moving to Las Vegas in 1953, where he became entertainment director at the Sahara Hotel. He subsequently worked in Miami and Los Angeles, and Judith Miller lived in all these cities growing up. Miller graduated from Barnard and received a master's degree in public affairs from the Woodrow Wilson School at Princeton. Before joining the *Times*'s Washington bureau in 1977, Miller worked for *The Progressive* and National Public Radio.

While in Washington, Miller had befriended Sulzberger, who was also working in the *Times* bureau there. She subsequently was sent to Cairo for four years before returning to Washington, where she served as an editor and a correspondent before moving to New York in the 1990s. In 2002 Miller was part of a team of *Times* reporters that won a Pulitzer Prize for explanatory reporting for stories about global terrorism. Between 2002 and 2005, much of Miller's reporting had focused on whether Iraq was developing or possessed weapons of mass destruction. Her stories were deeply flawed, highly partisan, and often wrong. She closely identified with her sources, including Ahmed Chalabi, whose exile group, the Iraqi National Congress, was the darling of Washington's most hawkish neoconservatives. During the walk-up to the Iraq war, several members of the Bush administration referred to her stories when justifying an attack.

Miller had been a divisive figure at the *Times*, supported by Sulzberger and former executive editor Howell Raines, but resented by many reporters who worked with her. They thought she was too close to her sources and too quick to embrace their ideology.

I wrote to her seeking permission to visit her in jail, and on September 22 we met for thirty minutes at the Alexandria Detention Center. Our conversation was largely about her incarceration and about friends we had in common. I told her that I admired her decision to engage in civil disobedience even though I thought Time Inc. had to turn over our notes after the Supreme Court refused to hear our petition. I didn't bring up the rumors I had been hearing, and Miller did not discuss her case, except to say that her source had been unwilling to give her the waiver that Matt Cooper had received from his sources.

A week later, Miller was out of jail. Sulzberger was there to meet her, jousting with her lawyers to be the first person she saw after leaving the SUV that had been used to ferry her past the detention center's gates. That night he hosted a small dinner, where, over steaks and martinis, they celebrated her release.

The next day, September 30, she appeared before the grand jury for nearly four hours. She testified that Libby was the source she had refused to identify and that he had first discussed Joseph Wilson's activities with her in June of 2003, a couple of weeks before Wilson's op-ed piece criticizing the Bush administration ran in the *Times*. Miller said that in their conversation Libby, who had played down the importance of Wilson's visit to Niger, had revealed that Wilson's wife might have worked on unconventional weapons at the CIA.

Miller said, however, that her notes did not show that Libby had identified Wilson's wife by name.

After testifying, Miller told reporters that she was a "journalist doing my job, protecting my source until my source freed me to perform my civic duty to testify." She subsequently said that a personal letter from Libby, followed by a telephone conversation with him, had convinced her that his waiver of confidentiality was voluntary and not offered at her behest or at the behest of her lawyers. She also said that she had been unwilling to testify until Fitzgerald agreed to confine his questioning to issues involving Libby, enabling her "to protect other confidential sources who had provided information—unrelated to Mr. Wilson or his wife—for articles published in the *Times*."

Miller's release from jail and her testimony raised serious questions. Some critics, within the *Times* and among opponents of the war, asked if she had gone to jail to seek martyrdom, to protect the Bush administration's efforts to squelch dissent, or to support the war in Iraq at the expense of the paper's credibility. Some insisted that Miller might have received the same waiver before she went to jail—and so wondered why she hadn't sought it at the time. Others were puzzled by her decision to negotiate her departure from jail, since she had told Judge Hogan upon sentencing that no amount of jail would make her talk.

Arianna Huffington, one of Miller's most persistent critics, wrote on her blog, *The Huffington Post*, "Any discussion of Miller's actions in Plamegate cannot leave out the key part she played in cheerleading the invasion of Iraq and in hyping the WMD threat . . . The inescapable fact is that Miller—intentionally or unintentionally—worked hand in glove in helping the White House propaganda machine sell the war in Iraq. And that includes Libby and his boss, Dick Cheney."

The *Times* editorial page had been Miller's most consistent supporter, running more than a dozen editorials in support of her position. It declared on August 29, 2005, "It's time for the authorities who jailed Ms. Miller to recognize that continued incarceration is not going to sway a reporter who believes she is making a principled sacrifice." It concluded, "If Judith Miller loses this fight, we all lose." But the paper's editorial for October 1, two days after Miller's release, seemed most intent on putting the episode behind it, saying, "Our chief reaction is relief that she is finally free."

The paper's news pages were much tougher on Miller. On October 16, the *Times* devoted more than two full pages to Miller, including Miller's lengthy reconstruction of her grand jury testimony. The main news story discussed many of the articles Miller had written before the war. Those stories, which argued that Saddam Hussein was developing weapons of mass destruction, were often based on information provided by anonymous sources within the administration and by people among the group of defectors, led by Ahmed Chalabi, that had been urging the United States to attack Iraq.

I had thought Miller one of those investigative reporters who needed tough, careful editing to keep her out of trouble. The *Times's* lengthy article confirmed my belief: "Interviews show that the paper's leaders, in taking what they considered to be a principled stand, ultimately left the major decisions in the case up to Ms. Miller, an intrepid reporter whom editors found hard to control."

The story made clear that Bill Keller, the paper's executive editor, and Arthur Sulzberger Jr., its publisher, "knew few details about Ms. Miller's conversations with her source other than his name." They had not reviewed Miller's notes, which referred in one place to "Valerie Flame" and in another place to "Victoria Wilson." Miller told the grand jury that she could not remember who gave her the name Valerie Flame, but that she did not believe it had come from Libby. She also said she was not sure whether Libby had used the name Victoria Wilson or whether she had made a mistake in "writing it on my own."

Keller sent a lengthy memo to his editorial employees the following Friday. In it, he said he had wished he had done a better job of debriefing Miller on the stories about purported WMD. He said that Miller had seemed to have misled the Washington bureau chief about the extent of her involvement in receiving leaks that were damaging to Joseph Wilson and Valerie Plame.

Keller said that he had concluded that the *Times* had to "fight this thing in court" in part because the press was facing the "insidious new menace" of blanket waivers that administration officials had been compelled to sign. "But if I had known the details of Judy's entanglements with Libby, I'd have been more careful in how the paper articulated its defense, and perhaps more willing than I had been to support efforts aimed at exploring compromises."

Keller then quoted from an e-mail from *Times* reporter Richard Stevenson that the editor said expressed a larger lesson:

I think there is, or should be, a contract between the paper and its reporters. The contract holds that the paper will go to the mat to back them up institutionally—but only to the degree that the reporter has lived up to his or her end of the bargain, specifically to have conducted him or herself in a way consistent with our legal, ethical and journalistic standards, to have been open and candid with the paper about sources, mistakes, conflicts and the like, and generally to deserve having the reputations of all of us put behind him or her. In that way, everybody knows going into a battle exactly what the situation is, what we're fighting for, the degree to which the facts might counsel compromise or not, and the degree to which our collective credibility should be put on the line.

Maureen Dowd's column of Saturday, October 22, was vicious. "Sorely in need of a tight editorial leash," she wrote, Miller "was kept on no leash at all." Dowd attacked Miller's reporting on the purported WMD and her willingness to attribute Libby's quotes to a "former Hill staffer" (rather than a senior White House official) because he once worked on Capitol Hill. "The implication was that this bit of deception was a common practice for reporters," Dowd wrote. "It isn't."

Dowd wondered whether Miller's "stint in the Alexandria jail was in part a career rehabilitation project." Dowd's column ended by saying that if Miller was allowed to return to the newsroom and to her old intelligence beat, "the institution most in danger would be the newspaper in your hands."

In the next day's paper, the *Times*'s public editor, Byron Calame, "the readers' representative," devoted his column to the paper's lengthy Miller story. Calame mentioned Sulzberger's "special support" of Miller, quoting Miller's statement that the publisher had "galvanized the editors, the senior editorial staff," around her. Calame's primary focus, however, was on the tendency of top editors to have moved too slowly to correct problems of coverage leading up to the war; Miller's journalistic shortcuts; and "the deferential treatment of Ms. Miller by editors who failed to dig into problems before they became a mess." Calame suggested that it might be a good idea for the paper to update its rules for granting anonymity, but he otherwise stayed away from Miller's decision to go to jail to protect her source. In his final paragraph, Calame opined that whatever limits were put on Miller, "the problems facing her inside and outside the newsroom will make it difficult for her to return to the paper as a reporter."

Although Miller had hoped to return to the paper, Arthur Sulzberger was no more able to withstand the pressure from his newsroom than when it had rebelled against the leadership of Howell Raines. He again gave in and a *Times* attorney, Kenneth A. Richieri, negotiated a severance agreement with Miller. She resigned November 9. The resignation story appeared on page 20 of the first section, but it did rate a brief mention on the *Times*'s front page. Miller had originally sought space on the paper's op-ed page to respond to her critics within the newsroom. The paper refused that demand but did agree to her writing a lengthy "To the Editor" letter explaining her position. In it, she said that she had chosen to go to jail to protect her confidential source but also "to dramatize the need" for a federal shield law.

Miller's letter denied that she had misled the *Times* Washington bureau chief, and she took exception to Keller's use of the word *entanglement* when describing her relationship with Libby: "I had no personal, social or other relationship with him except as a source, one among many to whom I had pledged confidentiality as a reporter for *The New York Times*." Miller had labored for years under rumors that she had slept with some of her sources.

In a letter to Miller following her retirement, Keller said his use of *entanglement* was "not intended to suggest an improper relationship, I was referring only to the series of interviews through which you and the paper became caught up in an epic legal controversy."

Miller said that criticisms from some of her colleagues had played a role in her decision, "but mainly I have chosen to resign because over the last few months, I have become the news, something a *New York Times* reporter never wants to be."

16

Waivers

The *New York Times* is the world's best newspaper, the one that sets the agenda for many other publications. Journalists elsewhere compare themselves to its reporters. In the days following Miller's departure from jail, the paper's coverage of her and itself was riveting to journalists across the country. Aside from one prescient story by reporter Adam Liptak, the *Times* didn't focus much on the circumstances surrounding Libby's waiver of confidentiality and the timing of Miller's decision to testify and get out of jail.

The waiver of confidentiality is a complicated issue for journalists, confidential sources, and lawyers. Waivers cannot be understood without some reflection on ownership of the "privilege" that enables reporters to keep the names of sources and some of the information they provide confidential. I believe the privilege results in a contract between the source, the journalist, and the journalist's employer, be it a publisher or a broadcaster. I also believe the source owns the privilege and that a reporter cannot grant confidentiality to a source without the source's agreement. Reporters and publishers should be free, however, to evaluate and determine the circumstances that might create a waiver of the privilege.

In doing so, however, journalists and publishers must keep in mind that the grant of confidentiality is an enforceable contract and that any publication that reveals the source's name can be held liable. In 1991 in *Cohen v. Cowles Media Co.*, writing for the majority in a 5–4 Supreme Court decision involving the Minneapolis *Star Tribune*, Justice Byron White held that the First Amendment can't be used to void a valid contract.

There is no consensus among journalists and lawyers about how and when a waiver should be sought, and how to determine whether a waiver, once granted, was voluntary or was gained through pressure or coercion.

Matt and I had felt persistent tension with some of our lawyers when we had asked how we might get a waiver from Karl Rove or his attorney. Matt's lawyer, Dick Sauber, who had favored Matt's getting a waiver from Libby, thought it much riskier for Matt to contact Rove directly to get a waiver. Although witnesses before a grand jury can usually speak to each other, they need to be careful not to say anything—conspiring, for example, to slant or lie about a prior conversation—that a prosecutor might consider improper or illegal. When I proposed that Sauber speak to Robert Luskin, Rove's lawyer, Bierstedt worried that such a conversation would inform Rove that he was Matt's source. I disagreed, but Bierstedt argued that Rove might face obstruction of justice charges if he didn't waive confidentiality after learning he was Matt's source—and that it was unfair for Matt to put his source, Rove, in such a quandary.

Many of these issues first surfaced in October 2004. Fitzgerald had issued a second subpoena seeking additional testimony from Matt, and Matt thought it might be a good time to contact Rove or his lawyer. But there was some concern about *Time* approaching Rove in the weeks before the election. Jim Kelly worried that the approach might be construed as an effort to interfere with President

Bush's reelection campaign, which Rove was managing. (One could have argued, of course, that not approaching Rove also interfered in the election.) The idea died, however, because Kelly, Bierstedt, and I all thought that election or not, we should exhaust all remedies in the courts before seeking a waiver from Rove.

Some prosecutors and legal scholars have argued that a source should not be allowed to remain confidential if leaking the information is a crime. If outing Plame had been illegal, then Rove and Libby would have been barred from asserting a privilege and the reporter could testify. By analogy, the lawyer-client privilege is waived if the lawyer learns that his client is committing a crime.

Sources, journalists, and their publications must also agree about what the waiver covers—confidentiality, anonymity, or both. Libby's lawyer, Joseph A. Tate, and Judith Miller both tried to assert that Libby's waiver was limited to confidentiality—that she could testify but couldn't write about her testimony. I had suspected that Robert Novak's primary source had made a similar stipulation, waiving confidentiality so Novak could testify, but not his anonymity, thus explaining why Novak hadn't identified him publicly.

Bill Keller and other *Times* editors argued that their readers had the right to know what Miller told the grand jury, and they insisted that she write about her testimony for the paper. Matt Cooper and I had concluded that the waiver granted by Rove's lawyer in the *WSJ* extended to the pages of *Time*, as well as to any future testimony before the grand jury, in part because witnesses are permitted to speak publicly about their own testimony.

Most journalists would reject the general waiver that Fitzgerald had obtained from members of Bush's White House, because it wasn't voluntary; the President had in effect ordered his subordinates to waive their right to confidentiality. Nonetheless, several reporters, including Cooper, NBC's Tim Russert, and *The Washington*

Post's Glenn Kessler, had obtained separate waivers from Libby that they construed as voluntary. Miller, however, said her insistence that "Libby voluntarily relieve me in writing and by phone of my promise to protect our conversations" could not have been satisfied "before I went to jail." She never explained why.

Writing in the *Times*, Liptak referred to three remarkable letters, written by Libby, Abrams, and Libby's lawyer, that, he proposed, "suggest that a similar deal may have been available for some time, raising questions about why Ms. Miller decided to testify."

Each of the letters had to do with Libby's willingness to waive his confidentiality. On September 15, 2005, Libby wrote Miller (who was in jail) that one of her lawyers, Robert Bennett, had asked him a few days earlier to "repeat for you the waiver of confidentiality that I specifically gave" to her other lawyer, Floyd Abrams, "over a year ago." Libby wrote he was "surprised" by Bennett's request, because Fitzgerald had "identified every reporter with whom I had spoken about anything in July 2003, including you. My counsel then called counsel for each of the reporters, including yours, and confirmed that my waiver was voluntary." He added that Abrams had "reassured us that he understood this, that your stand was one of principle or otherwise unrelated to us, and that there was nothing more we could do. In all the months since, we have never heard otherwise from anyone on your legal team, until your new counsel's request just a few days ago." Libby concluded the letter by stating his admiration for Miller's "principled fight with the government. But for my part, this is the rare case where this 'source' would be better off if you testified."

The next day, September 16, Libby's lawyer, Joseph Tate, wrote Fitzgerald a letter reiterating the points Libby had made in his letter to Miller. A copy of the letter was sent to Miller's lawyers. Tate wrote, "Our position has always been that it is in Mr. Libby's best interest for the reporters to testify fully. With regard to Ms. Miller, we provided the same assurances long ago. Her attorney and I had several conversations about this matter." Tate told Fitzgerald that he and Libby had "encouraged" Miller to testify, "believing that her testimony, when added to those of other reporters who have testified, will benefit my client." He then reminded Fitzgerald that Abrams had represented Cooper as well as Miller, and that Libby's waiver had been good enough for Cooper and the other reporters Libby had spoken to.

Those letters prompted Abrams to write Tate on September 29. His letter acknowledged, "It is true that in discussions with me last summer you told me that Mr. Libby had no objection to Ms. Miller testifying before the grand jury about her meeting with him in early July of 2003." Abrams added, however, that in their conversations "you did *not* say that Mr. Libby's written waiver was uncoerced. In fact, you said quite the opposite."

Abrams took issue with many of Tate's other points. He disputed as "inaccurate" Tate's assertion that Libby had "encouraged" Miller to testify: "As to the issue of Mr. Libby's waiver, the message you sent to me was viewed by Ms. Miller as inherently 'mixed.'" Abrams pointed out that neither Libby nor Tate had made any public or private response "in the face of repeated statements by Ms. Miller and myself to the effect that no satisfactory personal waiver had been obtained." He then acknowledged that while "other reporters may have been satisfied with representations from you about the voluntary nature of Mr. Libby's 'waiver,' Ms. Miller was not." Abrams's letter left unclear why Miller had required more specific assurances than had other reporters, including his other client Cooper.

The letters don't make Miller or Abrams look good. Libby's letter to Miller and Tate's letter to Fitzgerald both assert that Abrams had been told Libby's waiver was voluntary. Abrams's response leaves unclear whether he disputes their assertions or is saying that the waivers weren't specific enough for Miller, his client. First, he acknowledges that Tate had said Libby was willing to have Miller testify. As if to confirm that point he says later in the letter that, unlike other reporters, Miller wouldn't accept representations from Tate and they had to come from Libby himself. But he also complains that Tate didn't stipulate the waiver was "uncoerced" and, without elaboration, says Tate "said quite the opposite."

Robert Bennett also undercut Abrams in another *Times* article. In it, Bennett said that he had called Tate on August 31 and had been told that Libby had given Miller permission to testify a year earlier. "I called Tate and this guy could not have been clearer—'Bob, my client has given a waiver,'" Bennett said. The letters, and Bennett's comments, cast doubt on Miller's stated reason for her refusal to testify: that she was obligated to protect her source's confidentiality.

Miller's second reason for refusing to testify is equally suspect. She had said she could not get a guarantee from Fitzgerald to restrict his questions to Libby. Without that guarantee, she insisted, she could not protect the confidentiality of other sources. Abrams had supported that position, but I subsequently heard that neither he nor the editors at the *Times* spent much time reading and evaluating the notebooks. Bennett, however, performed an extensive review of all of Miller's notes from her interviews with Libby. According to the *Times*'s October 16 story, he had determined that Miller "had only one meaningful source," Libby, that would be of interest to the special counsel. Bennett gave Fitzgerald his personal assurance that Miller's notes didn't contain references to other sources important to the prosecutor, and Fitzgerald agreed to let Bennett redact the notebook. Fitzgerald also agreed to limit his questions to Libby and the Plame episode.

Although Bennett succeeded in getting his client out of jail, Miller looked bad. If Miller had been granted the same waiver that Cooper and others were, and if no other meaningful sources were in her notes that required protection, her refusal to testify and her decision to go to jail suggest she was willing to obstruct justice to protect a source, Scooter Libby, who didn't require protection. Had Miller stayed in jail under such circumstances, Fitzgerald would have had a strong case for having her held in criminal contempt.

The *Los Angeles Times* did not go that far, but in an angry editorial, it wrote on October 18 that it was "becoming increasingly clear" that Miller and *The New York Times* "have abused the public's trust by manufacturing a showdown with the government." The editorial declared that *The New York Times*'s October 16 story doesn't reveal "the *Times*' higher allegiance to the 1st Amendment, but its higher tolerance for the antics of a rogue reporter." The details of the Miller case "reveal not so much a reporter defending a principle as a reporter using a principle to defend herself."

The *Los Angeles Times* editorial also questioned why Miller changed her mind after eighty-five days in jail and decided to reveal her source. *The New York Times*'s own reporting after Miller was freed offered an account that tracked with what I had heard in early September about her desire to cut a deal to get out of jail. William Safire, a friend of Miller's, had said Fitzgerald had been warning her that she might stay in jail beyond October 28. Another friend, Claudia Payne, a *Times* editor, told the paper that once Miller realized that her jail term could be extended, "it changed things a great deal. She said, 'I don't want to spend my life in here.'"

The *Times* also reported something else I had been hearing in early September—that once Miller was jailed, "her lawyers were in open conflict about whether she should stay there." But in the end, Miller, saying, "I owed it to myself" to go free after two months in jail, instructed Bennett to contact Libby through his lawyer, Tate. Payne said that in seeking release, Miller's "paramount concern was how her actions would be viewed by her colleagues." After her release from jail, Miller told the paper, "We have everything to be proud of and nothing to apologize for."

Sulzberger, the *Times*'s publisher and one of Miller's biggest defenders, has refused to criticize her, although his public comments suggest some efforts to distance himself from her. He was quoted in the *Times*'s October 16 article saying, "This car had her hand on the wheel because she was the one at risk."

By then he had also moderated his criticism of my decision to turn over Time Inc.'s notes. Speaking in October 2005 at Harvard's Joan Shorenstein Center on the Press, Politics and Public Policy, he said he had been deeply disappointed by my decision, but that he had not criticized it. He said it was a tough decision that he was happy he had not had to make. When television journalist Judy Woodruff asked him what he would have done had the *Times*, like Time Inc., been held in contempt, he said he didn't know. The journalists would have told him not to comply, he said, and the lawyers would have told him to do what I had done.

17

Why We Need a Federal Shield Law

The best way to set right an injustice is to change the law. The courts provide the easiest way to seek redress, but legislatures provide greater certainty. For most of our history, the courts and the legislatures alike have been hostile to the notion that journalists have a right to keep their sources confidential. But nearly every state now offers journalists some protection, and the Supreme Court's refusal to hear our petition in the Plame case prompted renewed efforts to pass a federal shield law. The proposals differed in their specifics, but each would give reporters and their sources similar protections to those available in almost every state court in the country.

The need for a federal shield law has become even more urgent since then, as the Bush administration has sought to stifle dissent by going on the attack against reporters who have used confidential sources.

There were no state shield laws until Maryland's was passed in 1896. John T. Morris, a reporter for the Baltimore *Sun*, had been jailed for two days in the 1880s after refusing to tell a grand jury the sources for stories he had written about bribery of elected officials. It took a decade before the Maryland General Assembly passed legislation that provided limited protections to reporters. Over the next forty years, only two other states, Alabama and New Jersey, passed shield laws.

The courts were equally reticent, rejecting efforts to assert a reporter's right to keep sources confidential under the rules of evidence that courts had developed as a matter of common law or under the protections granted by the First Amendment. Writing for the majority in *Branzburg*, Justice Byron White noted that while "a number of States have provided newsmen a statutory privilege of varying breadth," by 1972, "the majority have not done so, and none has been provided by federal statute."

As our petition to the Supreme Court had noted, only seventeen states recognized a reporter's privilege in 1972, while forty-nine states and the District of Columbia now do. By 2005, thirty-one states and the District of Columbia had passed shield laws to protect journalists and their sources. The other eighteen states had recognized a reporter's privilege under common law, under interpretations of state constitutions, or under rules developed by the courts. Wyoming appears to be the only state where a reporter's privilege hasn't been considered.

These state laws and cases vary. Thirteen states and the District of Columbia give journalists an "absolute" privilege that protects them from divulging their sources. Some, such as New York, limit the protection to journalists whose sources have provided information confidentially, while others, such as the District of Columbia and Maryland, protect journalists from divulging the source for any information, whether or not the source has been promised confidentiality. Many state courts have held that the privilege belongs to the reporter, and that it cannot be waived by the source. Others protect both the reporter and the source.

Balancing tests are also considered important in many states. New Jersey, Ohio, and other states seek a balance between the rights of journalists and the rights of prosecutors or litigants. Some statutes define who is a journalist, while others leave it to the courts to decide case by case. Some states cover freelance writers, while others restrict coverage to full-time journalists employed by a publisher or broadcaster. Many shield laws contain exceptions favoring libel defendants and anyone seeking eyewitness testimony from journalists.

There were many efforts to pass a federal shield law in the years immediately following *Branzburg*. According to the Reporters Committee for Freedom of the Press (RCFP), as many as one hundred bills were introduced in Congress between 1972 and 1977. Interest among journalists waned, however, when it became clear that there was insufficient support for a law that provided absolute privilege. In addition, the push for legislation seemed less urgent as federal district and appellate courts began to narrow the scope of *Branzburg*, relying on Justice Powell's concurrence in that case or on the Department of Justice's guidelines to justify the imposition of balancing tests. As a result, few federal shield laws were proposed after the early 1980s.

The courts' willingness to narrow the import of *Branzburg*, however, became far less certain in the past decade, leading to a split between federal courts in the Northeast and the West, which tended to favor protecting journalists. Federal judges elsewhere, including Judge Richard Posner, the conservative Seventh Circuit justice, and, of course, Judge Hogan in Washington, were far more willing to rule against the press.

Soon after Hogan announced his decision, Senator Christopher Dodd, a Connecticut Democrat and arguably the press's best friend in Congress, introduced a federal shield law in the Senate. His proposed legislation, which garnered little support, would have provided near absolute protection for journalists and their sources.

A few months later, in February 2005, Republican Mike Pence, a conservative congressman who had been a radio broadcaster in his native Indiana, and Democrat Rick Boucher of Virginia introduced a comprehensive shield bill in the House of Representatives. Senator Richard Lugar, an Indiana Republican, introduced an identical bill in the Senate a few days later. Neither bill made much headway in the months following their introduction.

The Supreme Court's failure to hear our case led to editorials in *The New York Times*, *The Washington Post*, and many other newspapers calling for a federal shield law. Responding to the Supreme Court's order and to the jailing of Judith Miller, Senator Arlen Specter of Pennsylvania, who chaired the Senate Judiciary Committee, decided to hold hearings on the Lugar bill, and he wrote to ask if I would testify. I had first met Specter in the 1960s, when he was Philadelphia's district attorney and I was still in law school. During his years in the Senate I had thought him among the smartest and fairest legislators in Washington. I had discouraged journalists at *The Wall Street Journal* and Time Inc. who worked for me from testifying about proposed legislation, thinking that such a role was in conflict with our need to be impartial in our coverage of Congress, but I accepted Specter's invitation because I thought a federal shield law to be of such critical importance to journalists.

The hearings began on July 20, 2005, with opening statements from Senators Lugar and Dodd and from Congressman Pence. I was joined by five other witnesses: Cooper from *Time*; William Safire and Floyd Abrams from *The New York Times*; Lee Levine, a Washington First Amendment lawyer; and Geoffrey R. Stone, a respected constitutional law professor from the University of Chicago.

Abrams, Cooper, and I largely repeated what we had said in court filings and in articles and interviews. Safire argued that state shield laws had not harmed law enforcement but had "led to the exposure of corruption."

Levine said he could find no example between 1976 and 2000 where a "journalist was finally adjudged in contempt, much less imprisoned, for refusing to disclose a confidential source in a Federal criminal matter." In contrast, he said, an unusually large number of subpoenas seeking the names of confidential sources had been issued by federal courts beginning in 2001. "Indeed, three Federal proceedings in Washington, D.C., alone have generated such subpoenas to roughly two dozen reporters and news organizations, seven of whom have been held in contempt in less than a year." Levine said that these decisions had emboldened private litigants as well, since such litigants, like special prosecutors, aren't bound by the DOJ guidelines.

Professor Stone shared my view that the privilege should belong "to the source, not to the reporter. When the reporter invokes the privilege, she is merely acting as the agent of the source." As a result, if a source elects to waive confidentiality, the journalist has no independent authority to assert it.

Stone alone discussed standards for defining a journalist. He agreed with the majority in *Branzburg* that courts deciding the question as a matter of First Amendment interpretation would have to conclude that the liberty of the press is as much the right of "the lonely pamphleteer" as of a large metropolitan publisher. By extension, were courts to exclude the millions of bloggers now writing on the Internet, the result would be a licensing of the press that would be anathema to the traditions embodied in the Constitution.

Although the difficulty in defining a journalist might be a serious constraint for the courts, Stone said, "it poses a much more manageable issue in the context of legislation," since government often distinguishes among different speakers and publishers. "Which reporters are allowed to attend a White House briefing?" he asked. "Which are eligible to be embedded with the military? Broadcasting is regulated, but print journalism is not. Legislation treats the cable medium differently from both broadcasting and print journalism. Differentiation among different elements of the media is constitutional, as long as it is not based on viewpoint or any other invidious consideration, and as long as the differentiation is reasonable." In other words a legislature could define *journalist* any way it pleased.

Stone said if Congress wanted to limit the privilege of confidentiality, it should impose a balancing test, setting the source's need for confidentiality against the court's or the public's need for the information.

Using such a balancing test, Stone said that he would protect sources that had provided the Pentagon Papers to the media or that had leaked information about the Abu Ghraib scandal, but he wouldn't have protected the conversations Karl Rove had had with Matt Cooper about Valerie Plame because Rove wasn't a whistleblower in need of and deserving protection.

The Department of Justice was invited to testify, but no DOJ official appeared before Congress. Instead, James B. Comey, then the department's deputy attorney general, submitted a statement that took strong exception to the proposed shield law. Comey complained that the bill would shift authority to evaluate requests for subpoenas from the Justice Department to the courts. He warned that the bill would "create serious impediments to the Department's ability to effectively enforce the law and fight terrorism"—despite a provision that had been added to the bill that voided the privilege of confidentiality in the event of an imminent threat to national security.

Senator Richard J. Durbin, a Democrat from Illinois, was concerned that the only crimes that might void the privilege involved national security. He thought the law should also give prosecutors the power to learn the names of journalists' confidential sources when cases involved kidnapping and sexual predators.

The Department of Justice did send a representative to a second hearing, held on October 19, 2005. Chuck Rosenberg, the U.S. attorney for the Southern District of Texas and a former DOJ official, testified against passage of any new legislation. Rosenberg said the DOJ guidelines were adequate to protect the press and the public. He said that the Justice Department had issued a dozen subpoenas to the media in the previous fourteen years, and that each of these subpoenas had carefully been reviewed by senior officials and personally approved by the attorney general. But he failed to mention subpoenas by special prosecutors and by other branches of government such as the Securities and Exchange Commission and the Federal Communications Commission. And he made no mention of the huge increase in subpoenas filed in civil cases.

Judith Miller also testified at the October hearing, three weeks after getting out of jail. She focused on the importance of confidential sources for her work covering issues of national security. David Westin, president of ABC News and also a lawyer who had clerked for Justice Powell a few years after *Branzburg*, testified that when he first joined the network's news department a decade earlier, producers asked whether the story was right and important. Now, he said, he and his producers found themselves asking instead whether the story is worth the risk of "subpoena and coercive efforts by prosecutors or by civil litigants." His meaning was clear: these efforts were having a chilling effect on the freedom of the press.

By the end of the hearing, the bill's proponents clearly lacked the votes to get it passed. But equally clearly, Arlen Specter and others on the Judiciary Committee had heard enough to think it was worth another effort at drafting legislation. Over the next few months, the committee's staff worked with lawyers representing several news associations and companies, including Time Inc. and the New York Times Co. In May of 2006, five of the committee's senators—Specter; Lugar; Dodd; Lindsey Graham, a Republican from South Carolina; and Charles Schumer, a New York Democrat—introduced a new proposal for a federal shield law.

The shield law proposed by the five senators is deeply flawed, but it is better than no federal shield law, and it has a greater chance of passage than any other bill proposed to date. It envisions balancing tests, and appropriately, it proposes different standards for subpoenas issued by prosecutors in criminal proceedings, by defendants in criminal proceedings, and by litigants in civil cases.

The protections it would offer are inadequate. They do not cover, for example, nonconfidential information. Therefore, an "anonymous" source lacking "confidential source status" wouldn't be covered. In addition, a prosecutor could obtain a journalist's notes for stories if the source isn't confidential even if the material in the notes never appeared in the journalist's story. There are also exceptions for national security and for times when a journalist is a witness to a crime or engaged in activity that could lead to a civil lawsuit.

I regret that the proposed shield law doesn't stipulate that it would cover state and local jurisdictions, as well as federal cases. Under the "supremacy clause" in the U.S. Constitution, Congress could argue that journalism is a form of commerce that takes place across state lines and, as such, should be governed by federal law. States would then be precluded from creating a weaker privilege than the federal law would provide. The states could have stronger protections, of course. Some states might challenge such a provision, but the need for uniformity would justify trying to impose a federal standard.

The change of control in the Congress following the 2006 elections, together with continued pressure for a federal shield law from the media, will lead to introduction of new legislation in the House and the Senate. Republican congressman Mike Pence of Indiana, an early supporter of a federal shield law, said he would introduce a new law in the House with bipartisan support. Republican senator Richard Lugar and Democratic senators Chris Dodd and Chuck Schumer will sponsor a similar bill in the Senate.

Although many senators indicate they would support the new bill, it still faces an uphill fight in both houses of Congress. The Justice Department's continued opposition to any bill that makes it more difficult for it to get testimony from reporters and that shifts control from the DOJ to the courts creates a major obstacle. Public apathy or antipathy toward the press, however, is an even bigger problem. So long as the public remains wary and suspicious of the press, new legislation protecting the rights of the press will be difficult to enact.

18

Editorial Guidelines

Lovers should talk before they get in bed together. So should reporters and their sources.

Many reporters say that they never want to stop an interview to discuss ground rules with a source who asks to go "off the record." If you stop to explain the rules and the nuances, you'll spook the source, or so the theory goes. It's not true. Yes, reporting is an intricate form of seduction, but most sources, like lovers, are in fact more comfortable after having "the talk," learning the rules and dangers. The more inexperienced the source, or the lover, the greater the need for total candor.

Michael Duffy was working on revisions to our editorial guidelines in the months following my meeting with him and the rest of the *Time* Washington bureau. Duffy interviewed reporters and editors at many Time Inc. publications, and in the meantime I looked into how other news organizations handled sourcing. What I found was a perfect muddle.

Few news organizations bother to distinguish between the different types of unnamed sources journalists must deal with, and apart from the memo *The Wall Street Journal* had issued in the 1980s, when I was its managing editor, I could find no effort to distinguish between "anonymous" and "confidential" sources. There is also considerable confusion within the media about such basic terms as *on the record, not for attribution, background, deep background,* and *off the record.*

The term *on the record* rarely appears in guidelines, but the Associated Press stylebook definition is a good one: "On the record. The information can be used with no caveats, quoting the source by name."

In contrast, *off the record* (according to the AP) means that the information cannot be published at all, now or in the future. It is an extremely restrictive concept that reporters should rarely, if ever, agree to since there is no way the reporter can use the information. At best, it might inform a reporter about the background for a decision or give insight into a subject's character or personality. Whenever sources asked me to "go off the record," I always explained what the term meant and said that I didn't want to hear anything I couldn't use. Reporters and their sources, however, frequently confuse *off the record* with other terms that disguise the source but allow use of the information.

William Safire has written in his "On Language" column in *The New York Times Magazine* that the term *off the record* first appeared in a 1924 *Times* editorial and was picked up by Franklin Delano Roosevelt when he was governor of New York. Safire quotes from the diary of Harold Ickes, who served as secretary of the interior during FDR's presidency, who said that in press conferences the President answered every question, "although in some instances his answers were off the record." Safire also quotes S. Douglass Cater, a Lyndon Johnson aide who later taught journalism. Cater found that FDR stipulated three other ways information could be used: direct quotation, indirect quotation, and background.

Direct quotation is self-explanatory. *Indirect quotation* meant the source could be identified and the information paraphrased but not put in quotes. *Background* meant the information could be used without identifying FDR as the source. That definition, which has come to be interchangeable with *not for attribution,* prevails today.

Deep background came into use in the 1950s. Time Inc.'s Editorial Guidelines into the 1990s said *deep background* meant "not for attribution to any source at all." The definition of the American Society of Newspaper Editors (ASNE) was more detailed: "Deep background: You're allowed to write it but you must say it as though you know it. You can't even attribute to anonymous sources. Example: 'The president is known to think that . . .'" *Deep background* is also known as the Lindley rule. It was devised by Ernest K. Lindley, a *Newsweek* columnist and Washington bureau chief. Karl Rove agreed to speak to Matt on "deep background." Matt was not only wrong to treat the conversation as if it were "confidential," he also violated the rules for "deep background" when he attributed the information about Valerie Plame to administration officials.

I found little analysis in most editorial guidelines of the issue of challenges to the journalist's right to keep sources confidential. The ASNE Statement of Principles says only, "Pledges of Confidentiality to news sources must be honored at all costs, and therefore should not be given lightly. Unless there is a clear and pressing need to maintain confidences, sources of information should be identified." The Code of Ethics and Professional Conduct of the Radio-Television News Directors Association is similarly spare. It says, "Professional electronic journalists should: Identify sources whenever possible. Confidential sources should be used only when it is clearly in the public interest to gather or convey important information or when a person providing information might be harmed. Journalists should keep all commitments to protect confidential sources."

The Sacramento Bee, a McClatchy newspaper, focuses on issues of credibility in its guidelines. "Anonymous sources will be allowed only when the value of the story and the benefits of the information to our readership clearly outweigh the potential for skepticism and erosion of credibility that arises with use of such sources."

USA Today, the nation's largest-circulation newspaper, owned by

Gannett, wouldn't publish quotes without attribution at all in the first few years after it was founded, in 1982. Its founder, Allen Neuharth, was an absolutist on this point. Although *USA Today's* rules are a bit looser today, its guidelines still insist, "The identity of an unnamed source must be shared with and approved by a managing editor prior to publication." They also state, "Sources should understand that if information is attributed to them anonymously in the newspaper, an editor will know their identity. They should also understand they may be identified if their information proves to be false or unfounded."

The Washington Post too insists, "The source of anything that appears in the paper will be known to at least one editor." The *Los Angeles Times* declares, "In some cases, an editor may insist on knowing the source's identity in order to evaluate the reliability of the information provided." The *San Jose Mercury News* also requires that a reporter identify an unnamed source to his or her editor, and it adds, "Editors who learn the identity of the source will be bound by the same confidentiality agreement reached between the reporter and the source."

The Washington Post, the *San Jose Mercury News*, and other papers insist that an editor know the source to provide a needed check and balance on a reporter and the reporter's source. An editor also provides independent evaluation of the source's worth. And since an agreement to grant confidentiality to the source commits the publisher as well as the reporter, the editor makes sure that the publication believes the risk is worth the reward.

The New York Times, however, grants an exception. "In the case of exceptionally sensitive reporting, on crucial issues of law or national security in which sources face dire consequences if exposed, the reporter may appeal to the executive editor for total confidentiality." The *Times* guidelines add, "In such circumstances, intended to be extremely rare, the executive editor may choose to ask for only a limited description of the source and waive the right to know the full identity."

There are similar disparities with regard to a publication's responsibilities to a confidential source. Many publications don't address the issue. *The Dallas Morning News* is an exception, and it is precise:

> Unnamed sources must be aware that in rare instances (which, to date, have never occurred at the DMN) they could be identified if lawsuits involving coverage were pursued and efforts to keep them confidential were exhausted in legal disputes (known as "Mirandizing" a source). Discuss the sources and the situation with your supervising editor before any promise of anonymity is made. Remember that you are not making a personal commitment to the source. You are acting on behalf of the newspaper.

The *Los Angeles Times* guidelines say, "Promises to a source must be kept except under the most extraordinary circumstances." For example, the guidelines say, "If a source, acting in bad faith, were to succeed in using the newspaper to spread misinformation, we would consider our promise of anonymity no longer binding."

Duffy and I exchanged memos throughout the fall. We began with the Time Inc. Editorial Guidelines that Bierstedt and I had drawn up. Those guidelines made an important point—that the very publication of guidelines can create problems. "Lawyers will try to use them against us in litigation. Any discrepancy between what the guidelines say and what a journalist did in a particular situation will be highlighted in a lawsuit." Bierstedt and I thought, however, that the benefits outweighed this risk.

Although Duffy and I had come up with a draft for the revised guidelines by the end of the year, the new document wasn't released until February 23, 2006, about six weeks after I had stepped down as editor in chief. It was distributed to Time Inc. employees with a cover note by John Huey, my successor, acknowledging, "As it became clear last year, the use of confidential sourcing by journalists has evolved into a much more complex issue, legally and ethically, than we had ever imagined."

The new guidelines on reporting and sourcing were a distinct improvement. The "Sourcing" section gave precise definitions for the different terms of attribution, including *not for attribution, background, deep background,* and *off the record.* I was concerned, though, that this section also said, "In some cases, the requesting editor may agree to accept certain information about the source and not the source's identity." Carol Loomis, *Fortune's* most respected and most thorough reporter, was known to keep the names of her sources to herself, and there may be others. If there is an exception to the rule, it should be Loomis, but as I read the new guidelines, after stepping down as editor in chief, I think Time Inc. is making a mistake. There should be no exceptions.

At my urging, the difference between anonymous and confidential sources had been spelled out in a new section, "Confidential source status." The section reiterated Time Inc.'s policy not to reveal the identity of any confidential source, but it recognized that the privilege is not absolute. It explained that there might be occasions where a reporter might face a jail term for contempt of court and Time Inc. might face substantial fines. It also explained the consequences of a criminal contempt finding.

The new guidelines said that confidential source status should be reserved for sources who provide information "that is important, and in the public interest, to our readers, and by doing so are risking their lives, their jobs or reputations." It told reporters and editors they shouldn't agree to a source's request for confidentiality without the explicit approval, prior to publication, of the managing editor or Time Inc.'s editor in chief.

I think the new Time Inc. guidelines are as good as, or better than, any others I have read. But on further reflection, I would make them more anecdotal and more conversational, and I would be more specific about when a publication might defy a court order. I would remind journalists that the source, not the reporter, owns the privilege, and that the reporter, the publisher, and the source must all agree before the source is treated as "confidential." I would also make the point that journalists' promises of confidentiality should be "subject to the rule of law" and would explain what that restriction would allow and disallow. It also troubles me that the guidelines are not available to the public on the Time Warner and Time Inc. websites. (Many other news outlets publish their guidelines on their websites, though few make them easy for readers to find.) I would also require every editorial employee to read the guidelines and to sign a statement saying he or she has done so.

It is beyond dispute that many of journalism's most important triumphs couldn't have been written without confidential sources. But what about all the bad stories based on confidential information that would never have been written had the sources been known to editors and to the public?

The Washington Post's Watergate triumph fostered a culture there and elsewhere in journalism in which everyone wanted to be "Woodstein," coupling hard work, creativity, and confidential sources to bring down the rich and the powerful. One painful result was the *Post*'s story about an eight-year-old heroin addict, written by Janet Cooke, a young, ambitious reporter who was working under Woodward.

Cooke's story was published in September 1980 and it won a

Pulitzer Prize for feature writing—which the *Post* had to return after the story was exposed as a fake and the boy as a made-up character. The *Post* then published a lengthy analysis by its ombudsman, Bill Green, that attempted to explain how the story had gotten into print. During its preparation, Howard Simons, then the paper's managing editor and one of Watergate's unsung heroes, had decreed that the boy's real name couldn't be disclosed under any circumstances, presumably because he was a minor whose identity should be protected. Assistant city editor Milton Coleman told Cooke that she could promise the mother anonymity. Fair enough, but then Simons, Coleman, Woodward, then the paper's assistant managing editor for metropolitan news, and Bradlee all failed to learn the names of Cooke's sources, including the subject of the story.

Green, whose masterly dissection ran almost fourteen thousand words, wrote, "Coleman did not ask the mother's name or the family's street address. He had promised Cooke confidentiality for her sources. The jugular of journalism lay exposed—the faith an editor has to place in a reporter. Simons says an editor can ask the name of a source and if a reporter refuses to reveal it the editor has the option to reject a story. He did not ask Cooke or Coleman to reveal any details on identity."

Coleman, acting on instructions from Simons, did tell Cooke that the story would be controversial, that she might be subpoenaed because she had seen a crime, and that if she refused to name her sources, she might be jailed, but that "the *Post* will stand behind you 100%."

Doubts about the story were raised from the day it first appeared in the *Post*. Washington's mayor, police chief, and other citizens questioned the accuracy of the story and clamored for "Jimmy" to be identified and rescued from his family. They pressured the paper. After Cooke was awarded the Pulitzer, questions about Cooke's educational background were also raised, initially by the Toledo *Blade*, where Cooke had worked before joining the *Post*.

Green wrote that the *Post* "felt under attack." Charges of irresponsibility from the public were tough to take. Woodward said, "We went into our Watergate mode: protect the source and back the reporter." Lewis Simons, then on the Metro staff, told Green, "Pressures are so great to produce, to go beyond excellence to the 'holy-s---' story. Everyone knows that's what the editors want."

Finding another Watergate continues to be the goal for many investigative reporters. Speaking at a panel on the story in 1997, former Nixon White House counsel Leonard Garment—according to a story in *The Miami Herald*—said Watergate had made journalists cynical about government and politicians, setting loose "an uncontrollable monster on the land." Bradlee, who was also on the panel, as was Woodward, conceded that, for years, many new reporters approached stories with the idea that "give me two years, and I'll have Redford playing me in the movies." Woodward agreed that because Watergate began with a "third-rate burglary," many reporters treat even the most minor of transgressions out of proportion to their likely impact. As a result, every scandal is tagged with the suffix *gate* without any regard to its implications, Woodward said, resulting in a "politics of distrust."

The use of anonymous sources, of course, isn't restricted to major investigative pieces. It also plays an all-too-important role in routine coverage that has no bearing on the public interest or the public's right to know.

As an editor, I have been happy to let reporters take information from anonymous sources that provides background and guidance, but I have asked that, wherever possible, that information be confirmed by an on-the-record source. I also believe at least one editor must know the name of anonymous and confidential sources whose information appears in or informs a story. I am not so much worried that the information doesn't exist or the quote has been made up, although the Janet Cooke scandal and the more recent Jayson Blair scandal are chilling reminders that journalists tell lies just like everybody else.

My bigger concern is that many reporters get too close to their sources. Even the best reporters tend to "fall in love" with their sources and to trust them and the information they give more than they should. This is especially true of beat reporters who become reliant on the same sources for story after story. They can and often do believe a source solely because the source was accurate on a prior piece, without questioning anew whether the source is' telling the truth.

Investigative reporters, looking for stories that powerful people and institutions want to keep quiet, run the highest risk of manipulation. Sources are rarely altruistic. They usually have an agenda. That is not a reason to reject information from sources who won't go on the record, but it should raise the bar for judging the value of the information given without attribution, especially if the information cannot be corroborated.

Investigative reporters are usually the hardest working, most driven staffers in a news organization. I tend to think of them as half "passionate seekers of truth" and half "sociopaths." They should not be allowed to work without the supervision of strong editors—editors who are themselves blessed with schizoid personalities. The editor must help the investigative reporter shape a story and must encourage the reporter to pursue every possible lead as aggressively as possible. Once the story is finished, however, that same editor must assume an adversarial role, representing the reader or viewer, interrogating the reporters about the authenticity of quotes and documents, and about sources and their biases.

The best investigative reporters understand the challenges to their work and some thrive on it. But some of journalism's most embarrassing failures in recent years can be traced to editors who didn't do enough to challenge their most experienced journalists. Judith

Miller's stories on weapons of mass destruction, of course, come to mind. But she and the *Times* are by no means alone.

In 1998, CNN retracted a piece, a print version of which we had run in *Time*, claiming that the U.S. military had used nerve gas in a mission to kill American defectors in Laos during the Vietnam War. The piece had been prepared by some of the news channel's most experienced journalists, who had worked more than eight months on it. But CNN quickly retracted the story after realizing the assertion that nerve gas had been used was, at best, based on shaky, unproven allegations. In taking responsibility for the story, CNN News Group CEO Tom Johnson acknowledged that editors, producers, and executives were among those responsible for the report.

(Since the story was written by CNN employees and was based on confidential information that couldn't be independently verified, I thought we needed to treat the article the way we treated book excerpts—that is, we didn't try to fact-check the story. Time Inc.'s policy on book excerpts seems counterintuitive, but it reflects a 1991 federal appeals court decision in a libel suit brought by Jeffrey Masson, a psychoanalyst, against The New Yorker Magazine, Inc., writer Janet Malcolm, and Alfred A. Knopf, Inc. In it, the court ruled that "a publisher who does not already have 'obvious reasons to doubt' the accuracy of a story is not required to initiate an investigation that might plant such doubt." But when a doubt exists, the publisher must try to dispel it. "Thus, where the publisher undertakes to investigate the accuracy of a story and learns facts casting doubt on the information contained therein, it may not ignore those doubts, even though it had no duty to conduct the investigation in the first place." I think the court's decision absurd since it penalizes careful editing, but our lawyers thought we couldn't fact-check book excerpts, and after reading the court's opinion, I agree with their analysis.)

In January 2005, CBS News fired four employees, including three senior executives, for their role in preparing and reporting a disputed story from several months earlier about President Bush's National Guard service. The story, which CBS News anchor Dan Rather delivered on *60 Minutes Wednesday*, relied on an unnamed source, a former Texas National Guard official, whom Rather subsequently said had "misled" and "lied to" the network. Andrew Heyward, then president of CBS News, acknowledged that the network had rushed the story to air before the 2004 presidential election. A 234-page independent investigation of the story, prepared by former Associated Press president Louis Boccardi and former attorney general Richard Thornburgh, concluded that the network's senior executives hadn't been rigorous enough in challenging the story's producer, Mary Mapes. Mapes had gained great credibility within the network for her work in exposing the U.S. military's abuse of prisoners at Abu Ghraib, and her work on that story made her superiors less inclined to challenge her on the Bush National Guard story.

And so I have drafted still another set of Editorial Guidelines, a copy of which appears as an appendix. If these guidelines had been in place at Time Inc. in 2003, and if we had followed them, we would not have become enmeshed in the Plame case. I believe they can help publications avoid other pitfalls while making clear to sources and the public the rules by which we operate.

19

Scooter Libby's Indictment

Following Judith Miller's release from jail, developments, as Judge Hogan had said of our defense, became "curiouser and curiouser." The grand jury was set to expire October 28, and in the period between Miller's testimony and that date, the rumors ranged from Fitzgerald's taking no action to his indicting several administration officials, including Karl Rove.

Fitzgerald, however, issued only one indictment, on October 28. It charged I. Lewis Libby Jr., Vice President Cheney's chief of staff, on five felony counts, all related to perjury, obstruction of justice, and making false statements to the grand jury and the FBI. These were serious charges, obviously for Libby, but also for the White House. But the indictment didn't charge him or anyone else with leaking Valerie Plame's name or otherwise violating any laws involving national security. And it made no mention of Rove.

The twenty-two-page indictment alleged that Libby had told FBI investigators and the grand jury that he spoke to NBC's Tim Russert around July 10, 2003, and that Russert first told him that Wilson's wife worked for the CIA. According to the indictment, Libby further testified that he was only passing on what he had heard from Russert when he told Matt Cooper and Judith Miller about Plame's CIA connection, and that he wasn't even certain at the time that the information was true.

But the indictment alleged that Libby lied to or misled the grand jury, pointing to evidence that strongly suggested that Libby (far from simply passing on hearsay about the spouse of a person in the news) was at the center of an extensive White House effort to learn about and undermine the credibility of Joseph Wilson's trip to Niger. The indictment chronicled Libby's conversations with officials at the CIA, the State Department, and the White House, including, presumably, Rove. It charged that Libby had learned of Valerie Plame Wilson's CIA affiliation from at least four different government officials in June and July of 2003, before speaking to Russert, Cooper, or Miller. In contrast to what Libby told the grand jury, the indictment insisted that Plame's name had never come up in Libby's conversation with Russert, and that Libby had expressed no doubts about Wilson's wife working for the CIA in his conversations with Cooper and Miller.

Although the charges were limited to perjury, Fitzgerald made clear that he thought the leaks had caused damage. The indictment stated that disclosing the names of CIA employees, such as Plame, whose status was classified, "had the potential to damage the national security in ways that ranged from preventing the future use of those individuals in a covert capacity, to compromising intelligence-gathering methods and operation," endangering the safety of CIA employees and those who deal with them.

Fitzgerald gave an hour-long press conference, televised live, following the announcement of the indictment. Speaking without notes, he delivered a performance that prompted the *Times*'s Todd S. Purdum to write, "It was as if Mr. Fitzgerald had suddenly morphed from the ominous star of a long-running silent movie into a sympathetic echo of Kevin Costner in *The Untouchables*."

Fitzgerald made a strong argument for seeking to prosecute

Libby on the charges that he had lied under oath, even though the indictment didn't allege any violations through his leaks of information to journalists. In fact, he argued, Libby's lies had made it impossible for the grand jury to determine whether he had committed crimes involving national security.

Using a baseball analogy, Fitzgerald said, "What we have when someone charges obstruction of justice is the umpire gets sand thrown in his eyes. He's trying to figure out what happened and somebody blocked [his] view." He complained, "If you're asking me what his motives were, I can't tell you," adding, "The harm in an obstruction investigation is that it prevents us from making the very fine judgments we want to make."

Fitzgerald also sought to disabuse those who thought he should "take an obstruction charge less seriously than a leak charge. This is a very serious matter and compromising national security is a very serious matter . . . Anyone who would go into a grand jury and lie and obstruct and impede the investigation has committed a serious crime."

The initial reactions to the indictment were largely predictable. Newspapers and the news networks gave most of their Saturday coverage to it. Harry Reid, the Democrats' Senate leader, claimed, "The Libby indictment provides a window into what this is really all about, how this administration manufactured and manipulated intelligence in order to sell the war in Iraq."

The Wall Street Journal's editorial page, by contrast, took the position of many in the Bush administration. It said that Fitzgerald had "thrust himself into what was, at bottom, a policy dispute between an elected Administration and critics of the President's approach to the war on terror, who included parts of the permanent bureaucracy of the State Department and the CIA."

Journalists (and their lawyers) worried that a trial in which three prominent journalists would testify against their former source would set a dangerous precedent. Jane Kirtley, a professor of media ethics at the University of Minnesota, was among those who fretted that journalists would become an investigative arm of the government.

In his press conference, Fitzgerald had, however, tried to minimize the impact of the case on the media. He said that "no one wanted to have a dispute with *The New York Times* or anyone else" and that he "was not looking for a First Amendment showdown." He said, "I do not think that reporters should be subpoenaed anything close to routinely. It should be an extraordinary case." But, he argued, if the reporter is the witness to a crime, in this case Libby's alleged perjury, then as a prosecutor he had no choice but to demand the reporter's testimony. That is why Russert's testimony is so important to Fitzgerald's indictment of Libby.

James Goodale, the former counsel to the New York Times Co. who had worked so hard to undo *Branzburg*, predictably disagreed. "In order to get his case to this point, Mr. Fitzgerald has inflicted major damage on the journalistic community by jailing Ms. Miller," he argued, even though "Ms. Miller's testimony does not appear to be necessary for the indictment."

Gibson, Dunn's Ted Boutrous argued, "From Day 1, the crucial issue in this investigation has been whether Mr. Libby, Karl Rove or any other official knew Ms. Plame's status as a covert agent," and there was no need to subpoena any reporter to determine her status. If Plame wasn't a covert agent or Libby didn't know she was covert, Fitzgerald could have ended the investigation without ever getting to the perjury issue, Boutrous said.

Many other attorneys thought Fitzgerald was smart not to pursue possible violations of laws covering national security. There was no indication that the Intelligence Identities Protection Act applied, and Fitzgerald indicated at his news conference that he had spent little time trying to prove violation of that act. He hinted, however, that he had looked closely at the Espionage Act. He said that the act is "a difficult statute to interpret" and is much less precise than

Britain's Official Secrets Act. "The average American may not appreciate that there's no law that specifically just says if you give classified information to somebody else, it is a crime," he said.

Although perjury would be easier to prove than a threat to national security, it would still be a difficult case to win. Fitzgerald would have to prove that the recollections of reporters were better or more truthful than Libby's, and even more important, that Libby knew he was lying when he spoke to the FBI agents and testified before the grand jury.

On November 3, Libby's lawyers entered a plea of not guilty. Libby had resigned from Cheney's staff after receiving the indictment, and over the next month he had put together a formidable criminal defense team, including Theodore V. Wells Jr. and William Jeffress Jr., both of whom had successfully represented many federal officials in criminal cases. Wells made it clear that they would seek notes from all the reporters Libby had spoken to, setting off a new round of litigation with journalists over the confidentiality of their notes.

20

Rove Gets a Pass

Some wanted to compare "Plamegate" to Watergate. Bob Woodward was not among them.

On July 7, 2005, the day after Judith Miller went to jail, Woodward complained on National Public Radio about what he saw as the government's trying to force employees to sign waivers of confidentiality. A few days later, on CNN's *Larry King Live*, he praised Miller's willingness to go to jail to protect her sources. And on July 17, he belittled Fitzgerald's investigation on NBC's *Meet the Press*, saying that the special counsel "has discovered that there is an underground railroad of information in Washington."

But what America's most famous investigative reporter did not say was that a senior administration official had told him about Plame, her relationship to Wilson, and her position at the CIA in mid-June 2003, nearly a month before Robert Novak disclosed her CIA connection and well before Miller or Cooper had learned about it. Woodward, who, despite his title as an "assistant managing editor" at *The Washington Post*, spends most of his time writing books, told his boss, executive editor Leonard Downie Jr., of his knowledge in October 2005, a few weeks after Libby was indicted.

Having received a waiver of confidentiality from his source,

Woodward gave a two-hour deposition to Fitzgerald on November 14, in which he said he didn't believe the information was especially important or even classified. Woodward said, however, that he wasn't authorized to make his source's name public.

It was unclear what impact Woodward's deposition would have on Fitzgerald's case against Libby. Libby's lawyer Ted Wells called it a "bombshell" that undermined any assertion that Libby had been the first government official to discuss the Wilson-Plame CIA connection with a journalist. But others thought it wouldn't affect the perjury charges.

That Woodward had concealed what he had been told about Plame would be defensible were he just a book writer, but for a journalist who carries a lofty title at the *Post*, and whose first commitment is presumably to tell readers what he knows, his silence was disturbing. Many critics thought he had made too many deals in return for access to the Bush White House.

Mark Jurkowitz, then a prominent media critic at *The Boston Phoenix*, was one of many commentators who thought Woodward had traded his reputation for tough reporting in exchange for access. "The demythologizing of Woodward is occurring during a period when the kind of investigative reporting that built his legend faces a constellation of daunting obstacles, including declining newsroom resources, a secrecy-obsessed administration, and prosecutors and judges using subpoenas to poison the relationship between journalists and their confidential sources," Jurkowitz wrote. "The mounting critique of Woodward as access-seeking insider also corresponds to the growth of public skepticism about the mainstream media's methods and motives. Citizens frequently see journalists as biased, unaccountable and—perhaps most of all—part of a privileged power elite rather than a populist voice fighting for their rights and interests. In the end, playing into that corrosive public perception of the media as a cadre of elites may prove to be Woodward's biggest sin."

Arianna Huffington, after watching Woodward appear again on Larry King's show, pronounced his performance "laughable," particularly the way "he kept tossing in references to Watergate, strapping on those glory days like a protective armor. Over the course of 'the full hour,' he mentioned Watergate four times, Ben Bradlee three times, Deep Throat twice, and Richard Nixon and Katharine Graham once each. Memo to Bob: we get this, too. Your reporting once brought down a president. But that only makes your 'journalistic sins' on Plamegate all the more appalling and disappointing. It was pathetic watching the real-life Robert Redford reduced to holding up old headlines to fight off charges that he's just carrying water for the powerful."

Inside the *Post* newsroom, many journalists worried that their own credibility might be hurt by Woodward's decision not to report what he knew. Woodward apologized to *The Washington Post* on November 16: "I hunkered down. I'm in the habit of keeping secrets. I didn't want anything out there that was going to get me subpoenaed." Downie said that Woodward had "made a mistake" but that he remained comfortable with Woodward continuing to spend most of his time working on books, giving the *Post* first excerpts from them, and occasionally writing news stories. Woodward and Downie said they would speak to each other more than they had in recent years.

Woodward did provide a few additional details about his source to Viveca Novak, a reporter then working in *Time's* Washington bureau, who wrote a piece about her interview with him for the magazine's "Nation" section. (Viveca Novak is not related to Robert Novak.) He told her that despite his stated opposition to waivers, he had tried twice before, once in 2004 and again in 2005, to persuade his source to lift the confidentiality restriction, but that the source had refused. Then, after Libby was indicted, Woodward realized that Libby wasn't the first official to talk about Wilson's wife to a reporter. Woodward said he then called his source, who, this time, thought he had no alternative but to go to the prosecutor. Woodward told Viveca Novak that his source then released him to testify as well, but that the source still wouldn't let Woodward put his name in print or otherwise disclose it to the public.

I first met Karl Rove in the weeks before the 2004 presidential election. He came to the Time and Life Building in New York, where he provided background briefings to groups of *Time* journalists. I didn't see him again until the following February when, in one of life's more surreal moments, I interviewed him about his political and policy work in the Bush White House.

Dick Parsons and the Time Warner corporate communications staff had decided to hold a series of public programs in the company's new headquarters in New York's Columbus Circle. The programs, called "Conversations on the Circle," were to feature a newsmaker whom I would interview before an audience of political, business, cultural, and media leaders. Bill Clinton and Supreme Court justice Antonin Scalia would come later in the year, but Rove was Parsons's first selection for the series. Neither Parsons nor anyone on his public relations staff knew, of course, that Rove was Matt Cooper's confidential source. It was an awkward situation, but I didn't think I could delegate Parsons's assignment. Instead, I decided I should go ahead with the interview.

Sitting on the podium with Rove, I was reminded of his ability to take in massive amounts of information—his ability to read and respond to hundreds of messages a day is legendary—and his even greater ability to remember it. We did not discuss Joseph Wilson and Valerie Plame, and no one in the audience asked him about the grand jury investigation during the question-and-answer period.

Rove fielded questions on everything from the war in Iraq to which Ohio precincts had been crucial to Bush's winning reelection. He made a compelling case for President Bush as a hardworking chief executive, the nation's only president with an MBA (from Harvard no less), who spent his evenings reading briefing books. The skeptical members of the audience suddenly seemed credulous. When I asked Rove why he drove a Jaguar, the famed British make, he was quick to note that the Ford Motor Co.'s British subsidiary made it. Only one question, suggested by my wife, a scientist, gave him pause: whether his father, a geologist, believed in evolution, and if so, how that belief affected him. After a brief pause, he replied, "Yes, he did, but he also believed in God and so do I." Flawless.

I next saw Karl Rove at a conference in Aspen in early September 2005. We spoke for only a few minutes. By then Cooper had already testified before the grand jury, as had Rove. Our brief exchange was cordial, but Rove was quick to tell me how frustrated he was with Cooper. "Our ground rule was 'deep background,'" he said. "I never asked to be treated as a confidential source. Everyone would have been better off if Matt had just agreed to testify about our conversation." He went on to address a lunch crowd on the subject of Hurricane Katrina, and he again showed the mastery for detail he had shown in our interview at Time Warner's headquarters.

Watching Rove in Aspen reminded me of his extraordinary memory and his ability to absorb huge amounts of detail. He had to know he was a source for Matt. But perhaps he didn't know he was *the* source.

And then I learned about Viveca Novak's connections with Rove's lawyer, Robert Luskin.

Novak had joined *The Wall Street Journal*'s Washington bureau after I left the paper, and had done good work. Although I had nothing to do with her coming to *Time*, I was happy to see her in the magazine's Washington bureau, covering campaign finance and other subjects where her ability to develop sources often paid off.

One of her sources was Bob Luskin, whom she had met and befriended while covering one of his clients in 1996. They would get together occasionally to have a drink and swap stories at the Café Deluxe, a bar near the National Cathedral. At one of those meetings, in October 2003, Novak learned that Luskin was Karl Rove's lawyer. Over the next year, they met three or four more times. Novak subsequently recalled, in an article published in *Time*:

> Toward the end of one of our meetings, I remember Luskin looking at me and saying something to the effect of "Karl doesn't have a Cooper problem. He was not a source for Matt." I responded instinctively, thinking he was trying to spin me, and said something like, "Are you sure about that? That's not what I hear around TIME." He looked surprised and very serious. "There's nothing in the phone logs," he said . . . I was taken aback that he seemed so surprised . . . Luskin walked me to my car and said something like, "Thank you. This is important."

"Important" notwithstanding, Novak never told her bureau chief or anyone else at *Time* about that conversation. The subject did not come up again until "indictment week," the week Fitzgerald's grand jury was to expire at the end of October 2005.

During that week, Luskin called Novak and told her that he had "disclosed to Fitzgerald the content of a conversation he and I had had at Café Deluxe more than a year earlier and that Fitzgerald might want to talk to me." Luskin had apparently told Fitzgerald about his conversation with Novak in the hope that it would help Rove avoid indictment.

Luskin told Fitzgerald that his earlier talk with Novak led him and Rove on a search for evidence that Rove had been in contact with Cooper, something Rove had denied in earlier testimony before the grand jury. That search led to the discovery of an e-mail Rove had sent Stephen Hadley, then deputy national security adviser, telling Hadley about his conversation with Cooper. After finding the e-mail, Rove returned to the grand jury in October 2004 and told it that his failure to remember his conversation with Cooper in earlier testimony was an innocent mistake he was happy to correct.

Although Rove avoided indictment in October 2005, Fitzgerald called a second grand jury, and he wanted Novak to talk to him. Novak hired a criminal lawyer, Hank Schuelke, and—still not telling anyone at *Time*—she met for an informal meeting with Fitzgerald in Schuelke's office for two hours on November 10, 2005. (Prosecutors frequently interview potential witnesses informally before determining whether to take them before a grand jury for questioning under oath.) On Friday, November 18, as she was writing her article about Woodward's role in the Plame investigation, Novak learned that Fitzgerald wanted her to testify under oath. Over the weekend Novak finally told her bureau chief, Jay Carney, the story of how she had disclosed the cover of Cooper's source, Rove. I heard the story from Jim Kelly.

Novak met Fitzgerald again on December 8 and testified under oath. Novak told Fitzgerald it was widely known in *Time*'s Washington bureau that Rove was Cooper's source but that she couldn't remember who had told her. She was also unable to remember when she had told Luskin.

Novak then took a leave of absence from the Washington bureau, and in early 2006 she resigned from the magazine. Fitzgerald was not only doing a fine job of disrupting many reporter-source relationships in Washington; he was also laying bare the sloppy work habits of some of the town's best-known journalists, undermining the credibility of all journalists.

In June 2006, Luskin released a two-paragraph statement saying that Fitzgerald had formally advised him that he "did not anticipate seeking charges against Karl Rove." Although I had thought any charges against Rove would be difficult to prove, I had no doubt that Viveca Novak's conversations with Luskin about Cooper's confidential source played a critical role in Rove's changing his testimony and Luskin's convincing Fitzgerald that his client had made an innocent mistake, his bulletproof memory notwithstanding. If Rove's brief interview with *Time* got him in trouble, by a strange symmetry his lawyer's conversation with *Time* helped get him out of it.

Federal district judge Reggie B. Walton set Scooter Libby's trial for early 2007, but the sparring between Patrick Fitzgerald and Libby's lawyers began almost immediately after the indictment was announced. Libby's defense was built around the argument that he was too busy with urgent matters of state to remember casual conversations with reporters. To that end, his lawyers made extravagant demands for everything from the printed daily briefings given to President Bush to notes and other unpublished information obtained by reporters who had spoken to Libby. Fitzgerald, in contrast, worked to narrow the focus of pretrial discovery to the simple charge that Libby had lied about his conversations with Russert, Cooper, and Miller.

The myriad filings and cross-filings revealed a lot about the Bush White House's way of dealing with the media and about Libby's working relationship with Cheney and Bush. Most significantly, Fitzgerald disclosed that in July 2003 Bush had authorized Libby to leak classified intelligence about Iraq's nuclear ambitions—to Judith Miller.

The disclosure prompted outrage in the media and among Democrats, who accused Bush of hypocrisy for repeatedly criticizing government leaks by others while authorizing a leak of his own. Senate minority leader Harry Reid said, "President Bush must fully disclose his participation in the selective leaking of classified information." Jane Harman, the senior Democrat on the House Intelligence Committee, said the disclosure revealed that Bush was the "leaker in chief."

Fitzgerald's filing revealed that Bush—who has the authority to approve the declassification of information—did so through Cheney, who in turn encouraged Libby to discuss the National Intelligence Estimate with Miller, including details about Iraq's efforts to develop weapons of mass destruction. Libby acknowledged that the approval process was "unique in his recollection." He didn't say, however, that he had been authorized by Bush or Cheney to reveal Plame's name. About a week after Libby spoke to Miller, the White House published a declassified summary of the intelligence estimate.

According to Fitzgerald's filing, some White House documents "could be characterized as reflecting a plan to discredit, punish or seek revenge against Mr. Wilson." It said that Libby had asked Marc Grossman, undersecretary of state for political affairs, for information regarding Wilson's trip to Niger in late May and early June 2003. Grossman advised Libby shortly thereafter that "he had learned that Wilson's wife worked at the CIA and that State Department personnel believed that Mr. Wilson's wife was involved in the planning of Mr. Wilson's trip." Fitzgerald asserted that the central issue at trial would be whether Libby had lied when he testified he was not aware that Plame worked at the CIA before speaking with Tim Russert on July 10, 2003, and insisted that Grossman's testimony would show Libby knew of Plame's CIA affiliation more than a month earlier.

Another Fitzgerald filing included a handwritten note from Cheney to Libby on a photocopy of Wilson's July 2003 op-ed piece in the *Times*. The note from Cheney asked, "Have they done this sort of thing before? Send an Amb. to answer a question? Do we ordinarily send people out pro bono to work for us? Or did his wife send him on a junket?" The note strongly suggested that Cheney too knew Plame was a CIA agent—and made it appear likely that Cheney, and perhaps Bush himself, would be asked to testify at Libby's trial.

Libby's lawyers subpoenaed Miller and the *Times*, Cooper, and Russert, seeking a broad array of documents, including notes for dozens of stories they had written or had worked on that mentioned Libby. Although Judge Walton ruled that much of what Libby's lawyers sought was irrelevant to the case, he did order *Time* to turn over drafts of articles that Cooper had written, as well as many of Cooper's notes.

Since Cooper had already testified before the grand jury, it seemed futile to resist Walton's decision. The notes, which were turned over to Fitzgerald and to Libby's lawyers, did prompt an entertaining exchange of e-mails between Fitzgerald and Cooper's lawyer, Dick Sauber. Cooper had written that he was standing in the nude in his apartment when he got the call from Libby waiving his confidentiality and indicating Libby's willingness to let Cooper testify about their discussion of Wilson and Plame.

From: Sauber, Richard
Sent: Thursday, June 01, 2006 3:52 PM
To: Fitzgerald, Patrick J.
Subject: From Sauber

Pat- heard you called- email me when you are free and I will step
out of mtg and call your cell-

From: Fitzgerald, Patrick J.
Sent: Thursday, June 01, 2006 5:23 PM
To: Sauber, Richard
Subject: RE: From Sauber

I will save you the call. I was just calling to thank you for sending
over the documents and for the heads up on the discrepancy. And
then I was going to give you a hard time for not warning not to
read the materials over lunch, which was when I found out that
your client was au naturel for the relevant conversation.

From: Sauber, Richard
Sent: Friday, June 02, 2006 11:49 AM
To: Fitzgerald, Patrick J.
Subject: RE: From Sauber

At least the jury will be impressed by his transparency....

From: Fitzgerald, Patrick J.
Sent: Friday, June 02, 2006 12:53 PM
To: Sauber, Richard
Subject: RE: From Sauber

I have always made it a practice not to tell witnesses how to dress for court. You don't want to tell the incarcerated drug dealer to wear the orange jump suit and allow the defense to say you were trying to engender sympathy for the witness' plight. You don't want to tell him to wear a suit and endure the cross that you were trying to make him someone he is not. You always tell them to dress how they feel comfortable and let it be.

I am rethinking my policy . . .

21

The Government Escalates Its
Assault on the Press

The indictment of Scooter Libby was a milestone in the Plame-Cooper-Miller story. It exposed the Bush administration's efforts to manipulate the press while trying to destroy those who would criticize the President and his policies. But for those in the administration, battles with journalists were part of a broader effort to control leaks and to corral the press, which it had come to see as a part of the enemy forces it had to fight.

In the months following the Supreme Court's refusal to hear our case, the Bush administration made several attempts to intimidate and muzzle the press. Although the first salvo didn't appear to be aimed at the press, it quickly became part of the battle between the White House, the Department of Justice, and the media.

On August 4, 2005, the DOJ indicted two pro-Israel American lobbyists under the Espionage Act, charging them with conspiring to obtain and disclose classified information about national security to journalists and to Israeli government officials. The two lobbyists, Steven J. Rosen and Keith Weissman, had been working for the American Israel Public Affairs Committee (AIPAC) in Washington, D.C., when they allegedly obtained the classified information from Lawrence Franklin, who was then a top Defense Department analyst. The government secrets pertained to U.S. policy in Iran and to terrorism in Saudi Arabia and Central Asia. Franklin, who had already been indicted in the case, subsequently pleaded guilty to passing classified information to the two AIPAC employees and was sentenced to twelve years in prison.

Although the journalists who received the information weren't named or accused of wrongdoing, media lawyers understood the indictment's importance. The AIPAC case was the first in which the government sought to make the receipt of classified information a criminal act. Under the broad provisions of the Espionage Act, Rosen and Weissman, private citizens, were charged with communicating information about national defense "to any persons not entitled to receive it"—precisely what government sources do with journalists in Washington every day. Neither intent nor the value of the information to its recipients is an issue under the Espionage Act.

Floyd Abrams told *The Washington Post* that the AIPAC case is "the single most dangerous case for free speech and free press." The Reporters Committee for Freedom of the Press said, "The indictments in this case raise issues that could well affect the very nature of how journalism can be practiced." It added, "These charges potentially eviscerate the primary function of journalism—to gather and publicize information of public concern—particularly where the most valuable information to the public is information that other people, such as the government, want to conceal."

Rosen and Weissman both asserted that the First Amendment should have protected their conversations with Franklin, the Defense Department analyst. Their lawyers argued that no classified documents changed hands—the information was imparted orally—and that they didn't know Franklin was violating the law by discussing matters with them. Moreover, they said, they had no way of knowing what was classified and what wasn't.

The Justice Department said that as lobbyists Rosen and Weissman "have no First Amendment right to willfully disclose national defense information." It went on to say that journalists could similarly be prosecuted. But, it added, "We recognize that a prosecution under the espionage laws of an actual member of the press for publishing classified information leaked to it by a government source, would raise legitimate and serious issues and would not be undertaken lightly, indeed, the fact that there has never been such a prosecution speaks for itself."

Federal district judge T. S. Ellis III, in pretrial hearings for Rosen and Weissman, complained from the bench that the Espionage Act is overly broad, but he, nonetheless, seemed willing to rely on it in their trial. "We are a bit in new, uncharted waters, and that's why I'm going to consider this matter extremely carefully," he said. But in sentencing Franklin, Judge Ellis remarked that people "who come into unauthorized possession of classified information must abide by the law. That applies to academics, lawyers, journalists, professors, whatever."

Some of the best coverage of the ways in which the Bush administration used the Iraq war to expand its power, testing the limits of legality and secrecy, appeared in *The Washington Post*. The *Post* published more than a half-dozen page-one articles by Dana Priest in 2005 that detailed how the Central Intelligence Agency was dealing with suspected terrorists.

In January, Priest wrote about the CIA's and the Pentagon's long-range plans for indefinite imprisonment of the suspects against whom they didn't have enough evidence to charge in courts. In March, she wrote about a young Afghan detainee who had frozen to death in an abandoned warehouse that was used as a detention center—code-named the Salt Pit—while under CIA supervision. Later that month, she wrote that the CIA had done little to assure compliance with U.S. antitorture laws governing the transfer of suspected terrorists to other countries. In June and July, she wrote about how Italian and French intelligence services had helped the CIA deal with suspected members of Al Qaeda and other terrorist groups.

Then, in November 2005, Priest wrote two stories about the CIA's use of a hidden global network of prisons in more than two dozen countries, including nations in Eastern Europe. "CIA Holds Terror Suspects in Secret Prisons" appeared November 2, followed on November 18 by "Foreign Network at Front of CIA's Terror Fight." The covert prison system had been used since shortly after 9/11 to hide and interrogate important Al Qaeda captives. The counterintelligence centers enabled U.S. and foreign intelligence officers, working side by side, to "track and capture" suspected terrorists.

Priest's reporting relied heavily on confidential sources and classified information. The existence and location of the "black sites" used as prisons "are known to only a handful of officials in the United States and, usually, only to the president and a few top intelligence officers in each host country," Priest wrote. The *Post* noted that it had agreed not to publish the names of the Eastern European countries involved in the covert program, at the request of senior U.S. officials. Leonard Downie Jr., the *Post's* executive editor, contended in a note to readers that naming them wasn't important to readers and it might disrupt important intelligence relationships.

In reporting the stories on the intelligence centers, the *Post* said it "interviewed more than two dozen current and former intelligence officials and more than a dozen senior foreign intelligence officials as well as diplomatic and congressional sources," many of whom weren't authorized to speak publicly. Following publication of the articles, Democrats on the Senate Judiciary Committee demanded classified documents about the centers from the Justice Department and other agencies.

Vice President Cheney and the attorney general, Alberto Gonzales, made it clear that the administration believed the CIA had the right to maintain "black sites" in Eastern Europe and elsewhere and that no laws prohibited the harsh treatment the *Post* had reported at those sites. *The Wall Street Journal*'s editorial page wrote, "There is little doubt that *The Washington Post* story on alleged prisons in Europe has done enormous damage—at a minimum, to our ability to secure future cooperation in the war on terror from countries that don't want their assistance to be exposed."

In response to these concerns, the Justice Department and the FBI began interviewing officials at federal agencies engaged in national security and law enforcement. *The Washington Post* reported that the administration "has launched initiatives targeting journalists and their possible government sources. The efforts include several FBI probes, a polygraph investigation inside the CIA and a warning from the Justice Department that reporters could be prosecuted under espionage laws."

The New York Times editorial page has consistently been critical of the powers the Bush administration has asserted since September 11, 2001. But it was the *Times*'s news pages that most infuriated the administration when, in December 2005, the paper published a front-page article titled "Bush Lets U.S. Spy on Callers Without Courts." The lengthy story revealed that President Bush had secretly authorized the National Security Agency to eavesdrop on Americans and others within the United States without the court-approved warrants normally required for domestic spying. The monitoring, restricted to international telephone calls, was designed to search for evidence of terrorist activity. The story's authors, James Risen and Eric Lichtblau, said, "Some officials familiar with the continuing operation have questioned whether the surveillance has stretched, if not crossed, constitutional limits on legal searches." The story made clear it relied heavily on whistle-blowers, saying, "Nearly a dozen current and former officials, who were granted anonymity because of the classified nature of the program, discussed it with reporters for *The New York Times* because of their concerns about the operation's legality and oversight."

The *Times* reported that the White House had asked it not to publish the article, arguing that "it could jeopardize continuing investigations and alert would-be terrorists that they might be under scrutiny." After hearing the administration's concerns, the *Times* said, it delayed publication for a year to conduct additional reporting, and it omitted some of the information administration officials argued could be useful to terrorists. Many details in the article also appeared in a book by Risen published in January 2006, *State of War: The Secret History of the CIA and the Bush Administration*.

The Bush administration and its supporters were outraged by the NSA story, and they defended the President's actions. Attorney General Gonzales acknowledged that the Foreign Intelligence Surveillance Act (FISA) requires the government to obtain a court order before engaging in the kind of surveillance the *Times* had exposed. But he said that he and the White House "believe the President has the inherent authority under the Constitution as Commander-in-Chief to engage in this kind of activity" and that the Congress had confirmed that authority when it authorized the use of military force after 9/11. Moreover, he insisted that congressional leaders from both parties had been briefed on the NSA's surveillance practices.

The President described the NSA leaks as "a shameful act" that would help America's enemies, and he called on the Justice Department to investigate whether the disclosure of classified information involved criminal acts by the leakers and, possibly, the *Times*. Porter Goss, then head of the CIA, said that government employees who wanted to report abuses should do so through the process outlined under the Intelligence Community Whistleblower Protection Act, which enables CIA employees to report matters of "urgent concern" to the agency's inspector general, instead of going to the media. In an article entitled "Loose Lips Sink Spies," which appeared February 10, 2006, on the *Times*'s op-ed page, Goss wrote, "Those who choose to bypass the law and go straight to the press are not noble, honorable or patriotic. Nor are they whistleblowers. Instead they are committing a criminal act that potentially places American lives at risk." Goss had told a Senate Intelligence Committee hearing a week earlier, "It is my aim and it is my hope that we will witness a grand jury investigation with reporters present being asked to reveal who is leaking this information."

After *The Wall Street Journal* editorialized against the *Times*'s publication of the NSA story, *Times* executive editor Bill Keller wrote a letter to the *Journal* in reply. He explained that the *Times*'s editors had carefully weighed Bush's argument that the story shouldn't be published. But they had concluded that the administration's case "did not stand up to the evidence our reporters amassed and we judged that the responsible course was to publish what we knew and let readers assess it themselves."

That argument riled Bush supporters such as law professor John C. Eastman, who runs the Claremont Institute's Center for Constitutional Jurisprudence. Eastman, who clerked for Supreme Court justice Clarence Thomas after law school, says Keller's defense "is truly an extraordinary claim, that somehow *The New York Times* is entitled to weigh evidence and determine for itself whether to publish classified information—in other words, that *The New York Times* is above the law and can publish whatever classified information it sees fit, with impunity."

Eastman also rejected any suggestion that the First Amendment's freedom of the press provision creates "a special preserve for the institutionalized press, as opposed to ordinary citizens." Echoing *Branzburg*, he concluded, as a federal prosecutor no doubt would, that the "First Amendment does not afford any greater protection to the 'press' than it does to ordinary citizens."

The *Times* had several good responses, beginning with the obvious fact that the story was not likely to harm national security. It was already abundantly clear to Americans and to Al Qaeda that the government was wiretapping the conversations of suspected terrorists. The *Times* story, for all of its impact, wasn't about the wiretapping but about wiretapping without the warrants required under FISA. As the Open Society Institute's Morton Halperin has written, "All the story revealed was that the NSA was listening to some calls without a warrant—not how successful it was or even under what circumstances it was trying to listen in."

The Bush administration's battles with the press escalated in June 2006, when *The New York Times*, the *Los Angeles Times*, and *The Wall Street Journal* published stories about far-reaching government efforts to track global financial transfers by suspected terrorists.

The stories discussed the government's Terrorist Finance Tracking Program, administered by the CIA and the FBI under U.S. Treasury Department supervision. Using information from databases supplied by a Belgian cooperative, the Society for Worldwide Interbank Financial Telecommunication (SWIFT), the program traces wire transfers worth about $6 trillion daily between banks and other financial institutions.

The administration had made no secret of its efforts to track money transfers by terrorist suspects. There is no indication that the program, which operates under a series of U.S. subpoenas, is illegal in the United States, although a European Union panel held in November 2006 that the program violated EU data-protection rules. In any case, the program appears to have been effective. In fact, on this story and the one about warrantless surveillance, I was having trouble understanding all the fuss. Having been slow to question the rationale for the Iraq war itself, I thought these catch-up stories seemed relatively insignificant, as if a homeowner had used a rifle to kill a menacing intruder but had done so without a gun permit.

Neither the *Times* nor the government agrees with this assessment. The *Times* reported that the program has played a hidden role in domestic and foreign terrorism investigations since 2001 and helped in the capture of Riduan Isamuddin, better known as Hambali, the mastermind behind the Bali bombings in 2002 and, until his arrest, the most wanted Al Qaeda figure in Southeast Asia. And the Bush administration spent almost two months trying to persuade *The New York Times*—whose reporters, Lichtblau and Risen, had been working on the story for months—not to publish it, claiming that disclosure of the program could jeopardize its effectiveness. The Treasury enlisted several prominent officials, including Democrats and Republicans, to speak to the *Times* about the program's value. When the *Times* refused to withhold publication, the Treasury decided to brief reporters from the *Los Angeles Times* and the *Journal* who covered the "terror finance" beat. Such preemptive briefing is not uncommon if the government believes that it can help blunt the impact of an exclusive story it has been trying to suppress.

The administration immediately attacked the press following publication. Vice President Cheney criticized those in the news media who "take it upon themselves to disclose vital national security programs, thereby making it more difficult for us to prevent future attacks against the American people." A few days later President Bush condemned the *Times*'s disclosures as "disgraceful," adding that the story about the program "does great harm to the United States of America."

It didn't take long for conservative bloggers and talk-show hosts to pile on. One, Melanie Morgan, who has a radio program in California, urged that the *Times* be found guilty of treason and that its executive editor, Bill Keller, be executed. Congressman Peter King, then the Republican chairman of the House Homeland Security Committee, also called for criminal prosecution of the *Times*. King told the *New York Post* that he thought the *Times* had "disclosed classified information in time of war. They've compromised successful antiterror operations to further their own left-wing, elitist agenda."

Bill Keller posted a letter to readers on the paper's website saying that the paper decided to publish the report after concluding that there was no clear danger in doing so and that the public interest was served by reporting on the programs. He and Dean Baquet, editor of the *Los Angeles Times*, then wrote "When Do We Publish a Secret?"—an op-ed piece that appeared in both papers July 1, 2006. The piece noted, "Our job, especially in times like these, is to bring our readers information that will enable them to judge how well their elected leaders are fighting on their behalf, and at what price."

Priest, Risen, and Lichtblau were awarded Pulitzer Prizes, journalism's highest honor, for their stories on the CIA's detention centers and NSA eavesdropping. I shared the Pulitzer judges' assessment of Priest's work. I thought her stories were in the public interest and that they pointed to deceit, hypocrisy, and the possibility of serious wrongdoing by the Bush administration. Her stories met all my standards for the use of confidential sources—for these sources were whistle-blowers whose jobs and reputations would be at risk if their identities were made public.

President Bush had promised that the United States would stand behind the United Nations' Convention Against Torture following disclosure of the Abu Ghraib prison scandal in 2004. That convention, signed and ratified in 1984 and put in force in 1987, specifically held that "no State Party shall expel, return, or extradite a person to another State where there are substantial grounds for believing that he would be in danger of being subjected to torture." Yet the *Post* stories showed Bush's willingness to ignore that provision.

Although tensions between the Bush administration and the press remained high, the 2006 elections changed the balance of power in Washington. Congressional committees under the control of Democrats pledged investigations of many of the president's more controversial policies, and it appears that the change in political landscape has led to some moderation in the White House's positions. In January 2007 the Department of Justice surprised the press by announcing that it would end its policy of eavesdropping without warrants on Americans suspected of terrorist ties. Instead, it agreed to use the secret court that had jurisdiction over the NSA's wiretapping program all along.

22

Reviving the Espionage Act

War, and the need for increased security that accompanies it, has always exacerbated the tensions in government-press relationships. The nation's first curb on the press, the Sedition Act of 1798, was passed in the face of possible war with France. During the Civil War, President Lincoln ordered the arrest of many critics who wrote pieces or spoke against the war. He then suspended the writ of habeas corpus, precluding his jailed critics from seeking a judicial ruling on the legitimacy of their incarceration.

Although the current Espionage Act has been on the books since 1917, it has rarely been invoked against the media since 1918. The act grew out of President Woodrow Wilson's concerns about loyalty and secrecy during World War I. In April 1917, Wilson issued an executive order making "loyalty" a condition of government service. The Espionage Act was passed two months later and has been amended many times since then.

The sections of the act most pertinent to the media prohibit the gathering of information connected to national defense "with intent or reason to believe that the information is to be used to the injury of the United States, or to the advantage of any foreign nation." Although extremely broad, the focus is for the most part on gathering and copying, not on publishing. One subsection prohibits the retention or willful communication of documents and other material "relating to the national defense," even if the recipient had no reason to believe the material could endanger U.S. security.

The act also makes specific reference to publishing any information about troop movements or defense efforts. Although the section can be invoked only "in time of war," that term isn't limited to times marked by a formal declaration of war by Congress. It would almost certainly be held by the courts to include the military's actions in Iraq, just as it did President Truman's "police action" in Korea.

An amendment to the Espionage Act adopted in 1950 would appear to be most problematic for the *Times* and the story about the NSA's warrantless eavesdropping, since it specifically prohibits disclosure of classified information "concerning the communication intelligence activities of the United States or any foreign government."

President Wilson used the Espionage Act to punish publications by depriving them of their reduced-rate mailing privilege. As a result, more than seventy small newspapers and pamphlets, many of them published by the Socialist Party, were pressured into publishing nothing about World War I in the year after the act was signed into law. The press was further muzzled in 1918 when Congress passed the Sedition Acts, which made it illegal to speak against the government. About nine hundred antiwar protesters were arrested or imprisoned under the Espionage or Sedition Acts, including Eugene V. Debs, Bill Haywood, A. Philip Randolph, Max Eastman, and Emma Goldman.

The Sedition Acts were repealed in 1921, but the Supreme Court had already held in 1919 that the Espionage Act was constitutional when it ruled in *Schenck v. United States* that Charles Schenck, the Socialist Party's general secretary, was properly prosecuted for distributing an antiwar pamphlet. In the court's opinion, Oliver Wendell Holmes famously wrote:

The most stringent protection of free speech would not protect a man in falsely shouting fire in a theatre and causing a panic. It does not even protect a man from an injunction against uttering words used that have all the effect of force. The question in every case is whether the words used are used in such circumstances and are of such a nature as to create a clear and present danger that they will bring about the substantive evils that Congress has a right to prevent. It is a question of proximity and degree. When a nation is at war many things that might be said in time of peace are such a hindrance to its effort that their utterance will not be endured so long as men fight and that no Court should regard them as protected by any constitutional right.

During World War II, most publications engaged in some degree of self-censorship. The government, nonetheless, came close to seeking indictments against the *Chicago Tribune* under the Espionage Act in 1942. Colonel Robert R. McCormick, who had supported Jay Near and his *Saturday Press* more than a decade earlier, owned the *Tribune*. He was an isolationist who opposed President Roosevelt and his conduct of the war, and the *Tribune* editorialized against any efforts to censor his views or his paper's reporting on the war. Following the Battle of Midway, the *Tribune* published a story strongly suggesting that the United States had cracked Japan's naval codes. (It had.) Francis Biddle, Roosevelt's attorney general, brought the paper before a federal grand jury, but the case was dropped because the government couldn't prove any damage had been done.

Although the Supreme Court's decision in the Pentagon Papers was viewed, properly, as a huge victory for the media, a careful reading of the decision reveals dangers for the *Times* and the *Post* should the government seek to prosecute them under the Espionage Act. The Pentagon Papers case was about prior restraint, with the Court ruling, 6–3, in favor of the press. But two of the judges who voted in favor of continued publication made it clear in their concurrence that having published, the newspapers might be subject to prosecution.

Judge Gurfein rejected the government's effort to rely on the Espionage Act at the trial level in the Pentagon Papers case, ruling that Section 793(e) of the Espionage Act didn't prohibit "publishing," as other sections of the act did. Neither the Court of Appeals nor the Supreme Court ruled on the issue, but several of the judges, including Justice White, joined by Justice Stewart, disagreed with Judge Gurfein. Justice White wrote, "Prior restraints require an unusually heavy justification under the First Amendment; but failure by the Government to justify prior restraints does not measure its constitutional entitlement to a conviction for criminal publication. That the Government mistakenly chose to proceed by injunction does not mean that it could not successfully proceed in another way." The three dissenting judges in the Pentagon Papers case, Warren E. Burger, Harry Blackmun, and John M. Harlan, appear to have shared that position.

White and Stewart also made specific mention of Section 798, which "proscribes knowing and willful publication of any classified information concerning the cryptographic systems or communication intelligence activities of the United States as well as any information obtained from communication intelligence operations."

After the Pentagon Papers decision, the Nixon administration considered following up on what it saw as White and Stewart's invitation to prosecute the *Times* and, later, Daniel Ellsberg, who had provided the documents to the newspaper, under the Espionage Act. In his memoir, *United States Attorney: An Inside View of "Justice" in America under the Nixon Administration*, Whitney North Seymour, then the U.S. attorney in Manhattan, wrote that Deputy Attorney General Richard G. Kleindienst had urged him to convene a grand jury but that Seymour had refused.

Nearly two decades later, in 1989, Erwin N. Griswold, Nixon's solicitor general, made some startling admissions about the Pentagon Papers case in an article written for *The Washington Post.* Griswold, who had argued the government's case before the Supreme Court, wrote that he had hurriedly read as many of the documents as he could and had concluded that there were only eleven that might be worth keeping confidential. He then called Attorney General John Mitchell, who insisted that the government argue that all of the Pentagon Papers should remain secret, even though Mitchell admitted to Griswold that he had never seen the papers and didn't know what was in them. Griswold concluded that he had "never seen any trace of a threat to the national security from the publication. Indeed, I have never seen it even suggested that there was such an actual threat."

Largely in response to the Pentagon Papers case, Harold Edgar and Benno Schmidt Jr., both professors at Columbia Law School, wrote the definitive work on espionage laws, "The Espionage Statutes and Publication of Defense Information," for the *Columbia Law Review* in 1973. Their lengthy treatise delved into the legislative history of the Espionage Act, revealing that Congress had rejected a provision that would have permitted the president to prohibit newspapers from publishing information about the nation's defense.

Edgar and Schmidt argued that the Espionage Act was so vague that if taken to the Supreme Court in the present day (1973), it would be declared unconstitutional under the First Amendment. Testifying before a House Committee on Intelligence in 1979, Anthony Lapham, then the CIA's general counsel, appeared to agree when he said he couldn't explain our country's espionage laws: "I cannot tell you, for example, whether the leak of classified information to the press is a criminal act, or whether the publication of that same information by a newspaper is a criminal act, or whether this conduct becomes criminal if committed with a provable intent to injure the United States but remains noncriminal if committed without such intent."

Professor Geoffrey Stone has written that the Espionage Act, as applied to journalists,

> would unquestionably violate the First Amendment. Law regulating speech must be precisely tailored to prohibit only speech that may constitutionally be proscribed. This requirement addresses the concern that overbroad laws—laws that are not narrowly crafted—will chill the willingness of individuals to speak freely because of a fear that their expression might be unlawful. Not surprisingly, because the 1917 Act was drafted before the Supreme Court had ever interpreted the First Amendment, it does not incorporate any of the safeguards the Court has since held the First Amendment requires. For example, the Espionage Act provision is not limited only to publications that pose a "clear and present danger." For this reason, any prosecution of the press under this section would be dismissed out-of-hand because the statute itself is unconstitutional.

Although it will be difficult for this or any other administration to get convictions under the Espionage Act, the forces in Congress that want to limit press criticism of government are as strong or stronger than the legislators who favor passage of a federal shield law. The Bush administration has threatened to seek new legislation to prevent leaks. Republican senator Pat Roberts of Kansas, former chairman of the Senate Intelligence Committee, and his counterpart in the House, Congressman Pete Hoekstra of Michigan, have expressed interest in passing legislation similar to Britain's Official Secrets Act.

In the current climate, it is difficult to imagine the Senate passing such legislation, but another terrorist attack similar to the ones on September 11, 2001, might push the public to go beyond its support for the Patriot Act and other legislation that has encouraged the Bush administration to push the limits of the executive branch's power. In the meantime, we in the press have a hostile administration, a divided Congress, and a Supreme Court unwilling to revisit *Branzburg* and the laws covering the right to keep sources confidential. As a result, we are likely to see many more battles between the government and the media, similar to those involving the NSA and the CIA, in the years to come.

Absent new legislation, the Bush administration is likely to follow the path laid by Pat Fitzgerald in the Plame case. The Department of Justice will authorize the calling of grand juries and the pursuit of indictments against perceived media miscreants. The names of confidential sources will again be demanded. The ramifications for the media will be greater than those in the Plame case, even though many of the principles central to that case would be the same.

In response, the media will argue, as they have before, that leaking is ingrained in the culture of Washington and that government might function less smoothly without it. Not only has the President engaged in leaking, first declassifying the information to be leaked, when it suits him, but reporters friendly to the administration, such as Bill Gertz of *The Washington Times* and, in recent years, Bob Woodward, have also been the recipients of leaks that have been in the administration's interest.

Similarly, the *Times* has been quick to argue for the importance of leaks without much focus on the specifics of the laws governing secrecy in times of conflict. In an editorial published January 4, 2006, it said:

A democratic society cannot long survive if whistle-blowers are criminally punished for revealing what those in power don't want the public to know—especially if it's unethical, illegal or unconstitutional behavior by top officials. Reporters need to be able to protect these sources, regardless of whether the sources are motivated by policy disputes or nagging consciences. This is doubly important with an administration as dedicated as this one is to extreme secrecy.

Opponents of efforts to prosecute the media can also point out that so many documents are now "classified" that the term has lost all meaning. Moreover, much of what is classified is of dubious value to anyone.

Our culture of secrecy led to the classification of more than 14 million documents in 2005. Total documents classified in the first five years of the current Bush presidency—between 2001 and 2005—exceeded 64 million, up from fewer than 39 million documents in the prior five years. In contrast, fewer than 30 million pages were declassified in 2005, down from 204 million pages in 1997.

Although these trends were accelerated by a greater concern about secrecy after 9/11, many analysts and politicians are concerned that the higher level of classifications could backfire. Thomas H. Kean, chairman of the September 11 commission and a former Republican governor of New Jersey, told *The New York Times* in 2004 that he worried more about the barriers to sharing information among agencies and with the public than he did about leaks of sensitive information.

The Commission on Protecting and Reducing Government Secrecy, chaired by the late senator Daniel Patrick Moynihan, issued a lengthy report in 1997 that concluded excessive secrecy lessened government accountability, making it more difficult for the public to engage in informed debate. The Moynihan Commission recommended that the Confidential classification for documents be abolished, leaving only Top Secret or Secret classifications. It also acknowledged that secrecy is power and that many in government decide arbitrarily what to leak and what to keep confidential. The commission also quoted approvingly from a report the House Committee on Government Operations released in 1960 that concluded:

"Secrecy—the first refuge of incompetents—must be at a bare minimum in a democratic society, for a fully informed public is the basis of self-government. Those elected or appointed to positions of executive authority must recognize that government, in a democracy, cannot be wiser than the people."

Despite these obstacles, should the administration decide to use the Espionage Act to prosecute the media, it may find some support in the one prior federal court case involving the act and a publication. Although there are important distinctions, a defendant who relied on Edgar and Schmidt's theories and analysis lost his case.

The Fourth Circuit Court of Appeals upheld a conviction under the Espionage Act in 1988 in a case involving Samuel Loring Morison, a civil employee at the Naval Intelligence Center, who also worked on projects for a British military publication, *Jane's Defence Weekly*. In 1984, Morison stole classified pictures of a Soviet aircraft carrier that had been taken by a navy reconnaissance satellite. *Jane's* published the photos and sold one of them to *The Washington Post*, which republished it. After getting the pictures back from *Jane's*, the Justice Department found one of Morison's fingerprints on a photograph and indicted him under the Espionage Act, arguing that publication of the photographs enabled the Soviets to understand the satellite's reconnaissance capabilities.

Morison argued that the act wasn't intended to cover leaks to the press and that, in any case, the First Amendment allowed his communications with *Jane's*. The Court of Appeals held that the press was no more entitled to receive the photos than anyone else. In response to Morison's claim that his actions were protected by the First Amendment, Judge Donald Stuart Russell quoted Justice White's majority opinion in *Branzburg* that "it would be frivolous to assert . . . that the First Amendment, in the interest of securing news or otherwise, confers a license on either the reporter or his news sources to violate criminal laws." Although Morison's First Amendment argument was rejected, a concurring opinion by Judge J. Harvie Wilkinson III said, "There exists the tendency, even in a constitutional democracy, for government to withhold reports of disquieting developments and to manage news in a fashion most favorable to itself." In addition, he insisted the First Amendment "does not simply vanish at the invocation of the words 'national security.'"

The Supreme Court refused to review the Fourth Circuit decision and Morison was imprisoned until January 2001, when he received a pardon from outgoing president Bill Clinton. It is important to note that it wasn't clear in the case whether Morison was being tried as a government employee leaking information or as a journalist receiving it. Most of the court's language, however, would suggest that his guilt was more a function of his work for the navy, as would the fact that neither *Jane's* nor the *Post* was prosecuted.

23

Prosecutorial Excess

Mark Feldstein was reading some decades-old files in his Bethesda, Maryland, home when the Feds arrived. After flashing their badges, Special Agents Leslie Martell and Marcelle A. Bebbe told him the files were part of a criminal investigation and demanded access to them.

It was 9:15 a.m., March 3, 2006. Feldstein, who runs the journalism program at George Washington University, had taken a call from Martell the day before. She had told him that she needed to speak to him about files that muckraking journalist Jack Anderson had donated to the university before his death in December 2005.

Martell said the subject was too sensitive to discuss on an "open line" and that they had to meet in person. She suggested interviewing Feldstein at his home—she already had his Winnebago Road address—the next morning, and Feldstein agreed to the meeting.

Now Martell explained that the FBI needed to go through all the Anderson papers, many of which were more than twenty-five years old. Feldstein, expressing surprise at the agency's sudden interest in journalism history, asked what the agents were investigating. "Violations of the Espionage Act" by lobbyists for the American Israel Public Affairs Committee, AIPAC, he was told.

Feldstein says he told the agents that the Anderson papers were "ancient history," literally covered in dust, and that Anderson had pretty much ceased reporting and writing in the mid-1980s, when he had been struck with Parkinson's disease and then cancer. Since then he had relied on interns, reporters, and associates to report and write his columns, sharing the byline with him. Feldstein also said that he and some of his graduate students had reviewed Anderson's files from the Nixon era through 2004, the year he gave up his column, and had found no classified documents. Agent Martell said she and Agent Bebbe still had to see the documents, because they were searching for a "pattern and practice of leaking."

The agents also asked Feldstein for the names of former Anderson employees who were "pro-Israel in their views or who had pro-Israeli sources." When Feldstein told her that he was uncomfortable passing on secondhand rumors, Agent Martell replied that if he didn't want to name names, "she could mention initials and I could nod yes or no. That was a trick Robert Redford and Dustin Hoffman used in the movie *All the President's Men*. I didn't name any initials, either," he says.

Kevin Anderson, a Utah lawyer and the late columnist's son, said that Martell had contacted him a month before the meeting with Feldstein and said the "FBI had information that there might be 'classified' documents in Dad's papers that would help the government with a criminal investigation involving a Middle Eastern country." After hearing her request, Kevin Anderson agreed to arrange a meeting for her with Olivia Anderson, the columnist's ailing seventy-nine-year-old widow. "I was left with the impression that the FBI's investigation concerned terrorism," he says.

Kevin Anderson says that his mother, who had worked for the FBI in the 1940s, cooperated with the investigation. "She was anxious to tell me that Agent Martell's family had roots in West Virginia, where my mother was born and raised, and might be related to us," he says. Kevin Anderson later learned that his mother had signed a consent form giving the FBI permission to review the papers.

After complaining that his mother had been tricked—by the end of the meeting, Martell and Mrs. Anderson were calling each other "cousin"—Kevin Anderson had a conference call with Agent Martell, her division chief, and one of the U.S. attorneys general handling the criminal case. The FBI chief brought up the AIPAC case and said the agency wanted "Dad's documents to see if either Rosen's or Weissman's fingerprints were on any government documents." Kevin Anderson told the officials that he thought it unlikely his father's papers would be of much help.

He was then told that the FBI "intended to review all of Dad's papers, regardless of their relevance to the AIPAC case." In addition, he says, they repeatedly stated that they would be "dutybound" to remove any and all material they suspected might be "classified" and either keep it or return it in some redacted or edited form. Kevin Anderson says he thought "this would destroy the historic, political, and cultural value of Dad's papers."

He also worried that the agency's interest in Anderson's papers involved more than the AIPAC investigation. Anderson and his predecessor, Drew Pearson, had written many stories over several decades that had embarrassed the agency and its top officials, including J. Edgar Hoover.

In an effort to limit the agency's review of his father's papers, Kevin Anderson offered to review the papers personally to locate anything related to the AIPAC case. But he was told that "because I did not have security clearance, I could not review the documents."

After Feldstein and Kevin Anderson told the FBI that they would not turn over the documents, the agency said it would ask the Justice Department to take action. Instead, in November 2006 the FBI quietly dropped its efforts to recover Anderson's papers. Responding to a 147-page questionnaire from Arlen Specter's Senate

Judiciary Committee, Acting Assistant Attorney General James H. Clinger disclosed, "At this time the FBI is not seeking to reclaim any documents." Clinger said that the agency wanted to review the papers to determine whether public disclosure of any of them "would cause a risk to national security." He added, "Access was not sought because Anderson allegedly had information regarding former Director Hoover's personal life."

The FBI's efforts to retrieve classified documents from Anderson's archives seems trivial compared with stories about NSA eavesdropping or suspected CIA torture sites. The Anderson case—told primarily in Feldstein's and Kevin Anderson's testimony before the Senate Judiciary Committee—shows the depth and breadth of the Bush administration's efforts to intimidate the press.

As Kevin Anderson told the Senate Judiciary Committee, "Dad often said that documents would come across his desk classified as 'national security' secrets, but which really involved what he called 'political' secrets. They showed the misdeeds and manipulations of government employees who had abused the public trust and then tried to sweep the evidence under the secrecy stamp. Such information should not be hidden from the people."

The penchant for prosecutorial excess displayed in the Jack Anderson case isn't limited, alas, to the FBI or to Washington. An even more disturbing example of prosecutorial abuse involving two federal grand juries and the *San Francisco Chronicle* emerged at roughly the same time as the Plame case, beginning in 2003 and continuing through 2006.

The so-called BALCO case didn't involve national security or possible violations of the Espionage Act but the use of steroids and other performance-enhancing drugs by professional athletes. A federal grand jury began its investigation of the Bay Area Laboratory

Co-operative (BALCO), a Burlingame, California, nutritional-supplements company, in the fall of 2003. BALCO was suspected of distributing illegal steroids to some of the world's most famous athletes, including sluggers Barry Bonds of the San Francisco Giants and Jason Giambi of the New York Yankees (whose previous team was the Oakland A's), and sprinters Tim Montgomery and Kelli White.

In February 2004 the Department of Justice indicted four people, including BALCO's owners, Bonds's personal trainer, and an Olympic track coach, on charges that included money laundering and possession with intent to distribute illegal steroids. Two weeks later, prosecutors gave lawyers for the defendants thirty thousand pages of documents and grand jury transcripts. A week after the materials were turned over to the defense counsel, federal judge Susan Illston entered a protective order sealing the grand jury transcripts and other materials. The order also threatened anyone who violated the order with legal sanctions, including contempt of court.

The *San Francisco Chronicle* dominated the coverage of the BALCO story, publishing more than 450 stories on the impact of steroids on professional sports and on athletes playing at all levels, from the schoolyard to the major leagues. The coverage clearly served the public interest. It led Major League Baseball, finally, to acknowledge the pervasive use of steroids by its players, prompting it to outlaw the use of such drugs. It also prompted Congress to investigate the problem. President Bush, who was once a part owner of the Texas Rangers, praised the *Chronicle* for its reporting.

More than 125 of the *Chonicle*'s articles were written by Mark Fainaru-Wada and Lance Williams, including articles published in June and December 2004 recounting grand jury testimony about the use of steroids by Bonds, Montgomery, and others. Many of those stories were based on confidential sources. Shortly after the December articles were published, Judge Illston asked the Justice

Department to investigate the leaks, and the DOJ responded by impaneling a grand jury to do so.

All four defendants in the steroids case pleaded guilty in 2005, and some served brief jail terms. The grand jury investigation of the reporters continued, nonetheless, and in May 2006 subpoenas were served on the *Chronicle*'s two reporters and on the newspaper's custodian of records. Meanwhile, in March 2006, Fainaru-Wada and Williams published a book, *Game of Shadows: Barry Bonds, BALCO, and the Steroids Scandal*, based largely on their *Chronicle* stories. An excerpt of the book was published in *Sports Illustrated*, a Time Inc. publication, and shortly after that, the book made the best-seller lists. The reporters were honored with several journalism awards for their work, including the Edgar A. Poe Award of the White House Correspondents' Association and the George Polk Award.

The Hearst Corporation, publisher of the *Chronicle*, filed a motion to quash the subpoenas, making many of the points that Time Inc.'s lawyers had made litigating the subpoenas Fitzgerald had issued in the Plame case. The government replied with a lengthy brief essentially saying *Branzburg* required that the reporters testify because the case involved a grand jury.

But the Hearst motion raised some issues that clearly distinguish the BALCO case from the Plame case. There is no concern about national security or violent crimes, and the investigation of the reporters continued for more than a year following the defendants' guilty pleas. Since the reporters' testimony would therefore have no impact on the initial grand jury investigation, the subpoenas were issued solely to determine who might have violated the judge's protective order. Although a judge might want to punish anyone who did so, the alleged crime hardly seems to rise to a level to have justified a second grand jury.

More important, the issuance of the subpoenas would appear to contradict the Department of Justice's own regulations. Those guidelines didn't apply to Fitzgerald, a special counsel, in the Plame case, but they do apply to U.S. attorneys in federal courts.

The DOJ regulations have been in force since the 1970s and are meant to limit the use of subpoenas to compel testimony from the media. The statement of policy explains:

> Because freedom of the press can be no broader than the freedom of reporters to investigate and report the news, the prosecutorial power of the government should not be used in such a way that it impairs a reporter's responsibility to cover as broadly as possible controversial public issues . . . The approach in every case must be to strike the proper balance between the public's interest in the free dissemination of ideas and information and the public's interest in effective law enforcement and the fair administration of justice.

The regulations then stipulate that in criminal cases, "exigent" circumstances—defined in earlier versions of the *U.S. Attorneys' Manual* as situations "where immediate action is required to avoid the loss of life or the compromise of a security interest"—should govern subpoenas and the attorney general must personally authorize their issuance. In an effort to understand the Department of Justice's rationale for approving the subpoenas, Gibson, Dunn's Ted Boutrous wrote to Attorney General Gonzales on my behalf in December 2006, requesting, under the Freedom of Information Act, that he explain his actions. As of December 2007 I had not received a substantive reply.

Attorney General Gonzales did, however, defend his decision to allow a grand jury to be impaneled, calling it "the appropriate thing to do" in a interview with the *Houston Chronicle*, another Hearst newspaper. Showing a questionable view of "balance," Gonzales said that the government's interest in assuring that grand jury testimony be kept secret outweighed any positive results that followed publication of the leaked transcripts.

Hearst submitted several important affidavits in support of its motion to quash the subpoenas, including one from Mark Corallo, the former press secretary and public affairs director under Bush's first attorney general, John Ashcroft. Corallo testified that he would not have approved the subpoena and that he didn't believe Ashcroft would have done so either. Similarly, Jamie Gorelick, a former deputy attorney general in the Clinton administration, testified that she was unaware of any subpoena issued to the media calling on it to identify a confidential news source while she was at the DOJ. California attorney general Bill Lockyer testified that California's highly protective shield law would be undermined if disclosure was compelled.

The federal district court denied the reporters' motion to quash in August 2006, and on September 25, Fainaru-Wada and Williams were held in civil contempt and ordered imprisoned for up to eighteen months. If imprisoned for that length of time, each of their sentences would be longer than the combined sentences of all four convicted BALCO defendants. The *Chronicle* was also held in civil contempt in October and ordered to pay a daily sanction of $1,000 until it complied with the court's order to turn over its files.

The reporters and the *Chronicle* appealed the contempt findings to the Ninth Circuit Court of Appeals. But before the appeal could be argued, the Department of Justice announced that Troy L. Ellerman, an attorney representing one of the criminal defendants in the BALCO case, admitted that he had leaked the grand jury transcripts to the *Chronicle*. Ellerman agreed to plead guilty to four felony counts, and the DOJ said that it would withdraw the subpoenas it had issued to Fainaru-Wada and Williams.

Although I am convinced that the subpoenas should never have been issued and happy that the *Chronicle* reporters avoided a jail sentence, the details of how the stories were obtained are deeply troubling.

Ellerman, who represented James Valente, BALCO's vice president, had received copies of grand jury testimony after Valente was indicted in February 2004. He signed a protective order prohibiting him from disclosing the testimony to the press. Ellerman and Fainaru-Wada nonetheless met in Ellerman's office in June 2004. Ellerman let the reporter take verbatim notes of sprinter Tim Montgomery's testimony, and that testimony led to an important story.

I am not troubled by that meeting, given how frequently leaks from grand juries end up in the press. But after the story ran, Ellerman blamed the government for the leak. The lawyer filed a declaration with the court stating "he had no idea who" leaked Montgomery's testimony, then filed a motion to dismiss the charges against Valente, claiming that "repeated government leaks of confidential information to the media" made "a fair trial practically impossible anywhere in the country."

Under the *Los Angeles Times's* editorial guidelines, Ellerman's motion to dismiss would have voided his right to confidentiality since he was "acting in bad faith" by using the *Chronicle* to spread misinformation. His motion came close to turning the reporters into co-conspirators and may have given them adequate reason to waive the confidentiality they had granted Ellerman. At a minimum, if I were the reporters' editor, I would have prohibited any further contact with the lawyer. Instead, while Ellerman's motion to dismiss the indictment was still pending, Fainaru-Wada obtained additional grand jury testimony from the lawyer. That testimony led to stories about three baseball players, Bonds, Giambi, and Gary Sheffield. In doing so, the reporters appear to have aided the lawyer's efforts to obstruct justice. And they undercut many of the arguments in favor of their having the ability to protect the confidentiality of their source.

24

Mike Price Sues for Libel

Although criminal cases involving prosecutors and confidential sources get most of the headlines, most editors and publishers spend far more time and money defending themselves from subpoenas in libel, privacy, and other civil suits brought by plaintiffs. The cases may be more colorful than the criminal ones, but they are no less serious, especially since courts are increasingly adopting the rationale of *Branzburg* and applying it to civil cases. If testimony from confidential sources can be required in criminal investigations, many judges reason their information is also needed to assure that litigants in civil cases get a fair trial.

The strangest, most difficult libel case I dealt with in recent years involved Mike Price, who had been lured from Washington State to coach football at Alabama, only to be fired before he ever took the field with the Crimson Tide. Price had gone to Pensacola, Florida, on April 16, 2003, to play in the Emerald Coast Classic pro-am golf tournament. Reports about the hours he spent in Arety's Angels, a local strip club, and in a nearby hotel cost him his job.

A number of local talk-radio shows throughout the Southeast covered his visit to Pensacola. They reported that Price had spent hundreds of dollars on drinks, private dances, and tips for the dancers at Arety's, and that the following morning an unidentified woman had charged nearly $1,000 of hotel room service on the coach's credit card. Following a meeting of the university's trustees, Price was fired from his seven-year, $10 million contract as Alabama's coach, two weekends after his trip to Pensacola.

Sports Illustrated, the Time Inc. sports weekly known for its in-depth reporting, published a 1,868-word story entitled "Bad Behavior: How He Met His Destiny at a Strip Club." (The issue went to press the morning of May 8 and got to most of its readers before the May 12, 2003, issue date.) The "he," of course, was Price, and the double entendre "Destiny" referred to the stage name of Lori Boudreaux, a stripper who was the object of the coach's attentions at Arety's.

SI's report, written by Don Yaeger, claimed that Price had spent most of the afternoon in Pensacola buying dances from and drinks for Destiny, who, according to the story, said she "offered him a table dance. He tipped me $60. Then he asked [me] to take him to the semiprivate dance area. He got a little bad there. We have rules, and touching is not allowed." Destiny also told the magazine that he wanted her to meet him later that night at the Crowne Plaza hotel, where he had a room.

Price went to a dinner with the golf tournament's sponsors, but he returned to Arety's after dinner and bought $30 drinks for several dancers. Then, according to the *SI* article:

> At about midnight Price headed back to the hotel. He eventually met up with two women, both of whom he had earlier propositioned for sex, according to one of the women, who agreed to speak to SI about the hotel-room liaison on the condition that her name not be used. The woman, who declined comment when asked if she was paid for the evening,

said that the threesome engaged "in some pretty aggressive sex." She said that at one point she and her female companion decided to add a little levity to the activity: "We started screaming 'Roll Tide!' and he was yelling back, 'It's rolling, baby, it's rolling.'"

When Yaeger finally reached Price on his cell phone the day before the article's publication, Price said he had visited the strip bar only once—after the sponsors' dinner—and he denied having sex with two women in his hotel room or even inviting anyone to the room.

I read the story the same day. After doing so, I called the senior editor working on it to discuss the use of confidential sources. I signed off on the story after hearing that the story was "bulletproof" because we had three such sources.

Although Price was fired three days before our story went to press, he sued Time Inc. and Yaeger for $20 million for libel, slander, and outrageous conduct. (The article had mentioned that Price had already been fired.) In his suit, Price denied much of the SI story and claimed that SI had lied in its article about the existence of a confidential source or, in the alternative, had relied exclusively on a confidential source that it knew, or should have known, was untrustworthy. Although the case began in an Alabama state court, we succeeded in having it removed to a federal district court.

As we began to prepare our defense, our Alabama lawyer, Gary Huckaby, took a lengthy deposition, running over two days, from Price. Price admitted to drinking a lot during the evening, to being "intoxicated," and he was unable to recall whether he had bought drinks for the dancers at Arety's or to remember much of what else happened at the bar or in his hotel room. He did testify that a waitress named Tracy accompanied him from the bar to his hotel room, but he said they didn't have sex and that they both slept in their clothes on the room's one bed. Price said he woke up at 6 a.m., dressed for the golf tournament, and left the hotel, leaving Tracy asleep in the room. While on the golf course, Price said, he received a call from the hotel and was told a woman had charged more than $1,000 worth of liquor and some food to his credit card, which he had apparently left in the room.

In his deposition, Price also said that he had taken Viagra for four years for erectile dysfunction, that he didn't have his Viagra with him in Pensacola, and "with the alcohol that I had and the blood pressure, that it would be impossible for me to get an erection." It was the first time I had heard the "Viagra defense" used in a libel case.

Although Price's deposition strengthened our case—he did, after all, agree that he had spent a night in a hotel room with at least one woman, and his inability to remember much else undermined his credibility—we also encountered several serious problems. The biggest was Alabama's shield law. Although the law is strong, as written it covers newspapers and radio and television stations but doesn't mention magazines.

I thought we would be covered by the Alabama shield law. Any other result would be absurd. *Barron's*, after all, calls itself a magazine but appears on newsprint. *The Economist* calls itself a newspaper but appears in magazine format. *The New York Times Magazine* appears inside the Sunday *New York Times* newspaper. How could the quality of the paper stock or the physical size of the publication determine whether the shield law applied? We litigated the issues in a federal district court, lost, and then lost again when we appealed the decision to the Eleventh Circuit Court of Appeals.

Judge Edward Earl Carnes, who wrote the appellate court's unanimous opinion, said that Alabama courts gave statutes "their ordinary plain meaning. The term 'any dog' does not mean 'any dog or cat' unless a cat is a dog," he wrote. "Likewise, the term 'any newspaper' does not mean 'any newspaper or magazine,' unless a magazine is a newspaper."

The Eleventh Circuit's decision could have had dire consequences for us. If we couldn't get our confidential source to agree to testify, the trial judge would probably have found us in "default" and would have instructed the jury that our failure to produce the witness constituted an admission that we had libeled Price. The ensuing trial would have been conducted solely to determine the damages we owed Price.

I also learned that our sourcing was far from "bulletproof." Instead of three confidential sources, we had one confidential source who had told her story to three different journalists—Yaeger, a researcher, and a photographer—who were working for us. Moreover, our confidential source was also a named source in the story. And she had disappeared, making it impossible for our investigators and lawyers to discuss the possibility of a waiver.

When she did resurface, she did so as a witness for Price! In a sworn affidavit filed with the federal district court, Lori Boudreaux made clear that she was our confidential source, but she insisted that she had never gone to Price's hotel room. She said that she had heard that a couple of other women from the bar had gone to the hotel with Price, but that the women disagreed about whether any sexual acts had occurred. "I never told Don Yaeger that I was in the room or had any firsthand knowledge of what happened in the room," Boudreaux swore.

We couldn't agree about how to react to Boudreaux's sworn affidavit. Consistent with my belief that the source owns the confidentiality, not the journalists or the publisher, I insisted her affidavit on behalf of Price constituted a waiver of her confidentiality, enabling our three journalists to testify about what she had told each of them. But others, including some of our lawyers, argued that we couldn't confirm Boudreaux was our confidential source, even though she had said she was our source. Instead, they maintained that we couldn't name Boudreaux without a specific waiver from her.

Faced with these questions, we decided to settle the case before trial. Mike Price was subsequently hired as the head football coach at the University of Texas at El Paso, and we had learned that confidential sources can be as big a problem in libel cases as they can be in criminal matters.

25

Wen Ho Lee

Wen Ho Lee deserved an apology. He got one from a judge, but not from the press that had demonized him. Instead, he got what can only be called hush money from five media companies (none of them Time Inc.) in a significant case involving their use of confidential sources. Although I might have agreed to a similar payoff, I worry that the press will come to regret the Faustian bargain that led to it.

Lee, a naturalized U.S. citizen who had emigrated from Taiwan, was working as a scientist at the Los Alamos nuclear laboratory in 1996 when the FBI and the Department of Energy began a lengthy espionage investigation seeking to determine if he was spying for China. *The Wall Street Journal* first wrote about the investigation in a measured piece that appeared in January 1999. *The Washington Post* followed with a piece one month later. On March 6, 1999, however, the story took on epic status when James Risen and Jeff Gerth wrote a four-thousand-word article, "China Stole Nuclear Secrets for Bombs, U.S. Aides Say," for *The New York Times*. The article, which didn't name Lee, discussed the investigation. Although it relied heavily on confidential sources, it quoted Paul Redmond, a former spy hunter for the CIA, saying, "This is going to be just as bad as the

Rosenbergs." The reference was to a Soviet spy ring that included Julius and Ethel Rosenberg, American citizens who were convicted of stealing the first nuclear secrets out of Los Alamos at the dawn of the atomic age and were tried and executed as traitors in 1953.

The article began with the alarming assertion that "working with nuclear secrets from an American Government laboratory, China has made a leap in the development of nuclear weapons: the miniaturization of its bombs, according to Administration officials." The unnamed officials said the Chinese breakthrough "was accelerated by the theft of American nuclear secrets from Los Alamos National Laboratory in New Mexico" and that government investigators had "identified a suspect" at the laboratory.

Two days later, the government identified Lee by name when it fired him for "serious security violations." The *Times*, *The Washington Post*, the *Los Angeles Times*, CNN, and the Associated Press subsequently wrote about Lee and the government's suspicions, all relying on confidential sources. The *Times*'s William Safire joined the fray, blasting the Justice Department for not acting aggressively enough in its investigation of Lee, claiming this was "part of a pattern of averting exposure of Clinton's national-security laxity."

Although Lee was never prosecuted for espionage, he was indicted in December 1999 on fifty-nine counts, each a felony, of mishandling computer files. The Justice Department persuaded federal judge James A. Parker that Lee posed "a danger to the safety of this nation." He was held in solitary confinement for nine months and was shackled during weekly meetings with his family.

The government, which had threatened Lee during his incarceration with prosecution under the Atomic Energy Act (which carries a life sentence), subsequently withdrew fifty-eight of its counts, and Lee pleaded guilty to the remaining count of illegally downloading restricted data. He was released after being sentenced to time served.

Judge Parker apologized for allowing Lee to be held "under demeaning, unnecessarily punitive conditions," claiming that he had been pressured to continue such onerous confinement by the top decision makers in the executive branch, especially the Department of Justice and the Department of Energy. "They have embarrassed our entire nation and each of us who is a citizen of it," Judge Parker said.

The New York Times revisited its coverage shortly after Lee's release with a lengthy, unusual "public accounting." The assessment, couched in lawyerly terms, amounted to a remarkable apology. It said that the March 6, 1999, article "had flaws that are more apparent now that the weaknesses of the F.B.I. case against Dr. Lee have surfaced. It did not pay enough attention to the possibility that there had been a major intelligence loss in which the Los Alamos scientist was a minor player, or completely uninvolved."

The assessment concluded by blaming "those who directed the coverage, for not raising questions that occurred to us only later" for those instances where the *Times* fell short of its standards. "Nothing in this experience undermines our faith in any of our reporters, who remained persistent and fair-minded in their newsgathering in the face of some fierce attacks."

Lars-Erik Nelson, a columnist with the New York *Daily News* who had been highly critical of the *Times*'s coverage, thought the *Times* didn't go far enough. Nelson complained upon reading the *Times*'s mea culpa that the March 6 story "just didn't hold water on its own merits . . . There was no skepticism. They seemed to be captive of their sources."

After his release, Lee sued the Department of Justice, the Energy Department, and other federal officials for violating his rights under the Privacy Act by "leaking" information about him to the news media to cover up their own security failures. He then subpoenaed six reporters—Risen and Gerth from *The New York Times*, and one each from *The*

Washington Post, the *Los Angeles Times*, CNN, and the Associated Press—seeking the names of their confidential government sources.

The journalists refused to answer questions about their sources, asserting the same reporter's privilege that Matt Cooper and Time Inc. had asserted in the Plame case. Lee insisted that he had tried to determine the names of the government officials who had leaked information about him, but that he had been rebuffed, in part by assertions of law enforcement privilege. He said he couldn't pursue his case without the cooperation of the reporters. A federal district judge in Washington, D.C., agreed, as did the federal Court of Appeals for the D.C. Circuit. In doing so, the courts relied heavily on *Branzburg*.

Branzburg, of course, involved a grand jury investigating alleged crimes, as did our case. Wen Ho Lee was, in contrast, pursuing a civil case, and the reporters weren't even parties to it. The district and appellate courts, however, found support in a D.C. Circuit case from 1981, *Zerilli v. Smith*, for their finding that the reporters must testify in the Wen Ho Lee case.

On its surface, *Zerilli* appeared to be a case that was favorable to the media, and in many subsequent cases it was helpful to reporters. In that case, Anthony Zerilli and Michael Polizzi, two reputed members of the Mafia in Detroit, had sued the federal government under the Privacy Act, contending that employees of the Department of Justice had violated their constitutional rights by leaking transcripts of their wiretapped phone conversations with each other to *The Detroit News*. (I had written about "Big Mike" Polizzi while working in the *Journal*'s Detroit bureau on an unrelated story.) In an effort to determine who had leaked the wiretaps, Zerilli and Polizzi deposed Seth Cantor, a *News* reporter who refused to reveal his confidential sources. The appellate court held that "in this case the First Amendment interest in protecting a news reporter's sources outweighs the interest in compelled disclosure."

Zerilli had held that "where the public interest in effective criminal law enforcement is absent," *Branzburg* is not controlling. Instead, it laid out a qualified privilege based on a balancing test. The court required the plaintiff in a civil case to show that the information sought goes "to the heart of" his case and that the plaintiff had exhausted "every reasonable alternative source of information" before seeking the journalists' testimony.

In the Wen Ho Lee case, however, the courts concluded that Lee had met those requirements and ordered the reporters to testify. All of the journalists petitioned the Supreme Court, asking it to revisit *Branzburg* and to find that, at least in civil cases where they weren't defendants, they should be allowed to keep their sources confidential. The Supreme Court was expected to rule on the petitions in May or June of 2006.

Before the Supreme Court could announce whether it would take the case, Lee and the government settled for $1.645 million. The real story, however, was that the five news organizations that employed the reporters agreed to contribute $750,000 to the settlement to avoid contempt sanctions against them. (CNN, which had continued to represent one journalist, Pierre Thomas, even after he had jumped to ABC, refused to go along with the settlement. ABC agreed to pick up CNN's share.)

In announcing their decision to join the settlement, the five media companies said in a joint statement:

> We did so to protect our confidential sources, to protect our journalists from further sanction and possible imprisonment, and to protect our news organizations from potential exposure. We were reluctant to contribute anything to this settlement, but we sought relief in the courts and found none. Given the rulings of the federal courts in Washington and the absence of a federal shield law, we decided this was the best course to protect our sources and to protect our journalists.

The journalism in this case—which was not challenged by Lee's lawsuit—reported on a matter of great public interest, and the public could not have been informed about the issues without the information that we were able to obtain only from confidential sources. We will continue to vigorously fight subpoenas that seek to identify our confidential sources in the future.

The problem, of course, is that while the settlement protects the news organizations from fines and possible jail sentences for their reporters, it encourages plaintiffs in other Privacy Act lawsuits against the government to seek testimony from the media whenever leaks from confidential sources are involved.

Beyond the risk of more lawsuits, the Wen Ho Lee settlement raises other troubling issues. The media companies that settled still insist that the story was in the public interest and the public couldn't have been informed about important issues without the use of confidential sources. But the bigger truth is that the journalists granted confidentiality to sources who used it to smear a suspect when they didn't have the proof to support their suspicions. Instead of serving the public interest, reliance on confidential sources enabled the media, most egregiously *The New York Times*, to hype a story, and too much of the media were content to follow the *Times* without questioning its or their own judgments. Absent the hysterical coverage, it is unlikely that Wen Ho Lee would have suffered the loss of reputation and the harsh, solitary confinement and other indignities he endured for nine months.

Any cost-benefit analysis would mandate settling for $150,000, the amount, more or less, that each of the five media companies paid Wen Ho Lee—especially given the strong likelihood that the Supreme Court would refuse to hear the case or, worse, would affirm the lower court decisions. Although the risk of more lawsuits changes that equation a bit, it doesn't argue for continued refusal to settle.

But I don't see how *The New York Times* squares its decision to settle with its long-held policy of not settling libel suits in the United States for money. Perhaps something changed in the year following Arthur Sulzberger's ringing reaffirmation of Judith Miller and the Myron Farber case. Or perhaps the *Times* has also learned the truth of that old adage "Hard cases make bad law."

26

Libby Is Convicted

On March 7, 2007, Scooter Libby was convicted of lying to a grand jury and to the FBI. The six-week trial took place in the E. Barrett Prettyman Courthouse in Washington—the same courthouse where Judge Hogan had found Matt Cooper and Time Inc. in civil contempt.

Libby was found guilty on felony counts of obstructing justice, giving false statements, and two counts of perjury. He was acquitted on a fifth felony count when the jury, after almost ten days of deliberations, determined that he had not lied to the FBI about his conversation with Matt.

Ten of the eighteen witnesses who testified were journalists, and three of them—Cooper, Judith Miller, and Tim Russert—gave testimony that turned out to be essential to the government's case. The trial didn't address the possible violation of intelligence laws by Libby and others who leaked Valerie Plame's identity. But special prosecutor Patrick Fitzgerald convinced the jury that Libby was lying when he told the grand jury that he hadn't revealed Plame's identity to Miller or Cooper. Fitzgerald also established that Libby lied when he told the FBI and the grand jury that he had first learned Plame's identity from Russert.

Fitzgerald's case was relatively straightforward. By establishing that Libby knew Plame was a CIA agent before his conversation with Russert, he made clear that Libby had perjured himself by lying to the grand jury.

Robert L. Grenier, a former CIA official, and David S. Addington, a lawyer who worked for Vice President Cheney before succeeding Libby as the vice president's chief of staff, both testified about Libby's efforts to determine the circumstances surrounding Joseph Wilson's trip to Niger.

The *New York Times* columnist Nicholas D. Kristof had written (May 6, 2003), "The vice president's office asked for an investigation of the uranium deal, so a former U.S. ambassador to Africa was dispatched to Niger" in February 2002. Cheney had asked the CIA to check out reports about Iraqis buying uranium in Niger, but he didn't know the CIA had followed up by sending Wilson there. Nor did he know who had authorized the trip. After reading Kristof's column, he sought to determine which former ambassador had made the trip and who had sent him. A second Kristof column (June 13, 2003) cast doubt on assertions that the vice president's office learned of the Wilson mission only after reading his first column on the subject.

Former undersecretary of state Marc Grossman said he had told Libby (June 12, 2003) that Plame worked at the CIA and that she might have played a role in sending Wilson to Niger. Cathie Martin, Cheney's former communications director, said she told Libby in early July that her counterpart at the CIA had learned that Plame worked at the agency and that it had sent Wilson to Niger. Former White House press secretary Ari Fleischer testified that Libby told him Plame had sent Wilson to Niger. Libby did so over lunch at the White House mess on July 7, 2003, Fleischer said.

These dates were important, the prosecution argued, because Libby had told the grand jury that he had learned of Plame's connection to Wilson from Russert during a July 8, 2003, telephone call.

The defense's case, argued by lead attorney Theodore Wells, consisted of trying to show the jury that the prosecution witnesses had memory problems of their own and therefore their testimony was unreliable, making it impossible to establish Libby's guilt beyond a reasonable doubt. The defense called seven journalists as witnesses. Six of them—Bob Woodward, Walter Pincus, and Glenn Kessler from *The Washington Post*; syndicated columnist Robert Novak; *Newsweek's* Evan Thomas; and David Sanger from *The New York Times*—said that Libby had never mentioned Plame in interviews that took place around the time he was talking to Cooper, Miller, and Russert. The seventh, *Times* managing editor Jill Abramson, contradicted some of Miller's testimony when she said she couldn't recall Miller's proposing a story about Plame's role in arranging Wilson's trip to Niger. Their testimony did little to undermine the government's case. Although Libby and Cheney were expected to testify, neither did.

Pat Fitzgerald was the big winner. Although there had been no clear violation of intelligence laws and no clear need for naming a special prosecutor, he made a convincing case that once confronted with a senior White House official seen lying under oath in federal court, he had no choice but to prosecute him.

In addition to Libby, Vice President Cheney and the Bush administration were among the big losers. So was the press. Fitzgerald painted Libby as the administration's fall guy, who sought to shield the White House from criticism over the war—counting on the press to cover for him. The special prosecutor argued successfully that his investigation and the resulting indictment were worth the effort and that he couldn't try the case without testimony from the reporters Libby had lied to.

Fitzgerald suggested in his closing argument that Cheney had been his target but that Libby's lies had protected his boss. Cheney's office wanted to undermine Wilson's criticisms but it didn't want to be tagged with the smear. By claiming that he had learned of Plame's identity from a journalist, Libby covered up the vice president's deliberate effort to punish a White House foe by blowing his wife's cover. There is "a cloud over the vice president," Fitzgerald said in his closing argument. "That cloud is there because the defendant obstructed justice." Fitzgerald showed that Cheney had the motive and opportunity to control Libby's actions. During the trial, he played recordings of Libby's testimony to the grand jury in which Libby acknowledged that Cheney was upset by Wilson's column. He also showed that it was Cheney who got President Bush to declassify intelligence information, enabling Libby to use it in his meeting with Judith Miller. Libby said that Cheney had been among the first to tell him in mid-June 2003 about Plame's relationship with Wilson, but Libby asserted he hadn't thought it significant and had forgotten it. Early in the trial, Fitzgerald entered into evidence the handwritten note from Cheney to Libby, written on a copy of Wilson's *Times* op-ed piece of July 6, 2003, in which the vice president asked, "Do we ordinarily send people out pro bono to work for us? Or did his wife send him on a junket?"

Fitzgerald's closing argument to the jury also accused the White House of shading intelligence to justify its attack on Iraq, then trying to silence people who questioned that intelligence. "A critic points fingers at the White House and as a result his wife gets dragged into the newspapers," he said. Fitzgerald also suggested that Bush had reneged on a promise to fire any officials who had leaked Plame's identity to the press.

Although Libby's lawyers differed with the prosecution on most matters, Theodore Wells alleged in his opening statement that the White House was willing to sacrifice Libby to protect Karl Rove. (He never pursued that angle during the case.)

The journalists who testified were clearly uncomfortable acting as aides to the prosecution or to Libby. And a profession that likes to ask questions had some problems answering them. Some of the journalistic practices described or revealed during the trial served only to convince cynics that journalism is not a profession at all. Testimony from Cheney's former press person, Cathie Martin, showed how the administration sought to manipulate the media in order to reward friends and punish enemies. She told the jury that she had urged Cheney and the rest of his staff to demand anonymity in return for exclusive interviews and valued bits of information. Such manipulation isn't surprising, but her candor was.

Judith Miller further tarnished her reputation and that of the *Times*. She testified that she and Libby spoke three times in June and July of 2003. They met on June 23. That meeting was followed by a two-hour lunch in early July at Washington's St. Regis Hotel. Miller said Libby was agitated at the first meeting and critical of the CIA. She also said that he told her about Valerie Plame Wilson. That testimony was obviously damaging to Libby. But under cross-examination by one of Libby's lawyers, William H. Jeffress Jr., Miller admitted that she had failed to tell the grand jury about the June 23 meeting. When asked why, she said she "didn't remember" until she discovered a shopping bag full of her reporter's notebooks under her desk in the *Times*'s Manhattan newsroom. It was also at the St. Regis lunch, she told the grand jury, that she had agreed that Libby would be described in her article as a "former Hill staffer" instead of as a senior administration official. It was a telling example of her willingness to breach basic journalistic ethics in order to coddle her close sources.

Matt Cooper came off better than Miller did. He had his notes, although, under tough cross-examination, he sometimes had trouble making sense of them. He testified he had learned Plame's identity from Karl Rove on July 11, 2003, and that he had sought confirmation from Libby the next day. Cooper said he asked Libby about the Wilson-Plame-CIA connections and that Libby replied, "I heard that too." But there was nothing in his notes about that conversation, giving the defense the chance to question Matt's credibility.

Tim Russert was the prosecution's most effective witness. Libby had told the grand jury that Russert had told him Plame was at the CIA. Since he had said that he had forgotten that Cheney had already told him about her, Libby told the grand jury, "It seemed to me as if I was learning it for the first time."

Russert was careful in his responses and betrayed no uncertainty when denying that he had told Libby about Plame. He said it wouldn't have been possible for him to discuss Plame with Libby because their conversation took place before Russert read Robert Novak's story on July 14. Russert said he realized only when reading the story that the disclosure was "really big."

Although Russert's testimony was most responsible for Libby's conviction, his journalistic practices also took a hit. Most significantly, he testified that he assumed all phone calls from high government officials are confidential or on deep background. In doing so, he acknowledged one of the biggest problems with Washington journalism—a symbiosis between reporters and sources in which the reporters often think it is their first job to protect their sources and that informing the public comes second. (Glenn Kessler, a *Post* diplomatic reporter, said almost all his interviews were with officials who expected and were granted anonymity. "Almost every single conversation I have in Washington is on background," Kessler testified.)

Russert also suffered on cross-examination when he explained that at first he had resisted the government's subpoena to testify before the grand jury because he feared that testifying would chill his relationships with sources. But then he had to acknowledge that he had already told the FBI about the conversation he sought to protect by refusing to testify. That is, he invoked the need to keep his promises of confidentiality when he had already broken those promises. I think Russert was right to answer the queries from the FBI, since his conversation with Libby wasn't an interview on background. (Libby had called Russert to complain about the coverage on a different NBC program, *Hardball.*) But once Russert spoke to the FBI, it was difficult for him to make a convincing argument that he should be allowed to avoid testifying before the grand jury and at the trial.

The six journalists who testified that Libby had never mentioned Plame to them nonetheless showed the close relationship between reporters and the government officials they cover. Bob Woodward confirmed that he was the first reporter to learn Plame's identity and that he learned it from Richard L. Armitage, a former deputy secretary of state. The defense played a one-minute excerpt from Woodward's taped interview with Armitage in which Woodward asked why the CIA would have sent Wilson to Niger. "Because his wife's a [expletive deleted] analyst at the agency," Armitage replied. When Woodward ventured, "It's still weird," Armitage replied, "It's perfect. This is what she does—she is a WMD analyst out there."

The columnist Robert Novak finally acknowledged that Armitage was also his primary source on Plame and that Rove had confirmed her identity for him. (Michael Isikoff and David Corn had all but proved Armitage was Novak's source in September 2006 in their book, *Hubris: The Inside Story of Spin, Scandal, and the Selling of the Iraq War.*) Novak said that he and Armitage weren't friends and that it had taken him more than two years to get an interview with Armitage. In contrast, Novak said he spoke to Karl Rove—an ideological soul mate—two or three times a week.

Although Fitzgerald had known of Armitage's role since the earliest days of his investigation, he concluded that Armitage hadn't committed a crime in telling reporters that Plame was a CIA agent, presumably because he didn't know she was covert. The fact that Armitage was more hostile to Libby, Rove, and the architects of the Iraq war than to Wilson could have undermined the broad conspiracy theories that were advanced after Plame was first outed, but in the end, the perjury case stuck.

Times managing editor Jill Abramson's testimony suggested that editors can be as forgetful as reporters. Although Abramson contradicted her reporter, Miller, her own memory of conversations with the reporter was shaky. In very brief testimony about her work with Miller as Washington bureau chief, she acknowledged, "It's possible I occasionally tuned her out." Having worked with Jill at *The Wall Street Journal*, I doubt it was much of a "tune out," but her admission betrayed a larger problem at the *Times*. No one was giving Miller sufficient supervision, curbing her excesses.

The one journalist whose reputation was burnished by the trial was Denis Collins, otherwise known as Juror No. 1869. Collins, a former *Washington Post* reporter, was the only juror to speak after the trial, and it was clear that his methodical approach to questions of journalistic ethics influenced the other jurors. When questioned during the jury selection phase of the trial, Collins said he had worked for Woodward, knew Pincus, had been a neighbor of Russert's, and had gone to high school with the *Times* columnist Maureen Dowd.

John Dickerson, writing in *Slate*, described what happened next:

> For the next hour, lawyers for both the prosecution and defense turned the man around in their hands like a Rubik's Cube. Unbidden, he offered a view about memory that was straight from the Libby team's playbook. "Memory is a funny thing," he said. "I've been wrong and other people have been wrong. I'm skeptical about everything until I see it backed up." Would he be predisposed to believing testimony from

Bob Woodward above all others? "Let's face it—he's written two books about Iraq," said the man. "One contradicted the other in some ways. He was obviously wrong in some ways. I think he's capable of being human and wrong." Lawyers for both sides pressed and pressed on his impartiality until he turned into an evangelist for the profession: "One thing about being a newspaper reporter all those years, one thing that has always been important to me, was getting it right, checking all the facts . . . One thing that [Woodward] drilled into all of us is that you don't take anyone's word until you get the facts." To not judge the case fairly would "go against everything he taught us. I would find it shameful."

While the jury determined that Libby was guilty, Collins said afterward that Libby seemed like "the fall guy" who had been "pilloried" for a leak in which others at the White House had participated. "What are we doing with this guy?" Collins asked reporters after the trial. "Where's Rove" and the "other guys?"

Conclusion

Time Inc., on behalf of itself and Matt Cooper, spent millions of dollars fighting Patrick Fitzgerald in the courts, and we lost every round. When the Supreme Court refused to hear our plea, I folded our hand and turned over our notes to the grand jury. The decision was unpopular, but under the peculiar circumstances of our case, it was right.

Along the way, some ugly truths emerged about the ways in which prosecutors, politicians, and the press do their jobs. Karl Rove and our reporter Matt Cooper agreed that their conversation would be on "deep background." Matt broke one rule by dropping the "deep," attributing what he had heard to "administration sources." More seriously, he had decided, unilaterally, that Rove deserved confidential source status. That status demanded far more from Time Inc. and Matt than Rove had requested and far more than we should have been prepared to give. Then, in defiance of everything implicit in the word *confidential*, Matt put Rove's name in an e-mail to which dozens of Time Inc. employees had access. Cooper is an honest, hardworking reporter, doing what other honest, hardworking journalists do in Washington. But he was wrong in the ways in which he dealt with his sources. None of his editors, including this one, provided adequate guidance. One of America's most ferocious defenders of the First Amendment, Floyd Abrams, gave us less good advice than we deserved.

Some of Cooper's colleagues in *Time*'s Washington bureau also learned that Rove was his source from talk at the watercooler. One of them told Rove's lawyer about Cooper's supposedly confidential conversation with his client, and she never told Cooper or anyone else at *Time* what she had done. Luskin and Rove would have saved us and themselves a lot of trouble if they had told us what they knew. It is tempting to ascribe their silence to guilty conscience, but it is equally likely that they assumed we knew as much as our reporter had told them. In any case, had we known of that conversation at the time it happened, I would have insisted that we seek a waiver from Rove.

Judith Miller, a Pulitzer Prize–winning reporter at *The New York Times*, was ordered to cough up her notes, even though she had never used them for a story. She went to jail, saying that she could never disclose the identity of a confidential source. But she cracked after realizing she might be incarcerated much longer than the four months she had anticipated. After eighty-five days in the Alexandria Detention Center, she accepted a waiver of confidentiality from Scooter Libby. Libby insists he had made the waiver available to her long before she chose to go to jail. Miller says she needed a more clear-cut waiver than other reporters were willing to accept. In any case, neither her editors at the *Times* nor the paper's lawyers spent sufficient time with Miller before her incarceration discussing waiver issues with her. Nor did they spend enough time with her notebooks to determine whether she had anything on any other sources that couldn't be protected. She didn't.

The Supreme Court should have taken our case. That none of its nine justices wanted to do so is dispiriting, as is the resultant mess the press and the prosecutors are left with. Every state but one provides some kind of protection—usually through a shield law—for journalists and their confidential sources. But the federal courts do not. If a district attorney in Los Angeles wants the names of a reporter's sources for a grand jury, the reporter need not comply. But if a U.S. attorney down the street wants the same information for a federal grand jury, the reporter could face jail time for refusing to provide it.

Journalists in the United States need a federal shield law. If you don't believe me—as an editor, I am biased—ask the thirty-five state attorneys general who signed on to a brief submitted in our behalf when we petitioned the Supreme Court. They said the rules governing confidential sources are so confusing that they cannot make sense of them. They say a federal shield law will give clarity to the matter. But this administration's Justice Department opposes a federal shield law, and it will be difficult for Congress to pass one.

Some argument over the rules is inevitable. A federal shield law shouldn't be absolute. As the *Los Angeles Times* editorialized, "The cost of giving absolute legal protection to journalists' secrets is to make the government's secrets impossible to protect." That cost would be too high. There should be no privilege if there is an imminent threat to national security. Nor should most sources who break the law be protected, unless the law is so onerous or outrageous that it must be ignored. But once you say that the privilege isn't absolute, you need to develop balancing tests to determine when it can be breached. We should have different standards for criminal cases involving a grand jury, civil cases where journalists are defendants, and litigation where journalists are witnesses with information one side or the other might want.

Before the courts require the disclosure of an anonymous or confidential source, the prosecutors and plaintiffs should show they have reason to believe the information sought is essential. The criminal investigation must be important enough to merit disclosure. The information must be obtained in ways that don't trash the First

Amendment. It should be even more difficult for plaintiffs in civil trials to gain information from anonymous and confidential sources.

The leaks about Valerie Plame disgraced the administration and ruined her career at the CIA, and may have jeopardized national security. But they weren't against the law. So a special prosecutor should never have been appointed. Once Patrick Fitzgerald showed up for work, however, it was difficult for him to walk away from the signs that Scooter Libby and, perhaps, Karl Rove had perjured themselves.

Although Fitzgerald says he "wasn't looking for a First Amendment showdown," that is the precise result of his investigation. By issuing subpoenas that required reporters to betray their sources, Fitzgerald created the showdown, giving us no choice but to litigate as hard as we could, in any court we could. Because he prevailed, journalists testified against their will in the Libby trial, becoming tools of the prosecution or of Libby's defense team. Along the way, the reporting methods of journalists were also put on trial.

What remains troubling is Fitzgerald's continued refusal to release the affidavits he filed to justify compelling Cooper and Miller to testify. He has also refused to unseal all eight pages of Judge Tatel's opinion in which the D.C. Circuit Court of Appeals explained its rationale for supporting Fitzgerald's efforts to compel the reporters' testimony. Fitzgerald says the continuing need to preserve grand jury secrecy requires him to oppose the release. But the far greater risk is that Fitzgerald is hiding something that—had we known it at the time—might have changed the way we litigated on Cooper's and our own behalf.

Fitzgerald's successful conduct of his investigation has set a precedent that will encourage other prosecutors to seek testimony from the press, forcing many other journalists to betray their sources. Without the information that Fitzgerald is withholding, it remains difficult to say that his end justified his means.

Many of our most important stories—the ones that expose corruption, self-aggrandizement, and duplicity in high places—can't be reported or written without the use of confidential sources. Reporters Without Borders publishes an annual Worldwide Press Freedom Index. In 2006 the United States ranked 53rd out of 168 countries, embarrassingly behind Bosnia, Namibia, and the Dominican Republic. Without relief from continued assaults on the press, we shall fall further toward Russia (138) and last-place North Korea (168).

A federal shield law might protect reporters and their sources, but the law that Congress is considering has many limitations. A shield law should protect anonymous as well as confidential sources. Any shield law must deal with a couple of pesky issues: who is a journalist, and who should be protected? Congress can limit the shield law to so-called mainstream media, but it shouldn't. There weren't any big media companies when the First Amendment was passed. It was designed to protect "the lonely pamphleteer" of the eighteenth century, and it should protect the blogger in pajamas today.

The courts are already moving in that direction, at least in California, where a state appeals court ruled in May 2006 that online reporters are protected by the same confidentiality laws that protect traditional journalists. In doing so, it ruled against Apple Computer, which had hoped the courts would force bloggers to disclose who had leaked confidential company data to them. But a video blogger, Josh Wolf, now holds the U.S. record for a journalist being incarcerated. Wolf was jailed for eight months by a federal judge and was freed only in April 2007 after providing law-enforcement officials with videotape he shot of a San Francisco protest demonstration in 2005.

In addition to figuring out a way to control special prosecutors and their runaway investigations, government needs to make some other changes. Too much information is classified. Journalists shouldn't have to worry about accepting classified documents that aren't deserving of the "top secret" designation.

Journalists also have much to do. We need to distinguish between "anonymous" sources, whose names we leave out of stories, and "confidential" sources, whose names we won't disclose in litigation. The agreement with a confidential source is a contract between the reporter, the reporter's employer, and the source. The reporter should protect the source, but the source owns the confidentiality. The source can demand confidential-source status, but the reporter should rarely offer confidentiality to a source. It is, after all, in the reporter's interest to have the source on the record. We must also be more honest with our sources, and we must be vigilant to make sure our sources are honest with us. Reporters must explain that they cannot promise more than the law allows, and they shouldn't make promises that are against the public interest. Journalists aren't above the law, and we have to stop acting as though we are.

That said, there will inevitably be exceptions when reporters and their publications decide they must resist demands after exhausting every avenue of litigation. The consequences of such resistance are so great that journalists must do far more to resist using confidential sources. Deciding what merits the grant of confidentiality is, again, a balancing act. The source who seeks confidentiality should typically be risking livelihood, life, or reputation, and there should be no other way for the reporter to get the information than from the source. The information the source wishes to impart should be vital to the public interest. *The Washington Post*'s stories about CIA detention centers is one example where I think it would be appropriate to defy contempt findings to protect sources and their testimony. Confidential-source status should never be granted to government officials who are trying to spin a story, especially if they are breaking a law when they do so.

Individuals can engage in civil disobedience, but if the press defies the courts whenever we litigate and lose, then journalists are in fact asserting an absolute privilege for their sources and themselves.

It is more complicated for publicly held corporations. But there will no doubt be that rare case where they will also conclude that defiance of a court order is their only option.

There is an inevitable tension between the journalism and the law. I had accepted it in my own being from the time I could read. But as I immersed myself in the Plame case, forcing myself to understand the rules that govern the press and the courts, I finally was able to acknowledge that the lawyer in me had made me a better reporter and editor.

It is a tough time to be in the news business. Advertising and circulation are declining, and editorial budgets are being cut. Many of our best investigative stories do little to cure the public's apathy and distrust. Yet the need for public-interest journalism has never been greater. An imperial presidency is waging war on any institution that might challenge its authority. The Congress is paralyzed and the Supreme Court has been unwilling to acknowledge the consequences of failure to overturn *Branzburg*, a case that has had far more impact on the press than has Watergate or the Pentagon Papers.

We must continue to dedicate ourselves to holding government and other powerful institutions accountable. There will always be stories that rely on confidential sources, but we shall fail in our mission unless we fully understand their value as well as the dangers from their misuse.

Afterword

President Bush commuted Lewis Libby's prison sentence on July 2, 2007. It was a cynical cover-up and an outrage.

U.S. District Judge Reggie B. Walton had imposed a thirty-month prison sentence and a $250,000 fine on Libby after a jury had found him guilty of obstruction of justice and perjury in the Plame affair. Walton rejected Libby's request to remain free on bail while appealing his convictions. Then the President stepped in.

Thus Libby, the Vice President's chief of staff and a key figure in the administration's so-called "Iraq Team," got a pass from the President for lying in a case that began with concerns about a possible breach of national security. The lies resulted, most plausibly, from his efforts to protect Cheney, Bush, and others in the White House.

In a statement explaining the commutation, Bush tried to cast himself as a detached, neutral observer. He acknowledged that some people "point out that a jury of citizens weighed all the evidence and listened to all the testimony and found Mr. Libby guilty." But Bush said he thought Walton's sentence was "excessive," noting that it exceeded the recommendations of Libby's probation officer.

Beyond that, the President's statement relied on the views of "critics" of the case—unnamed Libby partisans who contended that a special prosecutor should never have been appointed and that the investigation should have been dropped after prosecutor Patrick Fitzgerald learned Libby hadn't leaked Plame's name to columnist Robert Novak, the journalist who first published her name and identified her as a CIA operative.

The President explained, "The critics point out that neither Mr. Libby nor anyone else has been charged with violating the Intelligence Identities Protection Act or the Espionage Act, which were the original subjects of the investigation."

Vice President Cheney also came to Libby's defense: "Scooter has dedicated much of his life to public service." Cheney said he had always considered Libby "to be a man of the highest intellect, judgment, and personal integrity—a man fully committed to protecting the vital security interests of the United States and its citizens."

Judge Walton released the texts of many letters from Libby's friends seeking leniency for him, including Donald H. Rumsfeld, Paul Wolfowitz, John R. Bolton, and several other architects and supporters of the war in Iraq. *The Wall Street Journal*'s editorial page, after criticizing Fitzgerald's "obsessive exercise," contended that Libby "got caught in a perjury net that we continue to believe trapped an innocent man who lost track of what he said, when he said it, and to whom."

While the President, the Vice President, and Libby's other supporters all sought to portray Libby as a dedicated public servant, they inadvertently succeeded in positioning Cheney's former chief of staff at the center of the administration, a figure essential to its war efforts and to its efforts to stifle dissent at home. In doing so, they only magnified the seriousness of the conviction of Libby and the immorality of Bush's decision to commute his sentence.

In his sentencing memorandum, Fitzgerald had asserted for the first time that Plame was a "covert" intelligence agent under the Intelligence Identities Protection Act. (Legislative assistants who drafted the act and I have disagreed with that assertion.) He said that classified information about Plame had been disclosed without authorization and that his investigation had sought to determine whether "other government officials" besides Libby, Karl Rove, and Richard Armitage had directed or approved their leaks "as part of a concerted effort to disclose this information."

Fitzgerald's memorandum reminded the court that Libby learned about Plame's "CIA employment in June 2003 directly from the Vice President." He also said that "there was an indication from Mr. Libby himself that his disclosures to the press may have been personally sanctioned by the Vice President." The special prosecutor argued that Libby's lies and obstruction of justice "made impossible an accurate evaluation of the role that Mr. Libby and those with whom he worked played in the disclosure of information regarding" Plame's employment "and about the motivations for their actions."

The special prosecutor said he didn't pursue a charge under statutes such as the Espionage Act and the Intelligence Identities Protection Act in part because "Mr. Libby's false testimony obscured a confident determination of what in fact occurred." He then quoted from Judge Tatel's concurring opinion in Judith Miller's, Matt Cooper's, and Time Inc.'s contempt case: "Insofar as false testimony may have impaired the special counsel's identification of culprits, perjury in this context is itself a crime with national security implications." In other words, Libby's perjury had worked—it had kept the special prosecutor from making his case and getting to the bottom of the Plame affair.

White House culpability in the Plame affair was further affirmed a few months later by the President's former press secretary, Scott McClellan. After leaving his position, McClellan began work on a memoir, *What Happened: Inside the Bush White House and What's Wrong with Washington*. In mid-November 2007 McClellan's publisher, PublicAffairs Books, posted its spring 2008 catalog on its website, with an excerpt from McClellan's chapter on the Plame affair:

> The most powerful leader in the world had called upon me to speak on his behalf and help restore credibility he lost amid the failure to find weapons of mass destruction in Iraq. So I stood at the White House briefing room podium in front of the glare of the klieg lights for the better part of two weeks and publicly exonerated two of the senior-most aides in the White House: Karl Rove and Scooter Libby.
>
> There was one problem. It was not true.
>
> I had unknowingly passed along false information. And five of the highest ranking officials in the administration were involved in my doing so: Rove, Libby, the Vice-President, the President's chief of staff and the President himself.

Peter Osnos, founder of PublicAffairs and its editor-at-large, subsequently wrote, "McClellan believes that Bush, at least initially, did not know he was telling his press secretary to relay a series of howlers about who said what to whom." But he declined to elaborate prior to the book's publication in April 2008.

Although Libby's sentence had been commuted, his conviction stood, and he announced in December 2007 that he was dropping an appeal. Neither that nor Bush's commutation of Libby's sentence, however, may be the end of the case. When asked if he might subsequently grant Libby a full pardon, the President would only say, "As to the future, I rule nothing in and nothing out."

The Bush administration's drive to establish an imperial presidency foundered in November 2006 when the Democrats gained control of the House and Senate in midterm elections. The change of control in Congress led to a series of investigations of the Justice Department and in September 2007 to the resignation of Attorney General Alberto Gonzales, whose interpretations of key points of law had enabled the Bush administration to pursue policies of questionable legality.

Under questioning by legislators, Gonzales performed so poorly when trying to explain the administration's controversial warrantless surveillance program that many legislators accused him of lying under oath. In December 2006 he claimed that several U.S. attorneys had been fired for poor performance. But it quickly emerged in congressional hearings that many of the firings were based on White House efforts to remove prosecutors whom the administration deemed disloyal to the Republican Party. D. Kyle Sampson, a Gonzales deputy, told the Senate Judiciary Committee in March 2007 that Patrick Fitzgerald had been on an earlier, larger list of U.S. attorneys targeted for removal, but that the idea was quickly dismissed.

In December 2007 Karl Rove, who had resigned as the President's adviser earlier in the year, and White House Chief of Staff John Bolton were found in contempt of Congress by the Senate Judiciary Committee for refusing to testify about the firings of the U.S. attorneys. Separately, the Justice Department began an internal investigation of Gonzales to determine whether the firings violated federal law.

Gonzales had not been a friend of the press. Quite the opposite. He had stretched or ignored the Department of Justice's own guidelines for subpoenas of journalists—I never did get a substantive reply from the DOJ to my Freedom of Information Act request in the BALCO case—and he had constantly threatened the press with investigation following stories involving leaks, especially leaks that were embarrassing to the White House.

I was relieved when I heard that President Bush had nominated

Michael Mukasey, a former federal judge, to replace Gonzales. Mukasey had gained a reputation for being tough on crime but careful about the law. He also pledged during his Senate confirmation hearings that he would restore a measure of independence to the Justice Department. In early January he opened a criminal investigation into the CIA's destruction of videotapes documenting the interrogation of two Al Qaeda terrorist suspects, appointing John Durham, a well-regarded federal prosecutor from Connecticut, to head the investigation. The investigation was commenced less than a month after *The New York Times* first exposed the destruction of the videotapes in a front-page story. The appointment of Durham acknowledged the possibility that the DOJ had played a role in that destruction.

I knew Mukasey as a young attorney in private practice. He had worked with Bob Sack on First Amendment cases while they were both at Patterson, Belknap, Webb & Tyler, and I hoped he would show a greater regard for press freedom than Gonzales had. The early signs, however, aren't encouraging. Mukasey has shown no inclination to drop the Justice Department's prosecution for espionage of the former lobbyists in the AIPAC case. The lobbyists had engaged in information-gathering that is similar to what journalists do in Washington every day. If they are convicted, in a trial scheduled to commence sometime in 2008, journalists will find it far more dangerous and difficult to do their jobs.

Mukasey also said during his Senate confirmation hearings that he opposed a federal shield law, arguing that the DOJ guidelines were adequate to protect the press and expressing concern that a shield law would make investigation of alleged terrorists more difficult. His comments echoed those of Patrick Fitzgerald, who had written an op-ed column for *The Washington Post* asserting, "Unlike state shield laws, a federal shield law poses unique obstacles to the protection of national security."

The Senate Judiciary Committee voted 15–2 on October 4, 2007, to support legislation establishing a federal shield law. The vote followed two weeks of hearings. Then, on October 16, the House of Representatives voted overwhelmingly, 398–21, to pass a similar shield law. There are minor differences between the two bills, but both are designed to establish standards that will enable journalists to protect their sources in federal court cases. Both versions include compromises. They require journalists to disclose information that would prevent acts of terrorism, significant harm to national security, death, or substantial bodily harm. Under the Senate Judiciary Committee's proposal, journalists who witness crimes are also required under the proposed legislation to testify to what they saw. The Senate and House versions of the shield law cover anyone who is regularly engaged in journalism, including, presumably, bloggers.

The proposed legislation doesn't provide an absolute privilege, and in many ways it is modeled on the Justice Department's own guidelines, seeking to balance the interests of the press, prosecutors, and plaintiffs. The shield law isn't perfect, but it goes a long way toward assuring that the federal courts will have the power to find a proper balance.

Despite these strong signs of support in Congress in 2008, there is no guarantee that a shield law will pass. As of early January 2008, Senate Majority Leader Harry M. Reid had not called for a vote on the House bill. Nor had he sought to create a House-Senate conference committee that could try to reconcile the two versions of the shield law before sending a compromise bill back to both chambers for a vote. Should a federal shield law emerge from Congress in 2008, it will almost certainly face a veto from President Bush. Although the votes in the Senate Judiciary Committee and the full House of Representatives suggest broad bipartisan support, we may need to have a new President in the White House before the legislation finally passes.

. . .

Absent a federal shield law, journalists and news organizations continue to face subpoenas seeking testimony about anonymous and confidential sources. In one notable case, Judge Reggie B. Walton, who presided over the Libby trial, ruled in August 2007 that five reporters must testify about their sources in a civil suit brought under the federal Privacy Act by a former Army scientist against the Justice Department.

The scientist, Steven J. Hatfill, was an expert on bioterrorism who had been identified by former attorney general John Ashcroft as a "person of interest" in the government's investigation of deadly anthrax attacks in 2001. Hatfill subsequently sued the government and, in a case that raised the same issues as Wen Ho Lee had raised, sought testimony from *Newsweek*'s Michael Isikoff and Daniel Klaidman, *The Washington Post*'s Allan Lengel, Toni Locy, formerly at *USA Today*, and James Stewart, then of CBS.

Sources for reports published in *Newsweek* and *The Washington Post* gave depositions to Hatfill after identifying themselves, but Stewart and Locy face contempt citations if their sources refuse to come forward and they refuse to testify.

The press continues to use anonymous and confidential sources when reporting important and often controversial stories, as it should. *The New York Times* said its report on the CIA's destruction of interrogation videotapes relied on information from several current and former intelligence officials. The article was clearly in the public interest and couldn't have been written without the grant of anonymity to the paper's sources.

The New York Times, *The Washington Post*, and other quality news organizations have also cut back on their reliance on unidentified sources, and the *Times* has been especially good about telling its readers why sources are granted immunity and what the source's motivation might be for providing information to the paper. Other publications are beginning to follow the *Times*'s lead.

That said, it is a rare day when one major publication or another doesn't engage in egregious misuse of sources. Howard Kurtz, *The Washington Post*'s media columnist, wrote a lengthy piece in December 2007 chronicling some of the worst excesses from the campaign trail. "Is it really necessary to allow operatives from one campaign to attack another candidate without their names attached?" Kurtz asked. He then cited examples from several publications, including *Newsweek*, *The Washington Post*, and the *Los Angeles Times*. They quoted "a Clinton strategist" calling Barack Obama "snack food" for Republicans; a "GOP consultant" questioning Fred Thompson's competence; and an "aide" to Mike Huckabee saying Mitt Romney's Mormonism "is definitely a factor in the race" because it is a "strange religion" that is not understood. In each case the reporters should have identified the source for the quote or it should have been deleted.

Two weeks later, *Time*'s Joe Klein wrote a critical column asserting that Mitt Romney is schizoid—negative, jingo-crazed, and smarmy about his opponents on television while trying to appear positive and moderate on the stump. He concluded that Romney was wildly unpopular among his peers.

Then Klein, too, fell off the wagon. Without attribution, he quoted a rival campaign manager saying, "I just hate the guy," adding, "If we can't win, I want to be sure he loses." Joe's editors thought the quote so good they highlighted it in a blurb accompanying the piece.

Appendix: Editorial Guidelines

Acknowledgments

Selected Bibliography

Index

Appendix

Editorial Guidelines

INTRODUCTION

We endeavor to serve the public interest by practicing the highest standards of professional journalism. Credibility is our most precious asset. It is arduously acquired and easily squandered. It can be maintained only if each of us accepts responsibility for it.

The ways in which we can discredit ourselves are beyond calculation. It is up to staff members to master these general principles and, beyond that, to listen carefully to their individual sense of right and wrong. If you know of anything that might cast a shadow on our reputation, you are expected to inform a supervising editor. This can be an uncomfortable duty; under some circumstances, it can do harm to one's relationships with fellow journalists. It is, nonetheless, a duty.

These guidelines contain useful principles for editorial staffers as well as freelancers. They apply to all the work we produce, in print, for broadcast, or on the Internet. They are, however, only guidelines, and there may be exceptions. You may encounter situations not described in these guidelines. At times, circumstances and good judgment may dictate different methods. Confer with your su-

---

These guidelines are based on Time Inc.'s new guidelines and, in many places, are identical to them. They also include small sections taken verbatim from the guidelines of the *Los Angeles Times* and *The Washington Post*. The section on confidential sources relies on Professor Geoffrey Stone's testimony before the Senate Judiciary Committee, and brief phrases are included from many of the news outlets whose guidelines are referred to in chapter 18.

pervisor or an editor, including, if necessary, the editor in chief, whenever you are uncertain about what to do. Do not be shy about asking questions. A robust, ongoing discussion of ethics at all levels is essential if we are to serve the public interest.

We are aware that the publication of editorial guidelines can create problems. Lawyers will try to use them against us in litigation. Any discrepancy between what the guidelines say and what a journalist did in a particular situation will be highlighted in a lawsuit. While recognizing this risk, we believe that these guidelines will help journalists conduct themselves in accordance with responsible journalistic practices and ensure that their work will be as accurate as possible.

REPORTING

A fair-minded reader of our news coverage should not be able to discern the private opinions of those who contributed to that coverage, or to infer that we are promoting any agenda. A crucial goal of our news and feature reporting—apart from editorials, columns, criticism, and other content that is expressly opinionated—is to be nonideological. Our stories may often make a point. But that point should be based on our reporting, not on our predetermined point of view. It may be difficult to fulfill our commitment to fairness. We must recognize our own biases and stand apart from them. We must also examine the ideological environment in which we work, for the biases of our sources, our colleagues, and our communities can distort our objectivity.

Investigative reporting requires special diligence with respect to fairness. Those involved in such stories should bear in mind that they are more credible when they provide a rich, nuanced account of the topic. Our coverage should avoid simplistic portrayals.

Keep in mind that there is always more than one viewpoint. People or groups that are under attack may refuse to discuss their views, but we should make every effort (and document those efforts) to get that side of the story, even if a refusal is a foregone conclusion. If the subject denies an allegation, that denial should appear in the published article. People who will be shown in an adverse light in an article must be given a meaningful opportunity to defend themselves. This means making a good-faith effort to give the subject of allegations or criticism sufficient time and information to respond substantively. Whenever possible, the reporter should meet face-to-face with the subject in a sincere effort to understand his or her best arguments.

When contacting a subject or a source, reporters and editors should routinely identify themselves and their news organization and state the purpose of their call. Exceptions to this policy should be approved by a senior editor.

When interviewing subjects or sources, note taking is essential. The better the notes, the easier it is to write the story. Many sources welcome the use of a recording device, which can be a valuable aid in verifying facts and quotes. It is impractical, however, to rely on a recorder alone, since transcription is time-consuming and recorders can malfunction. A combination of notes and a recorder is usually best.

Given the complexity of laws covering the recording of conversations, the legal department should be consulted if there is any uncertainty about its legality. In a majority of states (including New York and the District of Columbia), it is lawful to record a telephone conversation with the consent of only one party to the call—in this instance, the journalist—but in other states (including California) recording a telephone conversation without the consent of all parties is illegal and could subject the person recording the conversation to prosecution. Federal and state laws prohibit the undisclosed recording of telephone calls to which the journalist is not a party.

Reporters and editors should make every effort to authenticate any documents provided by sources in the course of reporting a story.

Reporters and photographers who wish to enter private property should not trespass. If a journalist pursuing a story is on private property and is ordered by the owner or owner's agent to leave, the journalist should leave. Even a place of public accommodation such as a restaurant may be subject to restrictions imposed by owners.

SOURCING FOR STORIES

We are committed to informing readers as completely as possible. We want to make our reporting as transparent as possible so that readers may know how and where we got our information. We should use anonymous sources only when we cannot otherwise provide information we consider reliable and newsworthy.

Reporters should make every effort to gather information and conduct interviews that are on the record. When we use an unnamed source, we risk undermining the credibility of the information we are providing. We must be certain in our own minds that the benefit to readers is worth the cost in credibility.

These standards are not intended to discourage reporters from cultivating sources who are wary of publicity. Such informants can be invaluable. But the information they provide can often be verified with sources willing to be named, from documents, or both. We should make every effort to obtain such verification.

We should not use such sources to publish material that is trivial, obvious, or self-serving. We should avoid blind quotations whose only purpose is to add color to a story. We should not use pseudonyms without telling the reader why we have done so. We must not mislead readers about the identities of people who appear in our stories. Sources should never be permitted to use the shield of anonymity to voice speculation.

Editors have an obligation to know the identity of unnamed sources used in a story, so that editors and reporters can jointly assess the appropriateness of using them. The source for anything that appears in the paper will be known to at least one editor. That source must understand this rule. If the source refuses to accept this rule, the reporter should refuse to accept information from the source. In the case of exceptionally sensitive reporting, the reporter may request that the source's identity be given solely to the editor in chief. In any case, the editor to whom the information is provided must be in a position to evaluate the credibility of the source—and must be prepared to protect the source's identity.

An unnamed source should have a compelling reason for insisting on anonymity. Readers and viewers should know why we have decided to grant anonymity to a source. The reporter and editor must be satisfied that the source has a sound factual basis for his or her assertions. We should recognize that some sources quoted anonymously might tend to exaggerate or overreach precisely because they will not be named.

GROUND RULES

Journalistic ground rules can be confusing, but our goal is clarity in our dealings with sources, readers, and viewers. Our ground rules should be explained to sources. Readers should be told as much as possible about how we learned the information in our stories. If a source is not on the record, it is important to establish ground rules at the beginning of a conversation. If the interview is recorded, it is preferable that recording also include discussion of ground rules. We should start virtually all interviews with the presumption that they are on the record. Inexperienced sources—usually ordinary people who unexpectedly find themselves the news—should clearly understand that you are a reporter and should not be surprised to find themselves quoted in your publication.

Journalists should not give the source more protection than is necessary. It is preferable to spell out the nature of the attribution in clear terms, instead of using vague and other terms that might be misunderstood. A primer:

- *On the Record*—The source can be named and identified by title, rank, job description, or other relevant information. Information can be used in direct quotation or indirect quotation.
- *Background*—The quote or information may be used for publication, provided the source is not identified by name. The anonymous source does require some attribution, such as a "senior White House official." How a source is described in print may be discussed with the source, but the source does not have the final say. We must try to balance our desire to give the reader or viewer as much information as possible about the source while striving to maintain the source's anonymity. When using this method of sourcing, every effort should be made to acknowledge the source's possible bias or agenda to help the reader put the information in perspective.
- *Not for Attribution*—Same as Background.
- *Deep Background*—The information can be used in or to inform a story and it can lead a journalist to other sources for confirmation. Nonetheless, the source providing information on Deep Background may not be identified in any way. Nor can the reporter say how the information was obtained. Sometimes known as the Lindley Rule (after *Newsweek* columnist Ernest K. Lindley), Deep Background is a favorite of government officials. It is a tricky category that should be avoided if possible, since there is no way to help readers understand where the information is coming from.
- *Off the Record*—The quote or information from the source may not be used in a story or for further reporting. The term is dangerous because so many people misuse it. Many sources, including some sophisticated officials, use the term when they really mean "not for attribution to me." We must be very careful when dealing with sources who say they want to be "off the record." If they mean "not for attribution to me," we need to explain the difference and discuss what the attribution will actually be. If they really mean Off the Record as we define the term, then in most circumstances, we should avoid listening to such information at all. Although Off the Record information may help us evaluate other data, we do not want to be hamstrung by a source who tells us something that is in most cases unusable. One alternative to Off the Record is For Guidance. A source may be willing to give us information for our guidance or to prompt further reporting, on the understanding that we

will not use his comments as the basis for putting something in the paper.

We do not allow sources to change the ground rules governing specific quotations after the fact. Once a quote is on the record, it remains there.

Sometimes sources will agree to be interviewed only if we promise to read quotations we plan to use back to the source before they are published. This can create difficult situations. We do not want to allow sources to change what was said in the original interview, but sometimes that cannot be avoided or can be avoided only at the cost of losing an on-the-record quote from an important source. If you find yourself in this gray area, consult with your editor.

We don't "cover the tracks" of anonymous sources by naming them elsewhere in the story and saying they wouldn't comment. It is preferable to paraphrase comments supplied on background to publishing full quotations from anonymous sources. Personal attacks given on background should never appear in quotes.

Reporters and editors should make every effort to confirm background information received from a source with other sources. They should also seek to confirm information gathered from an anonymous source with at least one other source. The second source should have firsthand or direct knowledge of the information. A second source who received the information from the primary source cannot be used to confirm information. A relevant document may serve as a second source. There will be times when we shall decide to publish information from a single, unnamed source, but we shall not do so without satisfying ourselves as to the source's reliability and the basis for the source's information. Reporters and editors must understand the risks—legal and to the publication's reputation—associated with printing a story based on one anonymous source.

Reporters and editors should apply special scrutiny to potentially defamatory or highly sensitive stories based solely on anonymous sources. Although the use of anonymous sources can be necessary and useful, we should rarely go to press with a potentially defamatory or highly sensitive story based solely on one or more confidential sources. Information gained from anonymous sources should be subjected to a level of scrutiny that is at least as rigorous as information obtained from on-the-record sources.

A publication can be sued for breaking a promise to a source. Other than agreeing to protect a source's name or other identifying details, you should not make promises or representations to a source—such as promising a cover story, assuring positive or favorable treatment, or promising access to a draft of the article prior to publication. As stated above, however, there may be occasions where reading quotes back to a source is permissible.

There is an inevitable tension between cases involving allegations of libel and those involving the need to protect confidential sources. In libel cases, the more notes, the better. But reporters and editors should be extremely careful about how and where they store information that might identify an anonymous source. Most electronic records, including e-mail, can be subpoenaed and retrieved in litigation. Moreover, such records are almost impossible to erase or delete. In addition, journalists' handwritten notes can also be sought in cases where the publisher is subpoenaed, and it can be very difficult to convince a court that a journalist's notes or other work product doesn't belong to the company. Code names for anonymous sources may help avoid discovery from electronic or handwritten records.

CONFIDENTIAL SOURCE STATUS

It is our policy not to reveal the name of any source who is not identified by name in the article in question. Our journalists and their sources, however, need to understand that a promise not to publish a source's name in a story (Not for Attribution or On Background) may be different from a promise of Confidential Source Status, which extends beyond the story. When a journalist promises confidentiality to a source, the journalist is not only making a commitment to the source but also committing the resources of the journalist's employer, whether a publisher or broadcaster.

Most conversations with unnamed sources are not "confidential." For the source to qualify as such, the journalist must either expressly promise confidentiality, or the circumstances and content of the conversation must be such that the source would reasonably assume confidentiality. If, for example, a source says, "I could lose my job if the information I am providing is traced back to me," reporters and editors should assume that the source is confidential.

Although journalists enjoy some legal protection from being compelled to testify about their newsgathering activities and the identities of their sources, we must recognize that the privilege of confidentiality is not absolute. There may be occasions in which the only way to keep a promise of Confidential Source Status is for the reporter to serve a jail term for civil contempt of court and for the journalist's employer to pay substantial fines. There is also a risk that a court might hold a reporter and the reporter's employer in criminal contempt of court. A finding of criminal contempt might subject the reporter to a felony conviction. If the employer is a publicly held company or a division of a publicly held company, it might be unable to accept a finding of criminal contempt without obtaining a supporting resolution from the corporation's board of directors.

In libel cases against a reporter or the reporter's employer, the refusal to identify a confidential source can result in a judge entering a default judgment against the company.

In general, Confidential Source Status should be reserved for sources who are providing information that is important and in the public interest, and who, by doing so, are risking their lives, jobs, or reputations. Reporters should alert editors as early as possible during newsgathering that they are collecting sensitive information from sources who may seek or expect confidentiality. Reporters and editors should refrain from granting Confidential Source Status without the explicit approval, prior to publication, of the publication's editor in chief. If the editors ultimately decide they cannot grant Confidential Source Status, the reporter or a top editor should inform the source that while we are willing to litigate vigorously to protect our sources, we cannot guarantee confidentiality. If the reporter, editor, and source cannot reach an understanding, the publication cannot publish the information. This procedure is undertaken for the protection of the source as much as the company, and it does not diminish the seriousness of our commitment to protect all our sources.

Reporters and editors should understand that they have no legal or moral right to promise confidentiality to a source beyond what is recognized in the law. Such promises should always be interpreted as "subject to the rule of law." It is the responsibility of the journalist, as well as the source, to understand that the journalist cannot legally promise more than the law allows. If a journalist expressly promises more than the law allows, the promise is legally ineffective, like any other promise that is contrary to public policy. A journalist who knowingly deceives a source by promising more than the law authorizes should be subject to professional discipline and civil liability to the source.

There may be cases where the law is unclear. It is unclear, for example, whether receipt of classified information is illegal under the Espionage Act and other laws. The importance of the information and the benefit to the public from its publication should provide the basis for deciding whether information should be accepted and published when the law is unclear. If the journalist and his or her employer decide it is legal to receive such information, they should be prepared to litigate the issue and to face jail or fines should they not prevail.

Acknowledgments

I am indebted to Jonathan Galassi, president and publisher of Farrar, Straus and Giroux, and to Paul Elie, who served as editor for this book. They and their colleagues at FSG showed admirable professionalism and passion for my story. No writer could have asked for more support.

I am similarly grateful to my agent, Lynn Nesbit, who served as Sherpa and sounding board.

I could not have written this book without the help of James Oberman and the Media Law Resource Center. Jim is a wizard. He can find obscure documents and ancient law-review articles in an instant. He did so on his own time while serving as *Time*'s head of research. MLRC Executive Director Sandra S. Baron and her staff provided daily and monthly reports on legal developments that concerned me. The materials made available to me through the center's white papers and the MLRC e-mail report, MediaLawDaily, were invaluable.

Fortune editor Tim Smith took my first draft and made it better. Paul Cappuccio, Richard Cellini, Nancy Conger, Greg Curtis, Clark Hoyt, Elma Kanefield, Sam Klagsbrun, Michael Mitchell, and William Whitworth also read drafts of the book. Their comments were invaluable.

The commitment to editorial independence at Time Inc. and Time Warner Inc. is greater than anything I have known of or experienced. John Huey and Ann Moore at Time Inc. and Richard Parsons and Jeff Bewkes at Time Warner Inc. gave me needed support after I turned over our notes to the special counsel, and then encouraged me to write this book. Robin Bierstedt, Matt Cooper, Michael Duffy, Jim Kelly, and John Redpath are friends and allies. They helped me wrestle with the issues and with the decisions I made, although I am solely responsible for the latter.

Gay and Nan Talese convinced me to write the book. Nan and Steve Rubin, Doubleday Broadway Group publisher, got me through its first draft.

My father, the late Raymond Pearlstine, was a lawyer's lawyer who influenced me in ways neither of us understood or appreciated.

Finally, my thanks to my wife, Jane Boon Pearlstine. As bad as it may have been to go to bed with an editor and wake up with a lawyer, it was nothing compared to serving as this first-time author's muse. She was a careful reader and a patient listener. Her suggestions were delivered with compassion and gentle humor.

Selected Bibliography

Abel, Elie. *Leaking: Who Does It? Who Benefits? At What Cost?* New York: Priority Press Publications, 1987.

Abrams, Floyd. *Speaking Freely: Trials of the First Amendment.* New York: Viking, 2005.

Bernstein, Carl, and Bob Woodward. *All the President's Men.* New York: Simon & Schuster, 1974.

Bickel, Alexander M. *The Morality of Consent.* New Haven: Yale University Press, 1975.

Blasi, Vince. "The Newsman's Privilege: An Empirical Study." *Michigan Law Review* 70:229 (December 1971).

Bradlee, Benjamin C. *A Good Life: Newspapering and Other Adventures.* New York: Simon & Schuster, 1995.

Branzburg v. Hayes, 408 U.S. 665, June 29, 1972.

Cohen, Dan. *Anonymous Source: At War Against the Media; A True Story.* Minneapolis: Oliver Press, 2005.

Cohen v. Cowles Media Co., 501 U.S. 663, June 24, 1991.

Dienes, C. Thomas, Lee Levine, and Robert C. Lind. *Newsgathering and the Law.* Charlottesville, Va.: Michie Law Publishers, 1997.

Edgar, Harold, and Schmidt, Benno C., Jr. "The Espionage Statutes and Publication of Defense Information." *Columbia Law Review* 73:5 (May 1973).

Ellsberg, Daniel. *Secrets: A Memoir of Vietnam and the Pentagon Papers.* New York: Viking, 2002.

Fainaru-Wada, Mark, and Lance Williams. *Game of Shadows: Barry Bonds,*

BALCO, and the Steroids Scandal That Rocked Professional Sports. New York: Gotham Books, 2006.

Farber, Myron. *"Somebody Is Lying": The Story of Dr. X.* New York: Doubleday, 1982.

Friendly, Fred W. *Minnesota Rag: Corruption, Yellow Journalism, and the Case That Saved Freedom of the Press.* New York: Random House, 1981.

Graham, Katharine. *Personal History.* New York: Alfred A. Knopf, 1997.

Isikoff, Michael, and David Corn. *Hubris: The Inside Story of Spin, Scandal, and the Selling of the Iraq War.* New York: Crown Publishers, 2006.

Kobre, Sidney. *Development of American Journalism.* Dubuque, Iowa: W. C. Brown, 1969.

Langley, Monica, and Lee Levine. *"Branzburg* Revisited: Confidential Sources and First Amendment Value." *George Washington Law Review* 57:1 (November 1988), p. 13.

Lively, Donald E., Dorothy E. Roberts, and Russell L. Weaver. *First Amendment Anthology.* Cincinnati: Anderson Publishing, 1994.

McKevitt v. Pallasch, 339 F.3rd 530, July 3, 2003.

Mnookin, Seth. *Hard News: The Scandals at* The New York Times *and Their Meaning for American Media.* New York: Random House, 2004.

Morrison v. Olson, 487 U.S. 654, June 29, 1988.

Near v. State of Minnesota, 283 U.S. 697, June 1, 1931.

Nestler, Jeffrey S. "The Underprivileged Profession: The Case for Supreme Court Recognition of the Journalist's Privilege." *University of Pennsylvania Law Review* 154:1, p. 201.

New York Times Co. v. United States, 403 U.S. 713, June 30, 1971.

Okrent, Daniel. *Public Editor #1: The Collected Columns (with Reflections, Reconsiderations, and Even a Few Retractions) of the First Ombudsman of the New York Times.* New York: Public Affairs, 2006.

Powe, Lucas A., Jr. *The Fourth Estate and the Constitution: Freedom of the Press in America.* Berkeley: University of California Press, 1991.

Prados, John, and Margaret Pratt Porter, eds. *Inside the Pentagon Papers.* Lawrence: University Press of Kansas, 2004.

Report of the Commission on Protecting and Reducing Government Secrecy. Washington, D.C.: United States Government Printing Office, 1997.

Report on the U.S. Intelligence Community's Prewar Intelligence Assessments on Iraq. United States Senate, Select Committee on Intelligence. July 7, 2004.

Risen, James. *State of War: The Secret History of the CIA and the Bush Administration*. New York: Free Press, 2006.

Stone, Geoffrey R. *Perilous Times: Free Speech in Wartime from the Sedition Act of 1798 to the War on Terrorism*. New York: W. W. Norton, 2004.

Ungar, Sanford J. *The Papers & the Papers: An Account of the Legal and Political Battle over the Pentagon Papers*. New York: E. P. Dutton, 1972.

United States v. Morison, 844 F.2nd 1057, April 1, 1988.

United States v. Nixon, 418 U.S. 683, July 24, 1974.

White Paper on the Reporter's Privilege. New York: Media Law Resource Center, August 2004.

Woodward, Bob. *Bush at War*. New York: Simon & Schuster, 2002.

———. *Plan of Attack*. New York: Simon & Schuster, 2004.

———. *State of Denial*. New York: Simon & Schuster, 2006.

Youngstown v. Sawyer, 343 U.S. 579, June 2, 1952.

Zerilli v. Smith, 211 U.S. App. D.C. 116, April 13, 1981.

Index

Made in the USA
Middletown, DE
28 January 2019